Living *Walden Two*

HILKE KUHLMANN

UNIVERSITY OF ILLINOIS PRESS

Urbana and Chicago

COMUNIDAD LOS HORCONES

# Living
## *Walden Two*

B. F. Skinner's Behaviorist Utopia
and Experimental Communities

Photo on page i: Sharing work is an important aspect of daily life at Twin Oaks Community. (Courtesy Twin Oaks Community.)
Photo on pages ii–iii: An old school bus serves as a communal means of transportation on group trips to the beach. (Photo by H. Kuhlmann.)

© 2005 by the Board of Trustees
of the University of Illinois
All rights reserved
Manufactured in the United States of America
C 5 4 3 2 1
∞ This book is printed on acid-free paper.

Library of Congress Cataloging-in-Publication Data

Kuhlmann, Hilke, 1969–
Living Walden Two : B. F. Skinner's behaviorist utopia
and experimental communities / Hilke Kuhlmann.
p.  m.
Includes bibliographical references and index.
ISBN 0-252-02962-3 (hardcover : alk. paper)
1. Utopias—United States. 2. Behavior modification—
United States. 3. Skinner, B. F. (Burrhus Frederic), 1904–
Walden two. 4. Communal living—United States. I. Title.
HX806.K84     2004
307.77'0973—dc22     2004020463

# Contents

# Acknowledgments

RESEARCHING communal experiments is a lot like poking around in other people's broken dreams. For this reason, I am particularly grateful to all of the current and former communards who shared their stories with me and often went out of their way to help me. Special thanks go to Twin Oaks Community for opening its home to me and teaching me the art of weaving hammocks, among other things.

On the academic side, I thank my advisor, Manfred Pütz, for first introducing me to *Walden Two* and seeing me through the Ph.D. process, and Kenneth Roemer and Donald Pitzer for their expert advice and support through all phases of this study. Most importantly, I am deeply grateful to Lyman Tower Sargent for always being there with advice whenever I needed it.

Research on the reception of *Walden Two* in intentional communities was made possible by a grant from the DAAD (German Academic Exchange Service) for 1998. My time as a participant-observer at Twin Oaks as well as shorter visits to Los Horcones, Lake Village, Sunflower House, and Dandelion Community deepened my understanding of these communities.

I thank Frank Cass for permission to reprint a modified version of an article that first appeared in the *Critical Review of International Social and Political Philosophy* 3.2–3 (Summer/Autumn 2000). I also thank the special collection on communities at the University of Virginia as well as the archive of the Center for Communal Studies in Indiana for opening their doors to me.

Above all, I wish to thank my family and friends for supporting me from the enthusiastic beginning to the exhausting end of this project, be it as listeners, proofreaders, or general support team.

# Introduction

B. F. SKINNER's *Walden Two* is arguably the most influential and hotly debated fictional utopia of the twentieth century. In the early summer of 1945, Skinner envisioned a society finally set free from war, suffering, and personal unhappiness. The psychologist's utopian vision as such was not unique, but his proposed technique for achieving the good life was: drawing on his laboratory experiments with rats and pigeons, Skinner thought that to change society effectively one had to change human behavior itself. To do this he suggested employing the techniques of behavioral engineering.

Although Skinner had done research almost exclusively on animal behavior at the time he wrote *Walden Two*, he was confident that the startling results his studies had produced in this area could also be applied to humans. Skinner's experiments suggested to him that animal and human behavior is always dependent on outward influences and that, contrary to popular belief, positive reinforcement is much more effective in handling behavior than punitive control, with its destructive side effects. Therefore, the perfect society should make extensive use of positive reinforcement in all areas of life. This led him to envision a society designed by behavioral engineers, who would condition people to live and enjoy the good life while being freed of such emotions as aggression, jealousy, or competition.

Whereas Skinner was convinced that he had found the key to world peace and happiness, almost nobody else seemed to think so in 1948, when the novel was first published. Far from being praised or even debated, the book was simply ignored. *Walden Two* only began to sell more than a dozen years after its publication. By then, Skinner had become a renowned scientist who was taken seriously in the academic world. His claim that human behavior can be studied scientifically and altered at will, which he had already expounded in 1945 in *Walden Two,* began to have considerable influence on many areas of thought in the 1960s and 1970s. His ideas not only became the foundation of a school of psychology but also had an immense impact on social reform in the United States and other western countries: if everything humans do, think, and feel is "learned" by responding to events in the outer environment, the possibilities for societal influence on individuals are endless. The treatment of juvenile delinquency, mental illness, and learning disabilities, the instruction children received in the public school system—all were affected by the apparent effectiveness of employing the techniques of behavior modification.

Yet Skinner's ideas were far from universally applauded. Although the soundness of his scientific work was seldom questioned, his far-reaching conclusions about human nature were repudiated by numerous influential critics. Noam Chomsky, Carl Rogers, Joseph Wood Krutch, and Arthur Koestler have repeatedly argued that Skinner's behavioral engineering reduces humans to laboratory rats and controlled robots, stripping them of dignity and free will. Skinner's refusal to pay attention to anything but observable behavior was thought to threaten a concept at the very root of western civilization: the individual endowed with inalienable rights and personal responsibility. His conclusion that societal survival could be ensured only by making conscious use of the techniques of controlling behavior to induce people to behave for the good of the group was rejected as totalitarian, as was his assertion that scientists could objectively arrive at values that ought to be adopted by society. As a result of the ongoing debate about Skinner's controversial ideas, which peaked in 1971 with his publication of *Beyond Freedom and Dignity,* interest in his early utopian novel—his only work of fiction—rose steadily. Quite suddenly, *Walden Two* was taken seriously.

Skinner gained fame during a time of social unrest in the United States. In the late sixties and early seventies, thousands of young people refused to follow the beaten path and set out to form intentional communities. With the heyday of behaviorism and communal living coinciding, it is perhaps not astonishing that *Walden Two* inspired some readers to try out Skinner's concept of the good life. In the 1960s and 1970s, while Skinner's controversial ideas were being widely debated, roughly three dozen intentional communities located almost exclusively in the United States proclaimed themselves to be Walden Two communities, or at least strongly influenced by *Walden Two.*

What did these experimental communities mean by "living" Walden Two? What were the social, political, and personal factors that played into the communards' interpretation of Skinner's novel, and how important was the utopian and communal heritage of their country in shaping their responses to *Walden Two?* What kinds of problems did the communards encounter while constructing intentional communities on the basis of *Walden Two?* And finally, how did these communards modify their interpretation of *Walden Two* on the basis of their experiences in trying to turn this work of fiction into reality?

In trying to understand what those readers who went on to establish communities found inspiring about Skinner's utopia, it is important to clearly differentiate between Skinner's writings in general and his only work of fiction. Contrary to the most common portrayal of *Walden Two* as a barely disguised vehicle for expounding on behavioral engineering, the novel is not, in fact, exclusively about behaviorism. Kenneth Roemer has argued convincingly that Skinner takes great care to present his controversial ideas in a way that aimed at making them acceptable to an American audience.

Throughout the novel, Skinner makes extensive use of literary strategies, characters, and images commonly encountered in utopian fiction. The utopian community is visited by six people from the outside, they are met by a guide called Frazier who is part of the utopian society, a subsequent tour with extensive dialogues between guide and visitors takes up the bulk of the novel, and, in the end, three of the six visitors decide to remain in utopia. To add to the nonthreatening picture, Skinner's utopia is essentially a large farm in contemporary rural America, populated by a thousand people engaged in meaningful work. This setting is strongly reminiscent of nineteenth-century experimental communities. Skinner frequently refers to Edward Bellamy's *Looking Backward,* both explicitly and implicitly, aligning himself skillfully with the most famous of all American utopias.

Most important in Skinner's attempt to win an American audience over to his ideas is perhaps the introduction of the guide, Frazier, who is also the founder of the fictional utopian community. Frazier has a very contradictory personality and is the most intriguing character in *Walden Two,* alternately wise, angry, lonely, funny, and jealous. He is, in other words, exactly the kind of person that Skinner would wish to obliterate in his behaviorally engineered utopia. As will be shown, the setting of the novel, the focus on the individualistic Frazier, and the conscious attempt to place *Walden Two* in the tradition of American utopianism and communal living are vitally important in understanding how the various groups approached their experiments in communal living and how the resultant communities changed upon encountering difficulties with taking *Walden Two* as a guideline.

The reception of *Walden Two* in intentional communities falls into two phases. During the first phase, several groups developed almost independently of each other and approached the building of a Walden Two in different ways: Lake Village, Walden Three, and Sunflower House were all initiated by behaviorists and share some characteristics; the distinctly different Twin Oaks Community in Virginia was founded by people barely knowledgeable about behaviorism but enthusiastic about income sharing; while the Mexican community of Los Horcones seems very much centered around its behaviorist cofounder, Juan Robinson.

Despite the differences among these pioneering Walden Two groups, there is also one important common thread. It appears that an unspoken assumption was at the core of these readers' understanding of *Walden Two:* most of them tacitly assumed that *they* would be the Frazier of their group. How did this unacknowledged identification with the novel's individualistic guide/founder, while on a conscious level being engaged in a cooperative venture with like-minded people, affect the development of the Walden Two communities? As might be expected, this setup caused profound problems in almost all of the communities, problems that were largely unforeseen by the pioneering communards and quickly forced them to reassess their reading of *Walden Two.*

Yet the impact of *Walden Two* on intentional communities went beyond the handful of pioneering groups and found its expression in a second wave of Walden Two communities encompassing more than two dozen groups. This second wave was largely inspired by Twin Oaks and the particular spin this one intentional community, and especially its cofounder Kat Kinkade, had given to its reading of *Walden Two.* Most importantly, these groups were excited about Skinner's proposed system of work distribution, the so-called labor-credit system, and the way Twin Oaks had adapted this system to fit its needs. In contrast to the often hasty dismissal of the sixties communities as chaotic and short-lived, Twin Oaks has attracted considerable attention over the years—both within and outside the communal movement—as a unique microsociety that appears to have succeeded in sustaining an alternative economic system. Twin Oaks is completely income sharing, requires all its able-bodied adult members to work an equal amount of time, and gives out an equal amount of benefits to all its members regardless of the quality of work performance.

Will people work willingly and joyously in the absence of personal incentives? On the surface, Twin Oaks appears to prove that a system can indeed be found that will induce people to work for the common good. Yet the fact that most of the Walden Two/Twin Oaks–inspired communities failed to survive in the long run indicates that there are perhaps other factors than the labor-credit system that have helped Twin Oaks to remain a vibrant community to this day.

Comunidad Los Horcones in Mexico differs from its northern siblings in several respects. Skinner wrote his fictional utopia with U.S. readers in mind, yet the communards in Mexico arguably come closest to having created a Walden Two in real life. Overall, it seems that cultural as well as specific personal factors facilitated the creation of a unique community that developed differently from all the other Walden Twos. Most importantly, Los Horcones is the only group still priding itself on being a Walden Two community.

# PART 1

# B. F. Skinner's
*Walden Two*

B. F. Skinner (right, at the 1978 American Psychological Association conference with Richard Graham of Dandelion Community) showed only peripheral interest in the "hippie communities" inspired by his novel. (courtesy Richard Graham)

# 1 *Walden Two:* A Behaviorist Utopia

*WALDEN TWO* BEGINS, like so many other utopian novels, with a journey. In the year 1945, a cynical professor is approached by a former student who has just returned from military service. The student, Rogers, reminds his professor of a utopian community he once mentioned in class. One of the professor's fellow graduate students, a man called Frazier, had always been planning to establish a community. Together they discover that Frazier actually followed through with his plan. Excited about the actual existence of a utopian community in their neighborhood, they write to the community and arrange for a visit. A few days later, a group of six—Professor Burris, his colleague Castle, Rogers, a fellow soldier from the war, and the two younger men's girlfriends—set out on their utopian adventure. Their goal is Frazier's community, Walden Two.

Reaching the community, located "about thirty miles from the largest city in the state" somewhere in rural America (11), involves no more than a train and then a bus ride. The visitors find themselves stranded along the highway: "An hour later our bus passed over a small bridge and hissed to a stop. We were left standing at the side of the road as the bus drew away in a popping roar" (11). Before they can decide what to do, they are greeted by a man who had been napping while waiting for them. This is Frazier, the founder of the community and their central guide throughout the novel. The group continues its trip in a station wagon by leaving the main highway, driving through farmland, and finally crossing a "creek on a small wooden bridge" (12).

Among gentle slopes, young pines, and a small pond they discover buildings of a "functional style" (12), which are, as Frazier informs them, part of Walden Two, a commune populated by roughly a thousand people. The visitors have arrived in Skinner's version of utopia. At the end of their short visit, three of them will join Walden Two, while three will return to the outside world. At the end of the novel we understand that the book was written by Burris, chronicling his development from cynical professor to useful new community member.

## Walden Two as an American-Style Utopian Community

Using a typical utopian strategy, Skinner presents his community as seen through the eyes of a group of visitors who are not (initially) part of the utopian world.[1] There are, however, several aspects of this introductory section of *Walden Two* that are noteworthy. First, Skinner places his utopia in the here and now rather than transferring it to a distant place or time. Second, he does not present a society of gigantic proportions but rather a community of a thousand members living on a farm. Third, reaching utopia does not involve a time machine, dream, or space craft in Skinner's novel but simply a train, a bus, and a station wagon. *Walden Two* is thus a classic example of what Robert Plank calls the modern "shrunken utopia."

The description of the Walden Two community, once the visitors have arrived, follows in a similar vein. The overall impression is of a pleasant summer resort, with various forms of the word "pleasant" appearing, as Kenneth Roemer has noted, at least forty-four times in the course of the novel (144). The utopians are shown drinking tea, engaging in intelligent conversation, and expressing an interest in the arts. In a typical passage, Burris describes a scene before him: "These were delightful people. Their conversation had a measure and cadence more often found in well-wrought fiction than in fact. They were pleasant and well-mannered, yet perfectly candid; they were lively, but not boisterous; affectionate, but not effusive" (24).

The description of happy and self-contained people is typical of utopian fiction, yet Skinner goes beyond the implicit reference to standards of utopian fiction by drawing explicitly on utopian images—and writers—that would have been familiar to an American audience: "'One advantage of cooperative housing,' Frazier said, 'is that we can deal with the weather. Edward Bellamy tried it, you remember. The streets of his Boston of the future were to be covered when it rained'" (19). In Walden Two, the main buildings are connected by covered passageways, which was more feasible than Bellamy's plan, explains Frazier, because of the smaller size of his community (19). Although these passageways are not a central aspect of Walden Two, they place the fictional community in the tradition of American utopianism.

Throughout the novel the reader is presented with ingenious little inventions aimed at making daily life more pleasant. These inventions include the aforementioned passageways, transparent trays that are easier to wash because they do not have to be flipped over to check for stains (41–42), and a tea service consisting of "tall glasses, set in braided grass jackets, to which loops of string were attached so that the glasses could be carried like pails," whose advantages over a conventional tea service are described at length (26–27). As Roemer has pointed out, these inventions give the community "an air of pragmatism that would appeal to many American readers" (132).

Other critics have observed that "*Walden Two* recalls in many ways the austere communism of many of the experimental communities of the nineteenth century" (Klaw 48). Skinner was well aware of his country's tradition of utopian communities. Just prior to writing *Walden Two* in a matter of weeks, Skinner had read Alice Felt Tyler's *Freedom's Ferment,* which deals with utopian communities from the revolution to the outbreak of the Civil War. Daniel W. Bjork reports that Skinner had read stories about the Shakers as a child and had visited the famous nineteenth-century utopian community Oneida during college (255). Prior to writing *Walden Two,* Skinner had also "'poke[d] about in the history of American communities, but never built up a formal bibliography'" (qtd. in Bjork 255).

Skinner's fictional communards wear sensible clothes "to avoid the waste which is imposed by changing styles." Mrs. Meyerson, a communard in charge of "Clothing for Women," further elaborates that the visitors "won't find half a dozen 'party dresses' among us" but that "each of us has something that would be in good taste except at very formal functions." Frazier adds that "[f]ull dress . . . is a form of conspicuous consumption which doesn't amuse us—except when we see it in others" (29–30).

Similarly, the communards eat tasty but healthy food (41), use their spare time for such pleasures as playing in a string ensemble or singing in a Bach Cantata Club (82), and, as mentioned above, they delight in drinking a cup of tea with each other. In one scene, the visitors are taken to a concert, and professor Burris feels that Walden Two might indeed have entered the "Golden Age" as he hears an excellent chorus sing the "Kyrie Eleison" (84–85). Incidentally, Julian West, the nineteenth-century visitor to Bellamy's utopian Boston of the year 2000, is similarly impressed by a musical performance (Bellamy 98).

Most important in reminding an American audience of their country's nineteenth-century utopian communities is perhaps Walden Two's attitude toward work and the distribution of property. Like many nineteenth-century utopian communities, Walden Two is fully income-sharing, resulting in the absence of classes or the division of society into rich and poor. All members of Skinner's utopian community engage in work, and Frazier points out to the astonished visitors that all adults, regardless of their profession, are required to put in two hours of physical labor a day. After dinner in the communal dining hall, an encounter between Frazier and a communard cleaning dirty dishes and trays is described: "A distinguished man with a full beard, who stopped Frazier to ask if he thought the library should acquire a more up-to-date musical encyclopedia, received the tray from the milk bath and placed it upside down on a set of revolving brushes which fitted the dishlike depressions" (43).

The communard is described as an educated man who is in no way inferior to Frazier and is not treated as such. It is explained to the visitors that nobody at Walden Two would ask somebody else to perform a task that they themselves would refuse to do (42).[2] Frazier adds: "'That's the virtue of Walden Two which pleases me most. I was never happy in being waited on. I could never enjoy the fleshpots for thinking of what might be going on below stairs.' It was obviously a borrowed expression, for Frazier's early life had not been affluent. But he suddenly continued in a loud, clear voice which could leave no doubt of his sincerity, 'Here a man can hold up his head and say, 'I've done my share!'" (51).

In explaining the system of labor distribution undergirding this egalitarianism and mutual respect among all members of the community, Skinner is again indebted to Bellamy. For the most part, the problem of work distribution is discussed in a few passages in chapter 8. The visitors thank Frazier for taking the time to show them around, to which Frazier responds that he is earning labor credits for doing so. In the longest passage about the work system used in Walden Two, Frazier explains, "'Labor-credits are a sort of money. But they're not coins or bills—just entries in a ledger. All goods and services are free, as you saw in the dining room this evening. Each of us pays for what he uses with twelve hundred labor-credits each year—say, four credits for each workday. We change the value according to the needs of the community. At two hours of work per credit—an eight-hour day—we could operate at a handsome profit. We're satisfied to keep just a shade beyond breaking even. The profit system is bad even when the worker gets the profits, because the strain of overwork isn't relieved by even a large reward. . . . At present it's about one hour of work per credit'" (45).

The credit value of a job is decided by how popular it is and how urgently it needs to be done: the less attractive a job is and the more urgently it needs to be done, the more rewarding it is to do that job. An "unpleasant job like cleaning sewers" thus has a higher credit value than "[w]orking in the flower gardens," ideally making every job equally desirable (46). Since the economic system at Walden Two does not aim at making a profit, the communards only work an average of four hours a day (53).

Frazier casually remarks that "'Bellamy suggested the principle in *Looking Backward*'" (46), and Bellamy's description of work in the year 2000 sounds remarkably similar indeed:

> It is the business of the administration to seek constantly to equalize the attractions of the trades, so far as the conditions of labor in them are concerned, so that all trades shall be equally attractive to persons having natural tastes for them. This is done by making the hours of labor in different trades to differ according to their arduousness. The lighter trades, prosecuted under the most agreeable circumstances, have in this way the longest hours, while an arduous trade, such as mining, has very short hours. There is no theory, no a priori rule, by which the respective attractiveness of industries is determined. . . . The principle is that no man's work ought to be, on the whole, harder for him than any other man's for him, the workers themselves to be the judges. (72)

In Bellamy's system, citizens also earn "credits" that can be exchanged for goods (83). Skinner's system of work distribution is thus clearly and heavily indebted to Bellamy.[3]

Skinner, like Bellamy before him, studiously avoids the word "socialism" in his discussion of his fully income-sharing, classless society made up of people working for the common good according to their abilities, with their needs taken care of by the community as a whole. In terms of making his utopia acceptable to an American audience, aligning himself with Bellamy—whose utopian vision has been called "as American as apple pie" (Plank 211)—is a good tactical move. Overall, however, Skinner expresses little interest in the economic aspects of Walden Two, so his use of Bellamy's model was perhaps more a matter of convenience than conviction or strategy. In fact, Roemer has remarked that Frazier's defense of the tea service "is almost as long and is more enthusiastic than his defense of Walden Two's economic system" (132). Also, in describing his utopians' attitude toward work, Skinner appears to argue not from the point of view of a revolutionary wishing to do away with capitalism but from the point of view of a middle-class intellectual who would love to get a daily dose of physical exercise as a matter of course. Frazier challenges his visitors to think of "'any "pure" scientist in our universities who wouldn't settle for two hours of physical work each day instead of the soul-searching work he's now compelled to do in the name of education,'" adding: "'It's fatal to forget the minority element—fatal to treat brawn as if there were no brains, and perhaps more speedily fatal to treat brains as if there were no brawn. One or two hours of physical work each day is a health measure'" (50–52).

Later on, Skinner describes at length how the visitors earn their share of labor credits by cleaning windows. After initial hesitation, both of the professors show enthusiasm for their job and agree at the end that the exertion was "better than grading blue books" or "reading term papers" and that it has put them "in a better condition for intellectual exercise" (67). In another credit-earning activity, Burris and the two young men chop wood, prompting Burris to remark later that the "boys were right about a spot of heavy work: it was just what I needed. A shower and a change put me in the pink. After lunch I could have enjoyed a nap, and I had rather planned to rest later in the afternoon. But a couple of hours on the woodpile had cleared my head after the strenuous discussion of the morning, and I was ready for more" (142).

Reading these descriptions of work at Walden Two, one wonders if what Skinner really had in mind when writing his utopia was not a pleasant retreat for burned-out academics on sabbatical. Almost the entire first third of *Walden Two*, just under a hundred pages, is devoted to this "'leisurely start,'" as Frazier calls it (15). Frazier only occasionally drops hints about the use of "cultural engineering" at Walden Two (44, 50, 51). Until late into the novel, all the reader is presented with is this description of a farm populated by very unfarmerlike people who are free of stress, too much intellectual exertion, and life's little annoyances. The visitors are shown around, they enjoy contributing their labor after initial hesitation, and they are impressed by the community's ingenious inventions aimed at making daily life more simple and pleasurable. Skinner's "vision of the good life," comments Krishan Kumar, seems to rest on the psychologist's happy memories of his childhood in Susquehanna, Pennsylvania, and strongly reflects his "small town, middle-class Protestant background" ("Utopia" 350).

## Behavioral Engineering at Walden Two: Child Education

The trouble starts when Frazier shows his visitors the community's nursery and school. As the visitors quickly discover, Frazier considers the educational system to be the real achievement of the community, and it is this system that leads to heated discussions between Frazier and his visitors (and that also incensed many critics). In this system, the children are kept in a completely controlled environment that is intended to weed out all behaviors considered unacceptable in utopia while fostering behaviors that make for self-confident, peaceful, happy, and productive members of society. This idea as such is not unusual in utopian fiction. Almost all utopian writers stress the importance of education, and proposals for carefully manipulating children's environment abound.

Skinner's proposal regarding education in utopia is unusual in that it affirms the use of behavioral engineering as the guiding principle in the educational process.[4] This system is so much at odds with the western conception of human nature that devoting the first hundred pages of the novel to a leisurely start does not seem exaggerated. It is not in the *depiction* of the good life that Skinner differs from other utopian writers but in his proposed method for achieving it.

Readers of utopian and dystopian fiction would be familiar with the concept of behavioral engineering as such, which had been described scathingly by Aldous Huxley in *Brave New World* (1932). In stark contrast to Huxley, however, Skinner applauds discarding outdated concepts of human nature and instituting a rigorous but well-meant regimen of conditioning for the children of his utopian world. The concept of applying behavioral engineering in the educational process is first explained at length in a discussion about jealousy and why it is an obsolete emotion among Walden Two children:

> "In a competitive world there's some point to [jealousy]. It energizes one to attack a frustrating condition. The impulse and the added energy are an advantage. Indeed, in a competitive world emotions work all too well. Look at the singular lack of success of the complacent man. He enjoys a more serene life, but it's less likely to be a fruitful one. The world isn't ready for simple pacifism or Christian humility, to cite two cases in point. Before you can safely train out the destructive and wasteful emotions, you must make sure they're no longer needed."
>
> "How do you make sure that jealousy isn't needed in Walden Two?" I said.
>
> "In Walden Two problems can't be solved by attacking others," said Frazier with marked finality.
>
> "That's not the same as eliminating jealousy, though," I said.
>
> "Of course it's not. But when a particular emotion is no longer a useful part of a behavioral repertoire, we proceed to eliminate it."
>
> "Yes, but how?"
>
> "It's simply a matter of behavioral engineering," said Frazier.
>
> "Behavioral engineering?"

"You're baiting me, Burris. You know perfectly well what I mean. The techniques have been available for centuries. We use them in education and in the psychological management of the community. But you're forcing my hand," he added. "I was saving that for this evening. But let's strike while the iron is hot." (93–94)

In order to change a behavior like jealousy, Frazier maintains, one needs to change the environment. In effecting changes in the environment, one must attend to the evolutionary needs of a culture. Rather than leaving environment and subsequent behavior to chance—"what is the virtue of accident?" (105)—one can actively influence the evolutionary process by using behavioral engineering. Striking while the iron is hot, Frazier proceeds by stating that the "'questions are simple enough'": "'What's the best behavior for the individual so far as the group is concerned? And how can the individual be induced to behave in that way? Why not explore these questions in a scientific spirit?'" (95).

Skinner devotes six chapters of *Walden Two* to an outline of the educational system, answering these "simple" questions. Yet he does not explain *why* the main question to be explored in a scientific spirit is so obviously how the individual can be induced to behave for the good of the group.

In contrast to most of his other writings, however, Skinner takes great care in *Walden Two* to point out the benefits of a behaviorally engineered society to the individual rather than placing his focus on society. In his defense of the Walden Two educational system, Frazier accuses other educational theories of consciously accepting that only the strongest will make it. He continues: "'In Walden Two we have a different objective. We make every man a brave man. They all come over the barriers'" (105).

Making all come over the barriers—for the sake of society—is achieved by completely controlling the children's environment and using techniques of behavior modification extensively throughout their childhood. To facilitate this process, children are raised communally at Walden Two. They live together in children's quarters, where they are cared for by professionals, while their parents live in adult quarters. This arrangement, argues Frazier, offers three advantages: First, the environment of the children can be completely controlled, thus making it possible to shield them from harmful influences such as infections or frustrating experiences; second, the behavioral conditioning of the children, which begins at a very early age, can be carried out effectively only in a controlled environment; and third, the development of the children is not dependent on the status and abilities of their parents.

While these living arrangements result in the abandonment of the nuclear family, they are not meant to discourage loving relationships between adults and children. The concept of loving one's children is simply expanded to everybody loving all children—"community love" instead of "mother love" (90). Apparently, Skinner did not think that abandoning strong emotional ties between children and their parents would be difficult to accomplish or in any way harmful. He has Frazier proclaim that "'[g]roup care is better than parental care. In the old pre-scientific days the early education of the child could be left to the parents, and indeed almost certainly had to be left to them. But with the rise of a science of behavior all is changed. . . . Even when our young mothers and fathers become skilled nursery-school workers, we avoid a strong personal dependency. Our goal is to have every adult member of Walden Two regard all our children as his own, and to have every child think of every adult as his parent. To this end we have made it bad taste to single out one's own child for special favors'" (132).

Early marriage is advocated, so that women can get childbearing out of the way and still be young enough to pursue careers. Furthermore, early marriages are intended to save teenagers the frustrations of unfulfilled sexual desires. At Walden Two, the babies born to these young parents are scrupulously cared for by the entire community, with all obstacles removed that could hamper a child's happiness. The newborns are kept naked on plastic stretchers in "aircribs," cubicles with adjustable heat and moisture, especially designed to make a child as comfortable and safe as possible while reducing the workload of those involved in nursery care. This control of the environment is gradually relaxed as the children grow older. The older children live together with roommates, the thirteen-year-olds take temporary rooms, still with roommates, in the adult building, while the maturing adolescent can decide at any point to take single quarters or joint quarters with his or her spouse (107).

The community's children undergo "ethical training" from age three to six (98). It is this training, teaching them self-control, perseverance, and tolerance for frustration, that enables them to go on to become good students, mature adults, and happy communards. While still in a completely shielded environment, the "ethical training" teaches the children methods to deal successfully with (artificially created) annoying experiences. The degree of annoyance increases over the years according to the increase in tolerance for frustration that builds up in the maturing children. Thus self-control is consciously and consistently taught. "'The sunshine of midday is extremely painful if you come from a dark room,'" runs Frazier's analogy for the educational process, "'but take it in easy stages and you can avoid pain altogether'" (97).

Frazier gives his visitors several examples of this easy-stages process: Children who have just returned from an exhausting hiking trip are confronted with bowls of hot soup they are forbidden to eat for a certain period of time. This is supposed to build up their tolerance for frustration, with the conditions of this little experiment becoming more frustrating as the children become more tolerant of frustration. Great care is taken to have all children master this exercise, which some may find easier than others. The person to emerge from that kind of education is to be self-controlled, strong, well-poised, and basically happy with his or her accomplishments.

Academic instruction, apparently the less important part of education in utopia, is individualized at Walden Two. Everybody can learn at his or her own pace, drawing satisfaction and reinforcement from individual accomplishments rather than competition. Children learn out of a natural curiosity that has never been stifled by overwhelmingly frustrating experiences (114). They do not need to be disciplined by teachers; teachers merely provide some kind of guidance and answer questions. Studying is a natural part of everybody's life at Walden Two, so the classroom is only the starting point of a lifelong undertaking. Once the children know the "techniques of learning" (113–14), they can do the actual studying by themselves. Education is also not restricted to the classroom but takes place wherever people work and children watch.

Throughout the description of the communal child-rearing program, which is designed to raise a new generation of self-confident and cooperative human beings, Frazier draws frequent comparisons to Christian ideals. In what appears to be an effort to "lend spiritual authority to secular reforms" (Roemer 141), *Walden Two* makes behavioral engineering sound like the culmination rather than the death of religion. The change from punitive control to positive reinforcement that is at the center of the educational system as well as the community as a whole is proclaimed by Frazier to be the scientific version of Jesus's accidental discovery of the power of loving your enemies: "'Jesus must have been quite astonished at the effect of his discovery. We are only just beginning to understand the weakness of force and aggression. But the science of behavior is clear about all that now'" (96–97).[5]

As shall be discussed later on, Skinner's efforts to make behavioral engineering in the realm of child education acceptable to an American audience generated strong reactions—as did his notions on government.

## The Governmental System

The Walden Two governmental system, described briefly in a few paragraphs in chapter 8—the same chapter in which the economic system is dealt with—explicitly places the guidance of the community in the hands of a few, thereby institutionalizing paternalism. Walden Two is not a democratic society, nor does it aim to be one. "'I'm not arguing for no government at all,'" explains Frazier, "'but only for none of the existing forms. We want a government based upon a science of behavior'" (182). The governmental system is thus a logical consequence of the educational system and builds on the same line of argument. Governmental affairs should be handled by those most proficient in the science of behavior: behavioral scientists. Frazier explains that scientists are best suited for the task of designing society because their aims are supposedly never selfish: "'What scientist worth the name is engaged, as scientist, in the satisfaction of his own basic needs? He may be thinking of the basic needs of others, but his own motives are clearly cultural. There can be no doubt of the survival value of the inquiring spirit'" (116). "Ordinary" members in Walden Two, as we will see, are neither capable nor interested in making sensible decisions based on the "needs of others."

In concrete terms, the government at Walden Two consists of a six-member Board of Planners (preferably three men and three women), which is responsible for providing living conditions that ensure the happiness of all members of Walden Two. Planners can serve a maximum of ten years. Frazier describes the role of the planners as follows: "'The Planners are charged with the success of the community. They make policies, review the work of the Managers, keep an eye on the state of the nation in general'" (48). The managers are one level below the planners in terms of importance and range of responsibility. Their job consists of ensuring that every aspect of Walden Two's economic system runs smoothly, and they are not necessarily well-versed in behaviorism.

In Walden Two neither planners nor managers are voted into office. Since competence is the main criterion for selection, Skinner thought that only those actually capable of judging competence for a certain job should be the ones to make decisions (48–49). Thus, planners and managers are appointed by their predecessors. The regular members of Walden Two do not vote, nor do they take an active part in governing the commune. They constitute the third group of members: ordinary people without "constitutional" rights.

As in Skinner's nonfictional writings, behavioral engineers are of pivotal importance to the design of an "improved" society because no scientist "worth the name" would even think of directing his or her actions toward personal profit or power. This point seems to be so obvious to Skinner that he does not bother to elaborate why a scientist's motives are "clearly" cultural, or why there can be "no doubt of the survival value of the inquiring spirit." Interestingly, however, Frazier is the only member of the utopian community who appears capable of even comprehending behavioral engineering. Skinner's frequent denial that Walden Two is run by behavioral engineers (*Matter* 321–23) thus seems in a way justified: the community is depicted as the brainchild not of a group of behavioral engineers but of one person, Frazier, with no evidence of how the community would function without him.

In stark contrast to the competence and ulterior motives assigned to scientists, Frazier talks about "ordinary people" in far less complimentary terms: "'Most people do live from day to day, or, if they have any long-time plan it's little more than the anticipation of some natural course—they look forward to having children, to seeing the children grow up, and so on. The majority of people don't want to plan. They want to be free of the responsibility of planning. What they ask is merely some assurance that they will be decently provided for. The rest is a day-to-day enjoyment of life. That's the explanation of your Father Divines; people naturally flock to anyone they can trust for the necessities of life. People of that sort are completely happy here'" (154–55).

The planner-manager system is based on the assumption that most people are not interested in the larger political picture as long as their own personal needs are satisfied. As a result of this attitude, the ordinary members of Walden Two are left completely unaware of the political decision-making process ruling their lives. An encounter between the visiting Professor Burris and an ordinary member of Walden Two is illuminating in this context:

> "You're visiting, aren't you?"
> "Yes, we're guests of Mr. Frazier."
> "Frazier? Oh, yes. I know who he is. Has a little goatee. A thin man. He thinks too much."
> I sat down on the grass, hugging my knees and looking at the flowers.
> "What do you think of Walden?" she asked. Like many members, she omitted the "Two."
> "I think it's fine," I said. "A beautiful spot. And everyone so perfectly happy." My face burned with shame at this obvious maneuver.

"Happy?" she said with evident surprise.

I looked up. Perhaps I had struck something.

"Why, yes. You all seem very happy. Aren't you?"

[. . .]

"Don't we look happy?"

"But you can't always tell," I said.

"You're kind of a gloomy fellow, aren't you? If you'll pardon me saying so."

"Why do you say that?"

"Oh, wondering are we happy—and things like that. You're a little like that What-do-you-call'im—the young man who comes around to see if you're satisfied with everything."

[. . .]

"What sort of work do you do?" I said.

"Cook. Pastry. Couldn't you tell?"

"What labor-credits do they give you for that kind of work?"

"Oh, I don't know. I just get out the pies and cakes. Have some good girls to help me. Mr. Engelbaum, too." (204–5)

This woman is characterized by Burris, who had set out to find fault with Walden Two (his "obvious maneuver"), as the "typical, middle-class house-wife" in utopia (204). Talking with her convinces Burris that there is nothing at all wrong with Walden Two and that, in fact, the members really are happy and satisfied with their lives, just as Frazier had claimed. The woman may prove Frazier's point, but she does more than that: she reveals that the "happy," ordinary members of Walden Two are ill-informed about the planner-manager and labor-credit systems. She recognizes Frazier mainly by his outer appearance, is only dimly aware of the function of the "What-do-you-call'im—the young man who comes around to see if you're satisfied with everything," and does not know how many labor credits she earns by making pastry. She is evidently quite happy not to think about anything too deeply, living up to what appears to be the Walden Two norm for ordinary members: happiness without inquiring into the why and how. This happy communard spots Burris right away for being planner material: " 'You're kind of a gloomy fellow . . . wondering are we happy—and things like that.' " Dangerously enough, the happy communard by whom Burris is so impressed recognizes Frazier only as the "thin man" who "thinks too much." She, the representative of the ordinary citizens of Walden Two, is obviously not in the least aware of Frazier's extraordinary position in either the founding or the governing of the community.

Castle questions Frazier about the undemocratic nature of Walden Two early in the novel, and he receives a short answer that is nevertheless right to the point: "'Then the members have no voice whatsoever,' said Castle in a carefully controlled voice, as if he were filing the point away for future use. 'Nor do they wish to have,' said Frazier flatly" (49).

In several encounters between Frazier, the visitors, and ordinary members (and even managers), the attitude that most people are not capable of comprehending the larger picture and should therefore not be involved in the decision-making process comes through clearly. One example is Mrs. Meyerson, in charge of women's clothing. The visitors and Frazier discuss beauty, and Frazier assures the visitors, "'We tried to get a representative sample—a true cross section. We failed in some respects, but I can't see how a selection could have been made, even unconsciously, on the basis of personal appearance. Do you think so, Rachel?' 'I'm sure you're right, Fraze,' said Mrs. Meyerson." As an afterthought, Burris adds, "though I am not sure she understood the point" (28).

Mrs. Meyerson then explains the community's attitude toward fashion: "'Well, I suppose the answer is we compromise. But it's not quite that. At least it's not just taking the easy way out—we spent a lot of time on it. We solved the problem by—experimenting, would you say?' She turned to Frazier. 'No,' he said flatly, without looking at her. 'Intuition.' 'By intuition, then,' Mrs. Meyerson cheerfully agreed" (29).

Mrs. Meyerson seems to be aware that the community favors an experimental attitude, yet she is clearly unsure about just what that entails. Frazier "flatly" puts her in her place by reducing her accomplishments to female intuition, to which she "cheerfully" agrees. Frazier reveals a similarly condescending attitude when the visitors ask the child-care worker Mrs. Nash a question:

> "What about the children who don't go [on a picnic]?" said Castle. "What do you do about the green-eyed monster?"
> Mrs. Nash was puzzled.
> "Jealousy. Envy," Castle elaborated. "Don't the children who stay home ever feel unhappy about it?"
> "I don't understand," said Mrs. Nash.
> "And I hope you won't try," said Frazier, with a smile. (91)

In a conversation with Burris, Mary Grove, one of the visitors who will ultimately join Walden Two, is depicted as not having understood Frazier's rather simple explanation of the labor credit varying from job to job according to desirability (63). Despite her lack of understanding—or perhaps precisely because of it—Mary will have her place in Walden Two. During a later scene, she introduces some communards to a new method of stitching. "It was evident from the general delight," reports Burris, "that Mary's contribution was appreciated, and I felt rather proud of her" (74–75).

The female characters that appear in *Walden Two* bake, stitch, care for the children, and can even achieve the position of being in charge of women's clothing. Skinner's utopia may be revolutionary in other respects; in terms of gender roles, it seems that Skinner was incapable of imagining anything but separate spheres for men and women, despite Frazier's claim that women bear children early so as not to be hampered in their careers.

If the women seem by and large incapable of comprehending anything that goes beyond intuition in Walden Two, the men—except Frazier, of course—are endowed with only slightly more analytical power. In an encounter with the dairy manager, it becomes apparent that even someone holding a managerial position is not expected to engage in abstract thought of any kind:

> Frazier let him take over, and the difference was surprising. Frazier's account had been highly selective. He preferred to talk about his beloved behavioral engineering or of man's triumph over nature—usually his more trivial triumphs at that. The Manager was unfamiliar with general principles. He was dealing with cows and milk and fodder and manure. A cream separator did not save labor or time; it got cream out of whole milk. Cows were not part of the cycle "from-grass-to-cow-to-man-to-grass"; they were Holsteins and Guernseys of certified health, giving so many pounds of butterfat annually. It was refreshing to get some plain fact. . . . While Frazier dreamt of economic structure and cultural design, he would get out the milk. (70–71)

The description of the dairy manager seems intended to stress the point that decision making is a profession like any other and should not be engaged in by people who are not good at it, just as Frazier accepts that he is not competent to speak about the dairy farm.

Almost all of the communards Skinner depicts in *Walden Two* are thus happily ignorant of the larger picture. They are, as Frazier had assured the visitors, "'free of the responsibility of planning.'" In contrast to the frequent portrayal of these ordinary members, scientists and planners are hardly mentioned throughout the novel. The longest passage about scientific experimentation is, interestingly, once again concerned with the improved tea service (25). In another passage, Frazier explains that he and "[o]ne of our

Planners, a young man named Simmons" (96), were mainly responsible for designing the educational system, yet he makes no further mention of Simmons. While describing the planner-manager system, Frazier mentions that the community "'supports a certain amount of research. Experiments are in progress in plant and animal breeding, the control of infant behavior, educational processes of several sorts, and the use of some of our raw materials'" (50). However, none of these experiments nor the scientists engaged in them are depicted in the novel.

Since Skinner does not believe that his governmental system could be misused, he provides for no safeguards. He reasons that members of Walden Two would accept the decisions of planners or managers only as long as they benefit from them. The only legitimization for a government at Walden Two is, after all, to sustain or create conditions that ensure the happiness of all members. It is, however, hard to see how a membership that is the very opposite of an informed citizenry could even keep track of the effect of economic or governmental conditions on their lives, let alone competently question decisions made by the planners.

Interestingly, while nobody can be pressured into obedience, "protest against the whole confounded system" is "unthinkable" at Walden Two, presumably because there is no cause for protest (32). In essence this means that there is no room for dissenting voices. Acceptance of the system is, however, based neither on punitive control nor propaganda. Since all members go through the Walden Two educational system, including the future planners and managers, it would not even occur to them to resort to punitive control, for this is a behavior that has been trained out of their behavioral repertoire. If anyone were to try it, he or she would soon discover that nobody at Walden Two can be pressured into obedience. "'We don't *propagandize,*'" explains Frazier. "'That's a basic principle.'" Unfortunately, while admitting that "'it would be possible'" (46), he does not give a reason for having adopted a no-propaganda policy. In view of the storm of protest over *Walden Two,* he may have done well to be more explicit on this point—among others.

## Behaviorism as Religion

Walden Two planners serve a maximum of ten years. "'Three of us,'" remarks Frazier casually, "'who've been on the Board since the beginning retire this year'" (48). Interestingly, then, Skinner places his novel at a turning point in the community's history: Frazier may be depicted as an outsider, but he is still the crucial figure in the community's founding and early development. He even admits as much:

> "But who's the dictator here?" said Frazier with what seemed like unbelievable naiveté.
> "Why, you, of course," said Castle.
> "I?"
> "Yes, you were the primum mobile, weren't you?"
> Frazier smiled.
> "I was? Well, I suppose you could say I gave the first push, but I'm not pushing now. There is no pushing, that's the whole thing. Set it up right, and it will run by itself." (219)

Is the fact that the visit to Walden Two takes place in the tenth year of the community's existence, the year Frazier will step down as a planner, an indication that Skinner himself was unable to truly imagine a society based on behavioral engineering running "by itself"? Talking to Burris, Frazier had called the members of Walden Two "his children" who are, according to his standards, "decently provided for." Do these metaphors not indicate that people are kept in a childlike state? What are we to make, then, of Frazier's assertion that he will not be an important figure in the community's future?

Skinner's solution to this question appears to be at odds with his demand that a permanently experimental attitude be adopted at Walden Two (106). Rather than educating his "children" about the basics of behavioral engineering and the labor-credit and governmental systems (thus ensuring that the community is functional without him), Skinner seems to suggest using the methods of organized religion to enforce the observance of a behavioral code. Thus, while Frazier, the founding father, is depicted as a knowledgeable behavioral engineer, the future of the community appears to rest largely on the perpetuation of the founder's ideas rather than on continued experimentation. Although Frazier repeatedly cites the use of scientific experimentation—especially in the area of human behavior—as the basis of all the community's practices, behaviorism comes close to being believed in religiously at Walden Two. Frazier describes service-like communal meetings that strengthen the communards' commitment to the "Behavior Code," something like the Walden Two catechism. Frazier explains that the community "'borrowed some of the practices of organized religion—to inspire group loyalty and strengthen the observance of the Code'" (185–86). These practices indicate that behaviorism is far more than a science for the Walden Two communards. Frazier even explicitly says that if "'the Code is too difficult for anyone or doesn't seem to be working to his advantage, he seeks the help of our psychologists. They're our "priests," if you like'" (186).

Perhaps Skinner meant to point out that once irrefutable scientific data have been gained, they have to be institutionalized in some way in order to have a long-lived influence on society. One could, however, interpret the need for an almost religious belief in behaviorism differently: with the vast majority of the members ignorant about behaviorism, what else can they do but *believe* in it *on faith?* The happy communard Burris talks to would definitely not have been capable of carrying out or even comprehending any scientific experiment whatsoever.

The impression of behaviorism taking the place of religion at Walden Two is further strengthened by a little scene at the beginning of the novel. The astonished visitors see a large flock of sheep that are only "kept together by a single length of string." Questioning Frazier's assertion that the sheep do not wander but respect the string as if it were an electric fence, Frazier makes an interesting admission: "'I should have told you,' said Frazier soberly, 'that no small part of the force of tradition is due to the quiet creature you see yonder.' He pointed to a beautiful sheep dog, which was watching us from a respectful distance. 'We call him the Bishop'" (16). Apart from the fact that a watchdog exists at all and is apparently still necessary as a last resort, it is noteworthy that the dog carries a name used in church hierarchies.

## Frazier: Founder and Leader?

A discussion of Skinner's utopian vision is not complete without a closer look at the community's founder. Frazier is a complex personality who is infinitely more interesting than any other character in the novel and "one of the most fascinating guides in utopian literature" in general (Roemer 134). It is, ironically, this fiercely individualistic person who pronounces the death of the individual in utopia. Throughout the novel, it is Frazier with whom the reader is confronted, not the utopians who benefited from behavioral engineering in their upbringing (and are thus threatening by implication to a humanist conception of the human being). In fact, since Walden Two has been in existence for only ten years, it would not be logically possible to present the reader with adult utopians raised in the behaviorist spirit. Yet this is probably not the only reason why it is Frazier who takes center stage in Skinner's novel: it is hard to see how a generation of people free of conflicting emotions could hold the interest of readers.

Frazier, on the other hand, is at the same time an ingenious scientist, a social reformer with pretensions to being god, and a social misfit. Throughout the novel, he is described as afflicted with "human" emotions. He is "slightly annoyed" when someone makes a good point that he had forgotten (19), he stands "alone and unnoticed against a wall" during a birthday party (33), he laughs "triumphantly" at his success in disconcerting the visitors (37), he snorts "in disgust" (38), shouts (55), smiles "with obvious delight" (58), is impatient (79), nervous (101), tender (131), and embarrassed (229). Frazier concludes that "'as a person I am a complete failure'" (234). Challenging Burris to admit that he does not like him, Frazier gives a good summary of his personality and how it relates to the utopian community in which he lives:

> "You think I'm conceited, aggressive, tactless, selfish. You're convinced that I'm completely insensitive to my effect upon others, except when the effect is calculated. You can't see in me any of the personal warmth or the straightforward natural strength which are responsible for the success of Walden Two. My motives are ulterior and devious, my emotions warped. In a word—of all the people you've seen in the past four days, you're sure that I'm one, at least, who couldn't possibly be a genuine member of any community."
>
> I still found nothing to say. It was as if Frazier were snatching the words away as I reached for them. He accepted my silence as assent.
>
> "Well, you're perfectly right," he said quietly. Then he stood up, drew back his arm, and sent the tile shattering into the fireplace.
>
> "But God damn it, Burris!" he cried, timing the "damn" to coincide with the crash of the tile. "Can't you see? *I'm-not-a-product-of-Walden-Two!*" He sat down. He looked at his empty hand, and picked up a second tile quickly, as if to conceal the evidence of his display of feeling. (233)

Skinner may have Frazier consider himself a failure because he lacks the self-control and equanimity resulting from the "ethical training" of the Walden Two educational system, yet many readers of *Walden Two,* such as Spencer Klaw, have not shared Frazier's sentiments: "For all that Frazier would be a most cantankerous and irritating companion, he is the only character in *Walden Two* one would care to spend any time with. It is likewise clear that it would be a dreary Utopia in which no one would ever grow up to be a cranky, stubborn, inventive iconoclast like Skinner" (51).

Klaw points out what Skinner has admitted: Frazier is in many ways a fictionalized version of himself, a point that has also been argued convincingly by Alan Elms (470–79). The fictional Frazier allowed Skinner to say things that he himself was not ready to say, while the narrator, Burris (Skinner's first name is Burrhus), represents Skinner's hesitance to let go of traditional values. *Walden Two* was, Skinner maintains, "a kind of self-therapy as the Burris side of me struggled to accept the Frazier side" (*Matter* 180).

Frazier may be an engaging character precisely because of his contradictory emotions, yet he is also the character who enraged readers more than any other in *Walden Two*. Although Frazier stresses repeatedly that the community is completely functional without him, his role in Walden Two is ambivalent enough to give readers the impression that he is crucial to its survival. While described as a social outcast most of the time, Frazier reveals himself as feeling almost godlike in "his heaven" (301). Frazier does not view his fellow communards as his equals. To Burris, he remarks that they "'are my children . . . I love them'" (282). It is hardly possible to express paternalism more clearly.

# 2 Behavioral Psychology and the Design of Society

SKINNER DEFENDED the social thinking that is at the root of *Walden Two* in numerous nonfictional writings. While I do not wish to equate Skinner's fictional with his nonfictional writings, I do think that a reading of *Walden Two* gains in depth when looking at Skinner's later writings.

The following discussion of Skinnerian behaviorism as expressed outside of his utopian novel will provide the context for the reception of *Walden Two*, which will be examined in the next chapter. *Walden Two* was his first explicit attempt at thinking through what his laboratory findings and experiments with animals might imply for the design of human society. By choosing the form of fiction, Skinner could let his protagonist Frazier "say things that I myself was not ready to say" (*Shaping* 297–98). Skinner remarks in the last volume of his autobiography that he "progressed mainly by becoming a convinced Frazierian" (*Matter* 206). In *Walden Two*, Skinner was still very much concerned with presenting his views in a way that would be acceptable to an American audience. In his later writings, this was not a concern anymore. Skinner's only published novel is, in several ways, more conciliatory in tone than his later, nonfictional writings.[6]

*Science and Human Behavior,* published in 1953, is a nonfictional version of the ideas expressed in *Walden Two.*[7] The book has a large middle section dealing in technical language with scientific experiments that Skinner had carried out with laboratory animals, thus attempting to give academic weight to his far-reaching conclusions concerning human behavior. Over the years, Skinner wrote several articles that are all variations of his basic theme: that society would benefit from placing the design of culture in the hands of those most suited for the task, behavioral engineers.[8]

None of his writings are as bold and outspoken as *Beyond Freedom and Dignity* (1971), a highly controversial book written in a popular style and intended for the general public. In fact, Skinner explicitly comments on his frequent use of the words "control" and "controller" in *Beyond Freedom and Dignity*—words he knew would incense his critics—by stating that "[n]othing is to be gained by using a softer word" (172).

Why this change of tone? Because, according to Skinner, nothing less than the survival of western society is at stake. Rather than asking what society can or ought to do for its citizens, he is concerned with how individuals can be induced to "behav[e] for the good of others" (*Beyond* 105). As Ernest Callenbach, a fellow utopian thinker mainly concerned with environmental issues (*Ecotopia*), observed in an interview: "It's true, however, that both Skinner and myself have recognized—which is not altogether easy in the hyper-individualism of American thought—that the primary issue has become survival, and that this is a species or social matter, not one of personal freedom or happiness. But granting priority to biological/social survival goes against the grain of the Protestant ethic, where it is the relationship between an individual and an extraterrestrial God that counts most" (393).

In placing survival first, the individual and his or her rights become secondary. Skinner is explicitly concerned with the welfare of the entire species, not with the individual. In *Beyond Freedom and Dignity,* Skinner makes his most explicit demand for a paradigm shift in how we think about ourselves. He maintains that his book is an effort "'to demonstrate how things go bad when you make a fetish out of individual freedom and dignity. If you insist that individual rights are the summum bonum, then the whole structure of society falls down'" (qtd. in Bjork 47). "Our culture has produced the science and technology it needs to save itself. It has the wealth needed for effective action," Skinner argues in *Beyond Freedom and Dignity.* "It has, to a considerable extent, a concern for its own future. But if it continues to take freedom or dignity, rather than its own survival, as its principal value, then it is possible that some other culture will make a greater contribution to the future" (173).

Skinner's perception of human society and its problems hinges on three basic assumptions. First, the humanist conception of the individual as a free agent responsible for his or her actions is a myth; human behavior is always subject to behavioral laws and can be studied and explained scientifically. Second, since there are no individuals who could make free choices, we must take charge of the environmental conditions governing human behavior rather than leaving these conditions to chance. And third, behavioral engineers, as the professionals who understand the laws of behavior, are best suited for the urgent task of redesigning society.

## The Concept of the Individual as a Myth

A central prerequisite for Skinner's proposed society is the negation of the idea of an individual possessed with freedom, dignity, and the ability to take personal responsibility for his or her actions, to choose between right and wrong. In Skinner's view, "[m]an is a machine in the sense that he is a complex system behaving in lawful ways" (*Beyond* 193). He realizes that the concept of man as a machine is at odds with major tenets of humanist thinking and maintains that humanism will have to be discarded in favor of a scientific view of human nature: "We are told that what is threatened is 'man qua man,' or 'man in his humanity,' or 'man as Thou not It,' or 'man as a person not a thing.' These are not very helpful expressions, but they supply a clue. What is being abolished is autonomous man—the inner man, the homunculus, the possessing demon, the man defended by the literatures of freedom and dignity. His abolition has long been overdue. Autonomous man is a device used to explain what we cannot explain any other way. He has been constructed from our ignorance, and as our understanding increases, the very stuff of which he is composed vanishes" (*Beyond* 191).

Skinner applauds the end of the construct of humans as free agents. He fully recognizes that most of his contemporaries find his conception of the individual "distasteful" (*Science* 449), yet he holds firmly to transferring his findings regarding animal behavior to human beings. He even maintains that "the highest human dignity may be to accept the facts of human behavior regardless of their momentary implications" (*Science* 449).

What, then, are the laws of behavior for which Skinner wishes to gain society's acceptance? Before turning to his ideas, it is necessary to briefly sketch the history of the then relatively young field of behavioral psychology on which Skinner built his own work.

In the late nineteenth century, instinct and environmental factors began to replace more mentalistic concepts of behavior. Skinner's most important immediate predecessors were Ivan Petrovich Pavlov (1849–1936) and John B. Watson (1878–1958). In a now famous experiment, Pavlov accidentally discovered the concept of the conditioned reflex. Working on the digestive processes of dogs, he noticed that after some repetitions, the dogs started salivating at the mere sound of a bell that they had previously heard immediately before receiving food. Pavlov became curious to uncover how a physiological process (in this case, salivation) can be triggered by a stimulus that is not naturally connected to it. In careful experimentation, he established a connection between an unconditioned stimulus (food) with a conditioned stimulus (the sound of a bell) and the process by which the conditioned stimulus can come to trigger the same response as the unconditioned stimulus.

While Pavlov, the physiologist, "stumbled" upon the idea of the conditioned reflex, Watson is generally credited with being the founder and main exponent of classical S-R (stimulus-response) behaviorism. His programmatic *Psychology from the Standpoint of a Behaviorist* (1919) became a "kind of manifesto of behaviorism" (Zimbardo and Gerrig 207). Watson stressed the importance of learning and the environment in the shaping of behavior and was not convinced of the importance of mentalistic concepts as well as pure instinct. He advocated a strictly experimental approach to understanding behavior rather than relying on introspection. Watsonian behaviorism was dominant during the 1920s and 1930s.

Classical behaviorism began to wane as experimenters felt the simple model of stimulus-response to be inadequate in describing complex behavior. Edward Tolman, among others, suggested that certain variables that influence behavior can not be studied directly, but their influence can be inferred from observable and measurable behavior. Neobehaviorism thus allows for a cognitive approach and is less rigid in its refusal of the inner life of a person as the proper subject matter of science.

B. F. Skinner's radical behaviorism—developed from the 1930s onwards—is much closer to Watson than to Tolman. Like Watson, Skinner focused on observable behavior to the complete exclusion of anything that was not measurable under laboratory conditions. As a main innovation, Skinner shifted his focus of attention to how behavior is shaped by its consequences and how to measure and influence these consequences. In classical conditioning as developed by Watson and Pavlov, the focus is on the connection between different types of stimuli (unconditioned and conditioned) and reflexes. In operant conditioning, the focus is on how spontaneously emitted behavior, so-called operant behavior, is shaped lawfully by its behavioral consequences.

After countless experiments with rats and pigeons, Skinner formulated three basic behavioral laws. First, behavior that is punished will be suppressed, but only as long as the threat of punishment is in place. As a means of achieving permanent behavioral changes, punishment is therefore ineffective. Second, behavior that is ignored will eventually cease to recur. And third, behavior that is reinforced will recur. The level of recurrence of behavior is dependant on the reinforcement schedule, that is, the means by which reinforcement is administered. For example, a pigeon pressing a lever may be reinforced for this behavior every thirty seconds (interval schedule), every fifth time it picks (ratio schedule), or randomly.

Skinner's research focused on the laws governing positive reinforcement, which he had determined early on as the most effective means of modifying behavior. In his laboratory, he experimented with various schedules of reinforcement and charted the behavioral responses of his experimental subjects; their responses indeed allowed an astonishing amount of precision in predicting behavior in other experimental subjects (*Science* 91–106).

## Planning Society Instead of Leaving Everything to Chance

Skinner's laboratory experiments led him to proclaim that human behavior, though more complex, will in time be similarly predictable. In analyzing western society with the concept in mind that human behavior is always determined by the environment, Skinner found much at fault with the controlling practices in place. If human behavior is controlled by the environment, then it does not make sense to view people as free agents responsible for their actions. Most importantly, it does not make sense to use punitive measures and expect any positive changes in behavior. As Krishan Kumar succinctly puts it:

> For [Skinner], the belief in punishment as the principal form of control is
> part and parcel of the whole historical and philosophical legacy which he has
> unremittingly opposed: the legacy of classical liberalism, and in particular the
> conception of the individual and his relation to society. Liberalism postulates
> the free, autonomous, rational individual. To this idea of freedom, Skinner
> contends, the concept of punishment is a necessary correlate. Individual free-
> dom implies the idea of individual responsibility, and responsibility requires
> the threat of punishment, for otherwise no credit attaches to the individual

for behaving well, nor can he be made to accept the consequences of behaving badly. What Skinner rather disparagingly calls "the literature of freedom and dignity" has, therefore, been responsible for giving philosophical underpinning and respectability to the otherwise barbarous idea of punishment. ("Utopia" 358)

Instead of holding on to the concept of free will and the idea of punishing or praising the actions of free agents, Skinner urges his audience to free human beings from the erroneous assumption that they can act any way they wish if only they decide to do so. Instead of punishing the supposedly freely chosen actions of free people, we should accept human beings as complex organisms who *always* act according to laws of behavior. In competitive societies that hold on to humanist concepts (free will, personal responsibility, and so on), people are not free at all: they do what they are told to do because they fear sanctions if they fail to do so. It is most likely punitive control that prompts children to do their homework, not enthusiasm for studying. Most adults go to work not because they enjoy doing so but because they might lose their jobs if they do not. Says Skinner: "Government has always been the special field of aversive control. The state is frequently defined in terms of the power to punish, and jurisprudence leans heavily upon the associated notion of personal responsibility" (Rogers and Skinner 1059). Though this arrangement may seem successful at first glance, it is oppressive and coercive by nature and harmful for the survival of our culture in the long run because most people resent punitive control. For this reason, life in modern society is characterized by aggressiveness and overconsumption, to name only two of the most important outlets for this resentment. Even worse, pollution, overpopulation, and the threat of nuclear warfare endanger the very existence of life as we know it (*Beyond* 144). As long as punitive control continues to be at the center of our personal, economic, and governmental environment, argues Skinner, it will be impossible to "live together peacefully, happily, and productively" (Foreword vi–vii). Only by moving beyond the legacy of humanist ideas like freedom and dignity can society finally find its way into a new age.

## Behavioral Psychologists Taking Charge

Since Skinner was firmly convinced that human behavior is *always* dependent—apart from genetic factors—on outward influences (or, rather, that outward influences are observable and reliable predictors of future behavior), the main question becomes who should take charge of these influences. "We cannot choose a way of life in which there is no control," he maintained time and again. "We can only change the controlling conditions" (*About* 190). Logically, then, Skinner asks what *kind* of controlling environment humanity ought to create for itself to ensure the survival of the human race, but not whether control should be instituted at all. "The real issue," he stresses, "is the effectiveness of techniques of control" (*Beyond* 70). In his view, wanting to choose freedom from control means to cling with "nostalgia" (206) to an outdated concept of human nature—which at this point in history is not only naïve but also dangerous because it stands in the way of redesigning western culture with a more rational and scientific understanding of human nature in mind (38–39). "To refuse to accept control," Skinner argued repeatedly, means "merely to leave control in other hands" (*Science* 439).

In Skinner's view, behavioral engineers are the obvious candidates for taking the control out of the hand of chance and/or politicians who operate with an outdated concept of human nature in mind. Since Skinner identified positive reinforcement as the most effective way of producing behavioral changes, these behavioral engineers, as the specialists with the most thorough understanding of the laws of behavior, will implement reinforcement schedules that will enhance their society's chances of survival. Punitive control is thus clearly not a feature of Skinner's new society. It may work in the short run, he stresses, but it provokes a negative reaction on the part of those controlled punitively, so that it ultimately backfires (*Beyond* 103). Positive reinforcement thus becomes an evolutionary necessity: "A culture needs the support of its members, and it must provide for the pursuit and achievement of happiness if it is to prevent disaffection or defection" (145). Positive reinforcement alone can produce stable behavioral changes and has the added advantage of avoiding problematic by-products such as resentment, aggression, and revolt.

Yet one has to ask how Skinner can be so sure about which behavior his behavioral engineers ought to reinforce. What is the guideline? Unfortunately, Skinner only answers this crucial question in passing. As Kumar points out, "Skinner has always been impatient with those who demanded to know what the social purpose or goal of his utopia is. To him, the goals of any perfected society are self-evident—better health, better education, greater knowledge, more fulfilling work and leisure, harmonious relationships. The problem of ultimate values is not a serious issue of contention." Assuming a consensus about the nature of the good life, Skinner is concerned with means, not ends ("Utopia" 349).

The question of how to determine the exact values that are to be reinforced by society's psychologists was often ignored by Skinner and certainly did not figure largely in *Walden Two*. At a later point, however, Skinner did provide a guiding principle for his new society: "Such a technology [behavioral engineering] is ethically neutral. It can be used by villain or saint. There is nothing in a methodology which determines the values governing its use. We are concerned here, however, not merely with practices, but with the design of a whole culture, and the survival of a culture then emerges as a special kind of value" (*Beyond* 143). The neutral technology thus becomes the means to an end—survival—according to which it can be evaluated. Designating the survival of a culture as the ultimate goal and value for societal reconstruction thus fulfills an important function in Skinner's thinking: If survival is paramount, then social practices can be measured by a seemingly clear guideline, simply by asking whether they promote or obstruct the survival of the species.

Skinner continues his argument by saying that since survival is the *only* valid ultimate value, a society employing an effective technology that will promote species survival is also scientifically sound. It is not an ethical agency but simply evolution that determines the value of a practice: "Things are good (positively reinforcing) or bad (negatively reinforcing) presumably because of the contingencies of survival under which the species evolved" (*Beyond* 99). A society based on scientific insight will therefore be able to determine how to enhance its chances of survival in the evolutionary process: "How will a more effective technology be used? By whom and to what end? These are really questions about reinforcers. Some things have become 'good' during the evolutionary history of the species, and they may be used to induce people to behave for the 'good of others'" (120). Skinner continues by outlining how science-oriented societal planners could proceed: "When a culture induces some of its members to work for its survival, what are they to do? They will need to foresee some of the difficulties the culture will encounter.... It may be enough simply to observe a steady increase in the number of people on the earth, in the size and location of nuclear stockpiles, or in the pollution of the environment and the depletion of natural resources; we may then change practices to induce people to have fewer children, spend less on nuclear weapons, stop polluting the environment, and consume resources at a lower rate, respectively" (144).

If survival of the species is paramount, and if the practices that promote survival in the evolutionary process are best determined scientifically—by observation, experimental changes, and evaluation of the changes according to their survival value—then it follows that scientists will be best suited for the task of redesigning society. And since the most fundamental problems of our time are rooted in human behavior, behavioral scientists ought to be the principal designers of the new society. With species survival as the ultimate value in mind, Skinner lays out the goal and methodology of the new society as follows:

> But for whom is a powerful technology of behavior to be used? Who is to use it? And to what end? We have been implying that the effects of one practice are better than those of another, but on what grounds? What is the good against which something else is called better? Can we define the good life? . . . It is usually implied that the answers are out of reach of science. Physicists and biologists often agree, and with some justification, since their sciences do not, indeed, have the answers. Physics may tell us how to build a nuclear bomb but not whether it should be built. Biology may tell us how to control birth and postpone death but not whether we ought to do so. Decisions about the uses of science seem to demand a kind of wisdom which, for some curious reason, scientists are denied. If they are to make value judgments at all, it is only with the wisdom they share with people in general.
>
> It would be a mistake for the behavioral scientist to agree. How people feel about facts, or what it means to feel anything, is a question for which a science of behavior should have an answer. (*Beyond* 96–97)

Behavioral engineers, according to Skinner, are the one group of scientists whose domain includes making value judgments. Biologists and physicists may not have more than "the wisdom they share with people in general" concerning value judgments, but behavioral scientists apparently do. Many critics have harshly disagreed with Skinner on this point. They stress the danger of placing too much power in the hands of a few; a theme they feel runs through all of Skinner's writings on society, starting with *Walden Two*.

# 3    Skinner's Utopian Vision and the Issue of Control

ACADEMIC AND PUBLIC REACTIONS to Skinner's societal proposals suggest that the behavioral psychologist was correct in assuming that he would incense many people. His social thinking, as expressed relatively cautiously in *Walden Two* and explicitly in nonfictional publications, has been attacked on many grounds by a multitude of critics. In the 1950s and 1960s, well-known critics, such as the humanist Joseph Wood Krutch, the psychologist Carl Rogers, the philosopher Arthur Koestler, and the linguist Noam Chomsky, all argued against Skinner's call for a society run by behaviorists.

Public debate about Skinner's ideas lagged behind considerably. It was only in the early seventies, peaking with the 1971 publication of *Beyond Freedom and Dignity*, that Skinner and his controversial ideas were a topic of intense public discussion. By then, many people had heard of the Aircrib (a cubicle designed by Skinner to provide maximum comfort for babies), the so-called Skinner box (an apparatus used in his experiments), and the concept of teaching machines (machines providing positive reinforcement for students as they go through a process of programmed learning). At the peak of his fame, Skinner's picture appeared on the cover of *Time* magazine on September 20, 1971, with a feature story presenting his provocative ideas in an article entitled "Skinner's Utopia: Panacea, or Path to Hell?" For a short time, Skinner became the "hottest item on national and big-city talk shows." Within a month, "millions of Americans had read or heard about B. F. Skinner and *Beyond Freedom and Dignity*" (Bjork 192).

Amid this newfound fame, *Walden Two* was suddenly read and taken seriously. Skinner had had considerable trouble even finding a publisher for his novel, causing a three-year delay in publication (Skinner, *Matter* 44). Between 1948 and 1960, only nine thousand copies of *Walden Two* were sold, while eight thousand were sold in 1961 alone. By the early 1970s, annual sales approached a hundred thousand (Bjork 162).

These new readers were presumably not interested in Skinner's skills as a novelist but read *Walden Two* in search of statements about behavioral engineering and the role Skinner envisioned for behavioral engineers. In the ensuing debate, the question of what Skinner is really saying has taken center stage, almost to the exclusion of *how* he says what he says. For many of the communards who were inspired by *Walden Two*, however, the fictional aspects of the novel—like its complex guide figure and the charming little details in the depiction of the rural community—were quite important. For the communards, *Walden Two* could not be reduced to a treatise on behavioral engineering as applied to society. These two widely divergent readings of *Walden Two*, both of which were to be found among the novel's enthusiasts, led to considerable misunderstandings within the communities trying to use Skinner's utopian novel as a model.

Despite the fact that much of the debate surrounding Skinner was virtually ignored in the communities movement, an understanding of the criticism is important, if only because much of what went wrong in the Walden Two communities can be explained in light of the points brought forward by Skinner's critics.

Most critics take issue with all of Skinner's basic assumptions: First, his denial of the existence of individuals as free agents; second, his advocacy of control for the good of society; and third, his contention that (behavioral) science can produce values.

## The Attack on Skinner's Notion of the Nonexistence of the Individual

Skinner's early attempt to put himself in line with American utopianism and thought did little to placate his critics. The title *Walden Two*—in reference to Thoreau's *Walden*, a classic of nineteenth-century American literature with utopian implications—leads readers to expect a text that is somehow a successor to *Walden* or otherwise closely related to it.[9] However, there is a stark contrast between the important role Thoreau assigns to the individual and the virtual dissolution of the very concept of individualism in *Walden Two*. *Walden* is a one-man utopia focusing on inner reform (Meyer 7), whereas *Walden Two* is in direct opposition to inner reform. Indeed, inner reform is an impossibility if there is no such thing as an inner person that could be reformed.

Critics of *Walden Two* jump on this point and frequently focus almost exclusively on the chapters depicting the child-rearing practices. The most influential of these critics was Joseph Wood Krutch. In his critique *The Measure of Man* (1953), he charges Skinner with confusing education with conditioning. He points out that "'conditioning' is achieved by methods which by-pass, or, as it were, short-circuit those very reasoning faculties which education proposes to cultivate and exercise" (208). Skinner's proposals, according to Krutch, are of a chilling emotionlessness, a point-blank disregard of all the values that differentiate human beings from animals, namely consciousness, language, feelings, and thoughts. According to Krutch, the children at Walden Two are not being taught to lead their lives as free agents of their actions. The result is a generation of people condemned to "automatic virtue ... [whose] desires, tastes, convictions, and ideals are precisely what the experimenter wants to make them" (209 and 204). Peter Wolfe, in his essay "*Walden Two* Twenty-Five Years Later: A Retrospective Look," agrees with Krutch by arguing that Skinner's methods turn "the individual into a colorless machine" and that "subduing the dreamer in him leaves but a ragged shadow" (21).

The intensely negative scholarly reaction to the fictional community's educational system foreshadowed the public outcry against the ideas expressed more brazenly in *Beyond Freedom and Dignity* two decades later. Skinner's social ideas, many people realized, threaten a concept that is at the very root of the American mentality: the individual. Skinner explicitly puts the survival of the species first, rejecting the idea that there even *is* such a thing as the individual—equipped with higher faculties and capable of personal responsibility, freedom, and dignity—that *could* be put first. Furthermore, Skinner does not lament the loss of the concept of the individual, he applauds it. In doing so, he puts himself in direct opposition to what Bjork has called the "basic national creed" (206), individuality as an "American birthright" (194). Bjork elaborates that there are concepts in *Beyond Freedom and Dignity* that "burrowed into the marrow of American belief, something that said that if the American people continued to embrace a creed whose bedrock was the pursuit of individual freedom and dignity, they would have an impoverished future if they had any future at all. *Beyond Freedom and Dignity* took level aim at the way many Americans saw themselves—past, present, and future—and argued that their views were not simply misplaced but socially dangerous. The book challenged what most Americans believed it meant to be American" (193).

## The Attack on the Advocacy of Control for the Good of Society

Arguing that there are no such things as individuals capable of making decisions and taking responsibility for their actions, Skinner urged society to accept that we are always controlled by our environment and that we should therefore take charge of the controlling circumstances instead of leaving them to chance.

However, many critics have asked who controls the controllers for which Skinner calls. As a safeguard against the misuse of power—presumably for those instances where a scientist goes astray—Skinner thought it might be enough to make "the controller a member of the group he controls" (*Beyond* 164). Furthermore, a scientist/designer would understand that the "ultimate strength of the controller depends upon the strength of those whom he controls," so he (the controller is never a she in Skinner's writings) would refrain from exploiting his subjects (*Science* 443).

The supposed safeguards against misuse of power have appeared strikingly weak to many readers and "evasive in the extreme" (Kumar, "Utopia" 374). Many critics therefore charge Skinner with taking "the totalitarian position which justifies all illiberal regimes: 'I know what is good for you'" (Bethlehem 93).

Consider for a moment that Skinner wrote his novel in the summer of 1945. His trust in the benevolence of scientists and omnipotent decision makers was apparently not shaken by the events happening around him in the real world. In fact, Skinner begins his introduction to the 1976 publication of *Walden Two* with the astonishing statement that the "early summer of 1945, when I wrote *Walden Two*, was not a bad time for Western Civilization." He continues by explaining that Hitler was defeated, Russia an ally, the bomb not yet dropped, and environmental problems were within bounds. The dissatisfactions that led him to write *Walden Two* were "personal": at forty-one, Skinner was a young professor who had just been forced to move and leave a group of musicians upon taking up a new job; he had to watch his wife's unhappiness with being a housewife and his daughter's unsatisfactory first year at school ("Walden Two" v).

In view of Skinner's potentially dictatorial planner-manager system, his statement that 1945 was "not a bad time" for western civilization seems rather baffling. It reveals a Skinner not very imaginative about the origin and nature of totalitarian regimes. Apparently the fact that the United States had won the war was sufficient for him not to bother with the details of recent history.

## The Attack on Skinner's Claim That Behavioral Science Can Determine Values

Skinner's introductory remark that "personal" dissatisfactions led him to write *Walden Two* is interesting in another respect as well: in his later writings, he puts great emphasis on the necessity of employing behavioral techniques in the design of society because survival is at stake. This is his final justification for placing the control of society into the hands of behavioral engineers. However, while writing *Walden Two* out of personal dissatisfactions, societal survival was apparently not yet a concern of his. Are we to conclude that behavioral engineers are the best decision makers in Skinner's view, regardless of whether or not survival as an ultimate value provides a supposedly objective guideline?

Take, for example, the issue of positive reinforcement versus punishment. Skinner's main argument for propagating positive reinforcement is its effectiveness (*Beyond* 70). The question of legitimacy does not enter into the equation. The new society rejects punitive control because it is inefficient and counterproductive in the long run, not because it is considered ethically unacceptable regardless of its (in)effectiveness. If his research had revealed that punishment was more effective, would that have justified its use?

As another example of value judgments being at the root of Skinner's supposedly neutral guideline, consider his explanation of whose survival is to be guaranteed. Skinner seems to use "my group," culture in general, western civilization, and mankind synonymously, leaving the reader to wonder just whose survival is paramount. Could not the survival of mankind be at odds with the survival of a certain group? What if the survival of the human race necessitated the demise of individuals? Skinner steers clear of all of these difficult questions by assuming that there is always a solution that is best for all. He tacitly assumes that humanity's survival is best guaranteed by having the United States take the lead in building peaceful and small settlements.

Leaving aside the question of which group's survival Skinner has in mind, the more fundamental question is why survival should be the ultimate value at all. It is generally acknowledged by most philosophers that values (and especially ultimate values) are beyond the realm of scientific reason. Anne E. Freedman, in her study of Skinner's societal proposals, points out that "scientific expertise is irrelevant in the realm of values" and that "Skinner, as a behavioral scientist, is no more nor less qualified than anyone else to decide what is right or wrong" (unit 6, p. 3).

Skinner, however, by calling the survival of a culture a "special kind of value," conveniently treats the value of *his* choice as if it were not a choice but a given: "Whether we like it or not, survival is the ultimate criterion. . . . Do not ask me why I want mankind to survive. I can only tell you why I want to breathe. Once the relation between a given step and the survival of my group has been pointed out, I will take that step. And it is the business of science to point out just such relations" (*Cumulative* 34).

Skinner thus treats survival as a value that is somehow obvious and also obviously paramount, without providing any explanation of why reincarnation or pleasing God (perhaps by dying a martyr) or eating popcorn could not equally be proclaimed the ultimate value by somebody else. Instead, Skinner introduces survival into his supposedly scientific construction as an intuitive given and sees little reason to fear behavioral engineers as those whose job it is to make value judgments for the rest of humanity. The rigorousness of the scientific environment, he argues, will induce them to remain honest:

> The scientist works under contingencies that minimize immediate personal reinforcers. No scientist is "pure," in the sense of being out of reach of immediate reinforcers, but other consequences of his behavior play an important role. If he designs an experiment in a particular way, or stops an experiment at a particular point, because the result will then confirm a theory bearing his name, or will have industrial uses from which he will profit, or will impress the agencies that support his research, he will almost certainly run into trouble. The published results of scientists are subject to rapid checks by others, and the scientist who allows himself to be swayed by consequences that are not part of his subject matter is likely to find himself in difficulties. To say that scientists are therefore more moral or ethical than other people, or that they have a more finely developed ethical sense, is to make the mistake of attributing to the scientist what is actually a feature of the environment in which he works. (*Beyond* 166)

Skinner seems to forget here that the ultimate value on which all of his assumptions rest—the survival of the human species—is something that he arrived at intuitively. As he said himself: "Do not ask me why I want mankind to survive. I can only tell you why I want to breathe" (*Cumulative* 34). This is hardly the description of a scientific experiment that can be subjected to "rapid checks by others." The basic problem remains: a scientist can tell you how to build a nuclear bomb but not whether to use it. A behavioral engineer may be able to tell you how to modify a person's behavior but not what modification is called for and what the limits of modification ought to be.

The extent of Skinner's naiveté regarding the misuse of power is hard to determine. It is not that he did not read his critics, at least initially. In his autobiography, for example, he quotes Karl Popper at length:

> "Skinner is an enemy of freedom and democracy. He has explained his con-
> tempt for freedom quite openly in his book *Beyond Freedom and Dignity.*
> He has expounded it many years before in a book *Walden Two*, which is the
> dream of a very kind but megalomaniac behaviorist who defends a behav-
> iorist dictatorship. . . . I regard these two books—especially *Beyond Freedom
> and Dignity*—as worse and more dangerous than the most fundamentalist
> religious tract: there is a mixture of naiveté, sheer ignorance, arrogation of
> omniscience, and Caesarean megalomania in these books, which is, in my
> opinion, far more urgent to combat than the churches." (Qtd. in *Matter*
> 391–92)

In 1956, Skinner engaged in a debate with the humanist psychologist Carl Rogers.[10] However, by the time *Beyond Freedom and Dignity* was published in 1971, Skinner showed a singular lack of concern about his critics' attacks on his social thinking. "'I never answer any of my critics,'" Skinner once told a journalist. "'I generally don't even read them. I have better things to do with my time than clear up their misunderstanding'" (qtd. in Rice 90). He has even suggested that his critics exhibit neurotic and even psychotic behavior in their attempt to cling to traditional concepts, claiming that there are "signs of emotional instability in those who have been deeply affected by the literature" of freedom (*Beyond* 157). Asked why he tends not to quote other authorities in his work, he explained that there had "'scarcely been any authority'" before the "'advent of an experimental analysis'" that he felt was worth quoting (qtd. in Bjork 200).

Skinner's disregard of his critics in his later life did little to convince them of the soundness of his proposals. Rogers saw in Skinner's proposals a "seri-ous underestimation of the problem of power" (Rogers and Skinner 1061). Furthermore, Rogers speculates that Skinner himself would not want to be a mindlessly happy and productive member of the society he proposes: "I can only feel that he was choosing these goals for others, not for himself. I would hate to see Skinner become 'well-behaved,' as that term would be defined for him by behavioral scientists. . . . And the most awful fate I can imagine for him would be to have him constantly 'happy.' It is the fact that he is very unhappy about many things which makes me prize him" (Rogers and Skinner 1061).

Skinner was comfortable discarding Rogers's concerns, yet many critics agree with the questions Rogers raised as early as 1956: "Who will be controlled? Who will exercise control? What type of control will be exercised? Most important of all, toward what end or what purpose, or in the pursuit of what value, will control be exercised?" (Rogers and Skinner 1060).

It was precisely these questions that tore many of the Walden Two communities apart.

## Notes

1. For an introduction to the history of utopian fiction, see Kumar, *Utopianism*.

2. The dinner scene in *Walden Two* is, once again, reminiscent of a similar scene in Bellamy's *Looking Backward* (124).

3. For all their similarities in the work system, Skinner and Bellamy differ fundamentally in their view of the worker for whose benefit the labor-credit system is instituted. While Bellamy also thought that his system was not due to a "moral new birth of humanity" but to "a changed environment" (196), an assessment very much in line with Skinner's thinking, he also proclaimed "that human nature in its essential qualities is good, not bad," and that humans were merely set free in the Boston of the year 2000 to live out their natural goodness (203). As will be discussed in more detail later on, Skinner's utopians have no "faith" in human nature at all, neither in "innate goodness" nor "evil" (*Walden Two* 182).

4. The principles of behavioral engineering will be discussed in more detail in the next chapter.

5. In contrast to the favorable comparisons between behavioral engineering and religious teachings in *Walden Two*, Skinner's tone in discussing religion is decidedly detached in *Beyond Freedom and Dignity*. Whereas a religious person may be inclined to at least entertain the thought of positive reinforcement as a secular version of "love your enemies" upon reading *Walden Two*, he or she would probably find little pleasure in reading the following passage in *Beyond Freedom and Dignity*: "A religious agency is a special form of government under which 'good' and 'bad' become 'pious' and 'sinful.' Contingencies involving positive and negative reinforcement, often of the most extreme sort, are codified—for example, as commandments—and maintained by specialists, usually with the support of ceremonies, rituals, and stories. . . . A person does not support a religion because he is devout; he supports it because of the contingencies arranged by the religious agency" (110–11).

6. Although *Walden Two* is Skinner's only published work of fiction, he was no stranger to literature. During college, his curriculum emphasized literature and com-

position. The young student thus resolved to be a writer, especially after receiving encouragement from Robert Frost, whom Skinner had met during a summer school session (Bjork 31–51). Skinner gave up on his plans to be a writer after a year, concluding in 1926 that he had "'failed as a writer because [he] had nothing important to say'" (qtd. in Bjork 55). By the time Skinner wrote *Walden Two* in 1945, he did have something to say, and he made good use of his knowledge of literary writing.

7. Skinner was asked to write *Science and Human Behavior* by his publisher Macmillan as a precondition for accepting *Walden Two* for publication (Bjork 153).

8. See Skinner, "Design of Experimental Communities," "Utopia as an Experimental Culture," and "News from Nowhere, 1984."

9. Skinner is not wholly responsible for associating his utopia this strongly with *Walden*, since it was his publisher, Charles Anderson of Macmillan, who finally chose the title (Skinner, *Matter* 44). Skinner, however, had intended to call his novel "The Sun Is But a Morning Star," the last sentence of *Walden*, indicating that he had aimed at drawing a connection between Thoreau and his own work (Bjork 147). Furthermore, *Walden Two* is not only the title of the novel but also the name of the fictional community, and the community's name was chosen by Skinner himself. Although baffling at first, there are indeed similarities between *Walden* and *Walden Two*, as Skinner also elaborates in an article entitled "Walden (One) and Walden Two" (1973). Skinner, like Thoreau, is suspicious of governments. Both advocate simplicity instead of mindless overconsumption, and both recommend pragmatism and making do with whatever is at hand (Bjork 147).

10. The debate was published as "Some Issues Concerning the Control of Human Behavior: A Symposium" (Rogers and Skinner).

# PART 2

# The Reception
# of *Walden Two*
# among Behaviorists

# 4 The Road Not Taken: Skinner, Experimental Communalism, and Token Economies

"ALMOST FROM THE MOMENT the book appeared," reports Skinner's biographer Daniel Bjork, there were "scattered efforts to start a behaviorally engineered community" (160). In 1948, a group of young people in Minneapolis, where Skinner had taught from 1936 to 1945, tried to set up an experimental community. A group at Yale made an effort to live communally along the lines of *Walden Two* in 1949, while another group led by Arthur Gladstone, again in New Haven, tried around 1955 (Skinner, *Matter* 9; Bjork 160). However, all of these early efforts were short-lived and remained largely in the planning phase. Several readers wrote to Skinner to express an interest in living at a Walden Two community but never followed through (Skinner, *Matter* 8).

During the first decade after the publication of his utopian novel, it appears that Skinner himself was the most committed Walden Two enthusiast around. In 1955, on sabbatical from Harvard, he seriously considered the feasibility of a real Walden Two: "I had time to dream, and a favorite theme was an experimental community. As a child I had particularly liked a song called 'Beautiful Isle of Somewhere,' which my grandmother and grandfather Burrhus played on their phonograph. It was the utopian dream—of an ideal world, not yet realized. *Walden Two* was different; it was, I thought, plausible here and now—more so, in fact, than when I had written the book" (*Matter* 83).

Ten years after he wrote his utopian novel, Skinner was "brimming with enthusiasm," feeling that Walden Two "'can be done, and that it will be the most reinforcing experiment in the century'" (qtd. in Bjork 160). Skinner wrote notes to himself about various aspects of the community that was to be called Lifeguild, which he carefully collected in a folder labeled "Design of a Culture" (Klaw 50). In the early 1960s, with steadily rising sales of *Walden*

*Two,* Skinner gave a "sort of recruiting talk" at several colleges and universities. An increasing number of people wrote to him about wanting to join a Walden Two community (Klaw 46).

Despite this rise in utopian activities, Skinner's interests began to veer in a different direction. He became more and more interested in education and put most of his energy into the development of a teaching machine, a device that would encourage students to master educational material in a step-by-step process at their own speed, with positive reinforcement for each completed step. This concept of "programmed instruction" became Skinner's "most ambitious attempt to apply positive reinforcement to society at large," slowly pushing plans for a utopian community into the background (Bjork 166). In his autobiography, Skinner notes that the "utopian dreaming" during his sabbatical had been "short-lived" (*Matter* 251). By the mid 1960s, he felt sure that his place was in the university, not a utopian community: "After long consideration I have decided that it would not be well for me personally to undertake an experimental community. I have a great many things planned for the next five years of an intellectual nature all of which bear, I think, on the eventual success of a radical reform of our way of life, and I do not feel that I should jeopardize those plans on the chance that something of a much more practical nature could be put through" (*Matter* 254–55).

Skinner's waning interest in founding a utopian community based on behavioral engineering never failed to baffle the enthusiasts *Walden Two* attracted in the 1960s and 1970s. Skinner, however, maintained that his interests were firmly of an "intellectual nature." Pressed about the topic, he usually added a more personal reason for not founding or joining a Walden Two community. "'I'd have to get a divorce right away,'" he said, because his "'wife doesn't believe in community'" (qtd. in Bjork 151). And indeed, Skinner's wife Eve commented in the 1971 *Time* article that catapulted Skinner to public fame that she and her husband "'had tremendous arguments about *Walden Two.* I wouldn't like it; I just like change and privacy'" (qtd. in Heyman 53). In 1967, Skinner gave a rather interesting third reason for not embarking on a Walden Two venture: "'Of course, I do need stimulation and a community of 1,000 would not be likely to have in it many other people interested in my field. Correspondence is not an adequate substitute'" (qtd. in Bjork 165).

Apparently, then, Skinner believed that an environment that he thought would be reinforcing enough for other people would fail to satisfy his own needs. The statement also reinforces the impression that Walden Two was not envisioned by Skinner as a society in which all members are equal partners in the scientific designing of a better society. If Skinner expected that there would not be many other people interested in his field—which is, after all, the field that is to be the very basis of the new society—then it follows logically that only a few of the people would be knowledgeable about behavioral science, and hence that only a few people would do the designing. However, since Skinner never did try communal living, how he would have acted in a communal setting remains a matter for speculation.

While Skinner slowly abandoned his plans for a utopian community, readers of *Walden Two* took up the idea. Behavioral science as formulated by Skinner reached its peak of societal influence in the 1960s and early 1970s, coinciding almost exactly with the heyday of communal living, and it was in this atmosphere of dual excitement that some behaviorists became serious about trying the good life as proposed in *Walden Two*.

In a 1968 survey of department chairmen at American universities, Skinner was "chosen overwhelmingly as the most influential figure in modern psychology" (Rice 27). In the late 1940s, Skinner and some of his colleagues had begun to formalize their field of study by founding academic societies and journals. By 1968, behaviorists were officially recognized as a separate division by the American Psychological Association, came together for conferences organized by the Association of Behavior Analysis, and published academic papers in two newly founded journals, the *Journal of the Experimental Analysis of Behavior* and the *Journal of Applied Behavioral Analysis*.[1] With these professional activities in the academic realm, behaviorists began to develop "'a new identity as an in-group, as a "movement,"'" recalls Schoenfeld, who was at the time a fellow behaviorist at Columbia (qtd. in Bjork 144).

Since behaviorism was a fairly new branch of psychology, the field was dominated by younger scientists who were at the beginning of their careers. With youthful optimism—and backed up by Skinner's often startling success in training pigeons and rats to perform tasks, which found much public attention—many of these scientists believed that the possibilities of behavioral engineering were boundless. Believing that they had the scientific expertise to revolutionize the world, combined with living during a time in which the media reported often about the upsurge of experimental communities and their rapid demise (McLaughlin and Davidson 92–93), it is perhaps not surprising that a number of young behaviorists were eager to rush to the aid of the utopian cause:

> In reading descriptions of past attempts at experimental living, one is struck
> by the frequency with which behavioral problems are mentioned. Many

people didn't do their share of the work, others weren't thrifty enough, tools and equipment were ruined, people were argumentative or cruel, and so on. The procedures that were used to control these problems included social ostracism, expulsion, and mutual criticism. Apparently, these techniques were not sufficient to solve the problems, which recurred and, reportedly, led to the dissolution of the experimental communities. Thus, some systematic techniques for increasing the occurrence of socially desirable behaviors and decreasing the occurrence of undesirable behaviors seem to be needed to create a successful Utopia. In short, what seems to have been missing in all of the attempts at creating a better community is a science of behavior—a set of techniques for engineering the desired behavioral and cultural changes in the members of the community.

B. F. Skinner, in his Utopian novel *Walden Two*, speculated on what a community based on such a science of behavior might be like. Such a science has clearly emerged since Skinner wrote *Walden Two*. (Miller and Feallock 74)

The above quotation indicates that these readers of *Walden Two* were behaviorists first, and they analyzed the problems of communal living from a behavioral point of view. This already points to a difficulty in pinpointing such readers' understanding of *Walden Two* and its influence on communal activities: this group of readers was very much aware of Skinner's scientific writings and drew no dividing line between *Walden Two*, Skinner's only work of fiction, and any of his other texts.

Also, many of these young behaviorists were engaged in setting up reinforcement systems, so-called token economies, in closed institutions such as mental hospitals, prisons, or classrooms for special education. Token economies are systems of reinforcement in which the occurrence of desired behavior—for example, sitting quietly or being on time—is reinforced by a member of the staff with a token that can be exchanged for privileges such as watching television (Ulrich, "Operant Conditioning" 31). It seems likely that these designers of token economies in closed institutions considered the implementation of token economies in utopian communities as well, and Skinner explicitly points in that direction in *Beyond Freedom and Dignity* by saying that "it should be possible to design a world in which behavior likely to be punished seldom or never occurs. We try to design such a world for those who cannot solve the problem of punishment for themselves, such as babies, retardates, or psychotics, and if it could be done for everyone, much time and energy would be saved" (62).

With regard to the impact of *Walden Two* on the majority of behaviorist readers, it therefore seems that wanting to create a functional utopia was closely connected in their minds to an activity they were already engaged in, creating controlled conditions in closed settings: "Ayllon and Azrin worked with a group of about 45 institutionalized 'mental patients' in a state mental hospital. This group, though made up of so-called 'abnormal' individuals, had many of the same problems that any community of 'normals' would have. . . . As these problems are common to any group-living situation, it can be argued that the technology developed by Ayllon and Azrin is relevant to experimental communities. . . . The experiment that we will describe in the following pages takes another step toward developing a behavioral technology for a voluntary community of adults" (Miller and Feallock 75).

It seems likely, therefore, that the atmosphere described in *Walden Two* was familiar to many of the behaviorist readers of the sixties and seventies who were involved in establishing token economies in mental hospitals, prisons, and residential centers for handicapped children. One could argue with considerable justice that the line of argument Frazier presents for his utopian community Walden Two is not fundamentally different from the approach taken in token-economy programs. Both are concerned with developing effective systems of reinforcing desirable behavior; both leave the task of *defining* desirable behavior to behavioral engineers; and both have, ideally speaking, the happiness of the recipients of reinforcement in mind without deeming it necessary to involve these recipients in fundamental decisions affecting their lives. In short, these behaviorists engaged in designing token economies had a position of authority that must have struck them, upon reading *Walden Two,* as remarkably similar to Frazier's: benevolent but absolute authority in clearly defined social settings.

Token economies found widespread societal acceptance in the late 1960s when used with people "who have devastatingly severe problems and who have not been helped by other therapies" (Ulrich, "Operant Conditioning" 22). The underlying ethical issues were often formulated only in hindsight, but they were recognized by many behaviorists actually involved in these programs: "First, in order to make tokens effective," reflects the behaviorist Roger Ulrich, "patients must be deprived of the things that tokens can buy. Second, the reinforcing power of tokens may be directed toward behaviors that represent, not the personal growth of the patient, but the patient's conformity to institutional or societal standards that are nontherapeutic" ("Operant Conditioning" 32).

During the peak of Walden Two activities among behaviorists, enthusiasm about the effectiveness of token economies seems to have outweighed the fear of possible misuse. It is hardly surprising that the widespread excitement of communal living, paired with the apparent success of the token economies that were being developed around the same time, led some of the behaviorist readers of *Walden Two* to believe that the time had come to transfer the reinforcement systems used in closed institutions to a "voluntary community of adults."

In keeping with their training, these academics approached the Walden Two project as they would any other scientific undertaking. They organized conferences, drew up proposals, sought out possible funding sources, and formed discussion groups and committees (Ulrich, "Experimental Living" 4, 10–11; *Modern Utopian;* Skinner, *Matter* 90).

The peak of this activity was the Waldenwoods conference in Michigan in the summer of 1966. Eighty-three adults and four children attended "to take part in the planning of a Walden II–type community" (*Modern Utopian* 4). The conference participants had been invited on the basis of the so-called Breiling list, a compilation of people who had expressed a serious interest in *Walden Two* by contacting Skinner and who had in turn been referred to the fellow behaviorist Jim Breiling (*Modern Utopian* 4). By 1965, this list had grown to 250 people (Bjork 160).

Skinner's own contribution to the conference was a taped message in which he proclaimed that in "many ways the successful design of an intentional community might be the most exciting and encouraging achievement of the latter half of the twentieth century" (*Modern Utopian* 5). Apart from being encouraging from a distance, however, Skinner did not get involved in this most exciting activity. By sending a taped message instead of making a personal appearance, he signaled interest and support on the one hand and detachment on the other hand. "My very warmest regards to you all and good luck," he proclaimed, and left the enthusiasts to work out the details (*Modern Utopian* 5).

Some common assumptions were shared by the behaviorists attending the Waldenwoods conference, setting them firmly apart from a second group of conference attendees with very different ideas about community who subsequently went on to found Twin Oaks Community, which will be discussed in more detail later on. An important assumption on the part of the behaviorist conference participants was the desirability and indeed necessity of outside funding. In fact, it seems that most of the participants were willing to embark on a communal experiment only if they were guaranteed "instant prosperity," as one attendee, Rudy Nesmith, put it.[2] Also, the behaviorist Walden Two enthusiasts considered a large membership an essential prerequisite for joining. The ideal community size was set at five hundred people, and on a questionnaire that was completed by forty conferees, only fifteen indicated willingness to join a community of at least fifty members (*Modern Utopian* 9–10).

Apart from money and size, the behaviorists shared the belief that the future community should be scientific and experimental (*Modern Utopian* 5), whereas the specific features of the minisociety described in *Walden Two* are hardly mentioned at all. Specifically mentioned is a discussion about "how the labor credit system should operate," without giving any details (6). This approach apparently earned Skinner's approval; he states in his taped message, "I don't know whether the pattern I drew up in *Walden Two* is the right one, of course. The book is fiction—I had to assume that I knew the results of a ten-year experiment and, of course, I didn't. But perhaps you will try the experiment and come up with the real results. If *Walden Two* helps to suggest some way to start, I shall be very happy" (*Modern Utopian* 5).

Following Skinner's cue, the Walden Two enthusiasts set about drawing up plans for their scientific experiment in communal living. As a means of developing communal behavior on the part of the participants, the communards oriented themselves toward Skinner's educational ideas. They developed a step-by-step program that would lead them gradually from a capitalist to a cooperative lifestyle. In order to assure success, each step was to be mastered successfully and reinforced before moving on to the next step. The Waldenwoods conferees thus developed a "three and one-half year plan" with "fourteen steps to be taken," ranging from the continuous meeting of subcommittees to the establishment and subsequent "evaluation of data" of a "summer training camp" to the "receipt of funds for permanent community" (*Modern Utopian* 8). The result would be an "orderly transition" from the present society to the community (7). The Skinnerian concept of programmed learning is clearly recognizable in this approach to building community.

The most important feature of the behaviorists' approach to building a Walden Two community, however, is the central position assigned to the designer: "The success of the community is contingent upon the successful engineering of human behavior. This implies the necessity of enlisting highly trained behavior engineers to contribute to the community design and development" (*Modern Utopian* 7).

Since the conference participants were such a group of highly trained behavior engineers, and since they were engaged in drawing up the initial design for a Walden Two, it seems likely that they envisioned themselves as the key to success for the new community. However, it is interesting to note that there was little discussion about who would actually participate in the experiment, apart from the designers. Some general characteristics were listed that potential members should possess, including commitment to rationality, a belief in the experimental method for gaining knowledge, non-authoritarianism, and the "willingness to change" (*Modern Utopian* 7). It remains unclear, however, whether there would be a clear division between those who designed the experiment and those who participated. It seems likely that the conference participants expected no fundamental difficulties from being experimenters and subjects at the same time, or from conducting a group experiment in which some but not all of the subjects are also the designers, and they simply saw no need to discuss issues of control, the potential misuse of power, or the nature of decision making in the new community. Apparently, the excitement to get started outweighed concerns about the control issue: "Another group discussed behavioral engineering and the negative emotions that such words as 'engineering,' 'conditioning,' and 'control' tend to produce in people. It was understood that conditioning and control could be used for good as well as bad purposes but that the 'Brave New World—1984' sounds as if it was upsetting. The discussion led to the question 'Why not start a community immediately?'" (8).

Behavioral engineering was clearly viewed as an ethically neutral technique, and it was regretted that dystopian novels had given it a negative connotation. However, behaviorists should not let themselves be deterred because behavioral engineering sounded to others "as if it was upsetting" in itself, regardless of the circumstances of its use. Instead of discussing these ethical concerns in detail, the conferees apparently agreed that the concerns could be dismissed and went back to discussing the best approach to establishing a Walden Two.

Despite the optimism and enthusiasm exhibited by the participants of the 1966 Waldenwoods conference—a feature they shared with almost all communal experimenters of the time, from flower child to Marxist revolutionary to anarchist squatter—almost none of the successive steps were actually taken. It seems that the main problems were the inability to find a funding agency and/or the academics' preference for theoretical plans over action. Whatever the reason, the fact remains that the excitement experienced during the conference slowly dissipated until little more than an occasional exchange of letters between participants remained.

Two of the conference participants, however, decided to go their own separate ways and to start Walden Two communities by themselves. The psychology professor Roger Ulrich founded Lake Village Community, and

Dr. Matt Israel at least came close to founding a community that was to be called Walden Three. The behaviorist and university professor Keith Miller also became involved in a cooperative housing project that he considered a major step toward the eventual establishment of a Walden Two community. The development of these three Walden Two experiments initiated by professional behaviorists will now be discussed in more detail.

# 5    Sunflower House

SUNFLOWER HOUSE is a student cooperative in Lawrence, Kansas, that was initiated by the behaviorist professor Keith Miller in 1969. Discovering funds left over from the dissolution of older student cooperatives in Lawrence, Miller led the way in the purchase of a house by the University of Kansas Student Housing Association (UKSHA), the agency in charge of the funds, for the explicit purpose of reestablishing a student cooperative (Sunflower House 11).

The house was named the Campus Improvement Association, commonly abbreviated to CIA House, and almost immediately turned into a "hotbed of student activism." Rather than being the site of orderly research, the house "was a crash pad, with dogs and guests outnumbering members." Routine housework was left undone, members failed to "share day-to-day chores and neglected management responsibilities." It became clear to the initiators, Miller and the UKSHA, that something needed to be done. As a result, the house was "shut down for a thorough cleaning and reorganization" and reopened in the spring of 1972 as Sunflower House (Sunflower House 11).

Part of the reopening was the introduction of a work-sharing system that was regarded by its initiators, Keith Miller and his graduate student Richard Feallock, as an important step toward the development of a behavioral technology that would serve a "voluntary community of adults": "Our goal was to develop a system for sharing the work, and, according to our analysis, the reasons that other experiments in living (particularly local 'communes') failed was that they did not have an effective system for sharing the work. Therefore, we focused on developing such a system, and we succeeded in doing so" (Miller and Feallock 86).

Miller and Feallock considered the implementation of an effective system of sharing household tasks as perhaps the most important requirement for the success of any attempt at alternative living. Developing a work-sharing system that could be generalized and then transferred to other groups besides Sunflower House filled the professor and graduate student with confidence that they were well on their way toward proving the feasibility of a Walden Two: "Our first step will be to use this set of specifications to replicate the present system with a similar group. Hopefully, we could then train other groups so that they could also start such a program. Our second step will probably be to extend the system to an adult living group involving families and children. If we are fortunate enough to move even part way along that path, a real, functioning, specifiable, *Walden Two* may not be too far off!" (Miller and Feallock 96).

Miller and Feallock were confident that they were at least on their way toward discovering a solution to the "breakdown of the equal sharing of housework as the major cause of the failure of communal experiments" by transferring the concept of "point economies from institutionalized to non-institutionalized settings and as an extension from dependent populations to legally competent adult populations" (Feallock and Miller 287). The student cooperative's work-sharing system as introduced in 1972 was "loosely based on a token economy—a system for distributing rewards contingent on desirable behavior" (Sunflower House 11).

In the case of Sunflower House, the desired behavior was housecleaning, the reward a reduction in the monthly rent. Students moving into Sunflower House agreed to pay rent that included the potential costs of a janitor and cleaning crew and subsequently were reimbursed if they partook satisfactorily in taking over the responsibilities of the nonexistent janitor and cleaning crew. This meant that every student had to earn a hundred credits every week in order to receive the monthly rent reduction. A list specified which jobs needed to be done every week and how much credit could be earned for doing them. The credit value was "based on the length of time that the job should normally take and the desirability of the job" (Miller and Feallock 78). The average job was set at fifteen credits an hour, so that students were most likely to work five to seven hours to earn the required amount of credits. Completed jobs were checked by an inspector, a fellow resident. If all of the components of the job were completed satisfactorily, the worker received full credit; if it was only partially completed, he or she received partial credit; and if it was completed to less than 50 percent satisfaction, the worker received no credits and was fined two dollars. In 1972, this system meant that residents paid a total of eighty-five dollars rent per month and received a monthly rent reduction of forty dollars, so that the monthly cost of living at Sunflower House came down to forty-five dollars for those who participated successfully in the work-sharing system (Feallock and Miller 279).

Experiments showed that the work-sharing system could not be maintained properly without "rent reductions as a back-up" (283). When students were given full rent reductions regardless of their participation in the work-sharing system, work performance dropped from 93 percent to an average of 67 percent in seventeen weeks: "When the condition was reversed to contingent rent reductions, the cleaning performance again increased to 94 percent of the outcomes passed. Thus, for the group as a whole, the percent of passed jobs was considerably higher with contingent rent reductions" (285).

The details of this system were refined in a series of experiments in which Sunflower House members were also asked to give input frequently in the form of questionnaires and at meetings. Additionally, many of the researchers were graduate students who also lived at Sunflower House.

For several years after the introduction of the work-sharing system at Sunflower House, Miller's students wrote their master's and doctoral theses based on experimental changes implemented in the work-sharing system designed to observe their effects on the workers (Couch et al.; Johnson et al.). Although the rent has naturally gone up since 1972, the basic work-sharing system is still used at Sunflower House, despite the fact that behavior analysts are no longer actively involved in the student co-op.

It is unclear, however, to what extent the results of the research done at Sunflower House are transferable to communal settings. Although a student co-op is certainly a "voluntary community of adults" (Miller and Feallock 75), and the successful introduction of a token economy outside of the closed settings in which they are most often used is noteworthy, a full-fledged community is a different matter. First of all, the students living at Sunflower House pay rent. When signing a lease, it is obvious that one is given some rights as a tenant, but not complete control. One powerful instrument of reinforcement is thus available to make the Sunflower House system work that is absent in income-sharing communities: money.

In essence, Miller and his graduate students posed the initial research question as, How do we get people to do their share of work? The more appropriate question in regard to utopian communities might have been, How do we get people to do their share of work *in the absence of monetary incen-*

*tives?* The "breakdown of the equal sharing of housework as the major cause of the failure of communal experiments," as rightfully observed by Sunflower House researchers, was arguably a consequence of the refusal of these groups to use money as a reinforcer but probably not a consequence of their inability to see that money might do the trick. In essence, the experiments show that Sunflower House students work in the household if they are given money for doing so and that they work harder if the amount of money they receive is contingent on their work performance. It is questionable whether incentives other than money would be equally effective.

Another aspect of Sunflower House as an approximation of a Walden Two experiment is worth mentioning. Initially, the work-sharing system that later proved to be quite successful did not get off to a good start. As the researchers admit candidly, "When the program was initiated, it was not democratic. That is, we set up a behavioral system without consulting with the residents (because they had not yet moved in). We tried to anticipate what target behaviors would be important and what type of consequence system would maintain those behaviors. This system was imposed on the people who moved into the house. Furthermore, we did not initially have any provisions for residents to make any input to this system." As a result, the "residents complained, rebelled, and lobbied for a voice in the system. The apparent satisfaction of residents with the group living program was very low. The house was clean and well fed, but unhappy" (Miller and Feallock 85–86).

As a result of these complaints, democratic control was given to the residents of Sunflower House—as far as this can be done in a housing situation that requires rent and is characterized by high turnover. At Sunflower House, the perennial question of who controls the controllers was perhaps not anticipated, but it was posed in hindsight, recognized as an important issue, and answered to the satisfaction of those involved in the experimental student co-op.

# 6  Lake Village

In the lab the experimenter tries to be a dictator. He tries to
achieve total control, changing individual variables at his
discretion. . . . As soon as the experimenter himself becomes a
subject, certain methodologies become far less practical and far
less attractive."

—Roger Ulrich, "Toward Experimental Living, Phase II"

DESPITE THE FACT that Skinner's utopia was eagerly discussed in the academic realm, few Walden Two communities were born directly out of academia. One of them was Lake Village, founded in 1971. Although the community departed rapidly from the behaviorist path, Lake Village was originally conceptualized as a scientific, behaviorist experiment, complete with funding, progress reports, and the collection and interpretation of scientific data. In keeping with the manner in which almost all of the communally oriented behaviorist readers interpreted *Walden Two*, the Lake Village group understood Skinner's utopia less as a blueprint for communal living than as an invitation to design its own version of a new, improved society that would make extensive use of the experimental analysis of behavior.

At the center of the founding group stood thirty-four-year-old Roger Ulrich, who became the head of the psychology department at Western Michigan University (WMU) in Kalamazoo in 1965 and quickly turned the department into a widely known center for behavioral research (Ulrich, "Some Moral" 36). Ulrich's research was mainly concerned with the relationship between pain and aggression in laboratory animals but soon expanded to the application of behavioral techniques in the field of education.

Together with a group of students, Ulrich founded a preschool program called the Learning Village. This preschool, located in a disadvantaged area of Kalamazoo, was designed to use behavior-modification techniques with young children who were likely to perform badly in school. Looking back, Ulrich recalls that he "really believed that behavioral engineering could make profound changes in human life, and that, with a little caution, those changes would surely be for the better" ("Some Moral" 37). The enthusiastic young teachers of the Learning Village were therefore surprised to learn that some of the people in the African American community they were primarily serving were somewhat resentful of the white teacher/black student setup, no matter how well-intentioned and progressive the teachers (Ulrich and Metheany 26–68).

These first hands-on experiences with people resenting the introduction of positive-reinforcement procedures without being asked to participate in the design left Ulrich and the other young teachers of the preschool unperturbed: "It was as if we had found a new religion. The entire universe was accessible and easily packaged. We used Science to explain everything just like some Christians use God" ("Experimental Living II" 58).

Soon after the Learning Village opened its doors in 1967, Ulrich was taking his enthusiasm for Skinner's new science one step further. If behavior modification was effective with students, why not apply it to society as a whole? Combining the ideas of teaching young children and living communally, Ulrich proposed a community of behavioral engineers who would take in abandoned children and give them a home. Not only would the new communards use behavioral techniques to improve their own behavior, they would also mold a generation of children free of aggression and eager to help solve society's problems: "Originally, as I attempted to get into doing an experimental community, I saw it as an extension of my earlier efforts in behavior analysis and modification. I thought, wrote, and said that I and my friends could, in a group living arrangement, apply the scientific analysis of behavior to our own lives. We could, at the same time, be both subjects and experimenters" ("Some Moral" 37).

It seems that the fundamental difference between a setting in which one modifies the behavior of other people and a setting in which one's own behavior is open to modification was not perceived at this point in the planning process, or at least not perceived as a problem. As will be shown later, the future communards were confident that science would provide objective answers about which behavior ought to be reinforced and by whom. This trust in science and the desirability of appointing scientists as omnipotent decision makers for the sake of utopia, strongly reminiscent of *Walden Two*, is spelled out clearly by Ulrich: "For the most part, Skinner was our leader. In the early summer of 1945, when he wrote *Walden Two*, he suggested that we could engineer a whole community. . . . Utopia seemed at times just within reach" ("Some Moral" 37).

By focusing on the education of abandoned children, the Lake Village group—consisting almost entirely of behaviorally oriented young teachers—adopted a plan for the community that helped to obscure the basic issues involved in placing the decision making in the hands of a few: it is unlikely that the teachers expected the children to suggest behavioral procedures designed to change their teachers' behavior. In a way, the Lake Village community as proposed by the teachers would have maintained a distinction between those who modify and those who are being modified, in practice if not in theory. The community indeed sounds like an unusual school rather than a microsociety encompassing all walks of life in a 1966 proposal for a Walden Two community presented by Ulrich:

> What I want to present today are some ideas for expanding the experimental laboratory into the less controlled environment of our everyday society. We can then start to attack some of our larger cultural problems—e.g. violence, population growth, pollution—with the same vigor that we have used in the experimental laboratory. . . . I personally have, for a long time, wanted to see what might be done if we could get children from birth and raise them in a controlled environment, in an environment in which we have been allowed to arrange certain conditions. . . . I believe the laboratory is now ready to expand into an experimental community. . . . Most important are the personnel who can get along with one another and, with trust and affection, direct the evolution for an experimental community. I have faith that such a group can evolve at Western [Michigan University]. ("Experimental Living" 5–8)

Of special interest in the above quotation is the use of the word "we." This "we" apparently encompasses a group of people who have worked in an experimental laboratory, are concerned about larger cultural problems, are capable of designing a controlled environment for children, and will direct the evolution of the experimental community with trust and affection. This seems an apt description of behavioral engineers engaged in the task of planners as envisioned by Skinner. This suggests that the Lake Village planning group consisted of people who saw themselves as gentle guides, with children conveniently playing the role of happy followers who are not involved in the decision-making process.

If there was little concern about the legitimacy of controlling the environment of children, several members of the Lake Village planning group wondered about the role Ulrich might envision for himself. He wrote in the plural "we," but since he was the main spokesperson for the group as well as the sole writer of the proposals, some people began to wonder just who he meant by "we," or rather, whether he really meant "I." While Ulrich's obvious position of leadership among the founders enabled the group to progress relatively quickly toward getting the community off the ground, feelings of dissatisfaction and powerlessness intensified in the course of the planning process, especially among the younger members. Marshall Wolfe, who held a certain amount of power and prestige in the preschool and was known to be trusted by Ulrich, insinuated during this prefounding time that Lake Village "would not be a democracy" ("Experimental Living" 19). Instead, the people who were in power in the outside world—the university and the Learning Village—would also assume power in the experimental living project (18–19). The schism between the younger people of the planning group, who were between twenty and twenty-seven years old and struggling for recognition, and the older people, twenty-nine to forty years old, well established, and mostly married with children, widened. The group began "fighting bitterly" (35).

Ulrich was urged to address the mounting concerns of his cofounders regarding the position he envisioned for himself at Lake Village. "I found myself," says Ulrich, "talking to a lot of people, all of whom seemed to be a little bit uneasy about the future" ("Experimental Living" 19–20). In a subsequent written statement, Ulrich used the term and concept of "leader" frequently, stating that leaders were "necessary" and that what made people leaders was the willingness and capability of taking on responsibility. He expected, so the statement said, that the hierarchical structure of the founding group would slowly evolve into something new and as yet unforeseeable once they had actually started the experiment of living communally (20–21). Looking back on the situation, Ulrich is more aware of his own motivations during the founding phase of Lake Village. He admits freely that

> [b]ecause of its history, and its current circumstances, the group was informally, but highly stratified. At the top stratum was me, the professor, the fund raiser, and I thought, the leader. In part society had placed me in that position. Truthfully, I wasn't willing to abdicate for a number of reasons. For one, if I truly abdicated and announced to the university and the funding sources that I now had relatively little to say about the direction of the group, financial support would cease and the whole effort would come to a halt. Second, I guess I felt qualified to be leader since I had some ideas I thought were pretty good. Finally, I guess I just couldn't give some things up. I had worked hard to get the group going and headed on a certain course and I was unwilling to let go. Also, to be honest, at the time I was enjoying some of the fruit of my work in the form of money, material goods, travel, and

so forth. I was trying to share these things, but, again, couldn't really give up control. . . . Although we often preached cooperation, it was a competitive situation. People were keenly aware of their position. I'm afraid I didn't do much to discourage the competitiveness. Perhaps I felt it made people work harder. Perhaps I enjoyed the idea that I was able to confer status on people—that people would compete for status in the organization that I had established. ("Experimental Living" 16)

On one level, the Lake Village group was engaged in a cooperative effort to start their model society/school populated with themselves and abandoned children, while on another level, Ulrich was clearly the central figure, one who enjoyed holding power without officially admitting to it.

In hindsight, Ulrich recognizes that in a way they had been deceiving themselves by taking *Walden Two,* with its similarly unclear distribution of power, as a model. And indeed, Ulrich clearly spells out similarities to the positive aspect of the elevated position Frazier holds in the fictional community by saying that everybody at Lake Village "wanted to be Frazier. We were all wanting to love one another, to be kind to one another, to be reinforcing" (Ulrich, Interview 14). Since this is Ulrich speaking, it can at least be said with certainty that *he* wanted to be Frazier.

Despite these increasing discussions about power, which were still theoretical at this point because the group had not started living communally, the group continued to draw up proposals for their community to obtain funding. These proposals centered on the role innovative child-rearing practices were to play in the community ("Experimental Living" 22–24). However, the financial optimism held by Ulrich and his group of communal-living enthusiasts was soon squashed. The Lake Village experimental living project never did get funding, and this lack of money caused serious financial problems for the academics and teachers ("Experimental Living" 5 and 17).

Rather than accepting the unavailability of funds for their Walden Two, the Lake Village group declared the preschool in which most of them were teachers a "major step toward experimental living" ("Experimental Living" 11), arguing that the proposed experimental community was simply another step toward a new society in which child education was rightfully at the center of attention, and thus justified using funds specifically intended for the preschool to get their community started. The experimental living project was thus brought under the auspices of the Behavior Development Corporation, the nonprofit organization under which the Learning Village operated and through which it received its funding. This allowed the communards-to-be to legally draw on the funds designated for the preschool to finance the initial down payment of thirty thousand dollars on 115 acres along the shore of Long Lake on the outskirts of Kalamazoo and pay the thousand-dollar monthly installments. As the funds for the preschool were drastically cut shortly afterwards, apparently for unrelated reasons, this solution for the financial basis of the experimental community was of relatively short duration ("Experimental Living" 35).

During this delicate time, the survival of the Long Lake property as the future site of the experimental community was greatly supported by the willingness of one family with independent financial means, the Hrens, to move onto the property in the summer of 1971 and help renovate the farmhouse. Jim Scherrer, one of the younger members of the corporation, also moved into a room of the one existing house. After months of planning, the experiment of communal living was actually beginning.

Parallel to the orderly process of planning a Walden Two, the young academics involved in the design of the experimental community were very much aware of the social upheaval happening around them (Altus 53). "'We were hippies,'" explains Ulrich, "'and all of the things that means—anti-Vietnam, pro–civil rights, learning to get back into balance with nature'" (qtd. in Falda). Most importantly, it seems that during the time when Lake Village was more plan than fact, from 1966 to 1971, Ulrich metamorphosed from a serious young scientist to a drug enthusiast rebelling against academic norms and rules (Altus 53). Looking back on his state of mind in the late sixties and early seventies, Ulrich remembers that there were times when he was reduced to nothing but a "confused junkie" (interview with the author, June 10, 1998).[3] Says Ulrich about his abundant use of drugs and the effect on the community:

> At this time I'd also gotten more and more into heavy drugs and although it wasn't the sole reason for any kind of great change, it was a fantastic happening. I had been mainlining cocaine and one night I decided that in addition to the cocaine, I'd drop acid at the same time. I was taken on the trip of my life. My mind started rushing faster and faster through the whole history of evolution and I was intermingled with it. A certain terror started to overtake me. Paranoia started to grab hold of me. At the time, my marriage was falling apart, I was having trouble with the lady I was dating at the time, our group had just lost a number of grants and we were hurting. . . . This went on and on and then I died. Something just broke. Instead of dying and then going to hell, I had gone to hell and then died. (Ulrich, Interview 15)

Ulrich's drug-induced experiences suggested to him that human behavior—at least his own—was far more complex and mysterious than he as a behavioral scientist had previously assumed. "It's a bit hard to have a good healthy dose of LSD put in you," Ulrich realized, "and still think that you can manage the universe" (14). Although this kind of "instant enlightenment" (interview with the author, June 10, 1998) brought about by drugs apparently did not affect the experimental design for Lake Village, it did produce a somewhat schizophrenic setup. It is difficult to conceive how the Walden Two community discussed by the Lake Village people in their writings could be populated by hippies on LSD. It seems, however, that these conflicting interests and leanings of the young academics coexisted and that the designing of a science-oriented community continued somewhat on its own momentum.

Ulrich's increasing use of drugs also had tangible effects. In 1967, two years after he had become head of the psychology department, his colleagues strongly suggested that he resign his position and become instead a research professor with far less responsibility and visibility ("Experimental Living" 8–9). It was apparently felt that Ulrich's unorthodox ideas, especially his increasing willingness to self-experiment with drugs, were beginning to have a detrimental effect on the entire department. Ulrich fought this factual degradation yet decided in the end to take the position offered, which at least allowed him to remain a professor.

Despite these departmental disagreements, or perhaps because of them, Ulrich rallied around him a strong group of supporters. While his interactions with his fellow professors became "minimal" after 1967 ("Experimental Living" 11), he turned increasingly toward students, younger faculty members, and teachers of the Learning Village in his search for people who shared his ideas; it was from these groups that Ulrich recruited the Lake Village cofounders.

The group was faced with serious problems, as it became clear that their approach to founding a community was hampered by lack of funds. Lake Village was originally conceptualized as a model society in which abandoned children and the children of the founding group would be shaped into model citizens—free of aggression, eager to solve society's problems, and cooperative—through the conscious use of behavior modification. When it became apparent in 1971 that the founding group could neither obtain funds nor convince child-care agencies to place abandoned children in their care, the central purpose of the envisioned community was lost. This loss of a common vision highlighted the fact that the founding group, most of whom were teachers in the behaviorally oriented preschool Learning Village, had agreed upon the usefulness of a method, behavior modification, but not to what end they wanted to use this method beyond modeling child behavior.

Not coincidentally, discussions about Ulrich's role at Lake Village intensified around the same time that the aim of the community became less clear. With the need to reformulate the design of the experimental community, questions that had surfaced earlier became more pressing: Who was to decide which direction the experimental community ought to take? Which data could they collect that would point them in the right direction? How would they, as scientists, decide which step to take next?

Being inspired by *Walden Two*, Ulrich and his friends initially felt confident that they could solve any problems as long as they approached them scientifically, with a "proper respect for data and how to gather it": "Perhaps the most important single consideration is that we have individuals who are willing constantly to strive toward modifying the behavior of themselves and others through a strategy of positive reinforcement as opposed to punishment. . . . The experimental community must include . . . individuals whose basic assumptions are that behavior has reasons, that behavior is a natural phenomenon just like other natural events, that we are lawfully operating organisms doing what we have to do as part of a more general universe of realities" ("Experimental Living" 25–28).

True to this behavioral approach to problem solving, several members of the founding group took it upon themselves to solve the question of what Lake Village ought to be like. They drew up a questionnaire, collected the data by having all of the people interested in living at Lake Village fill it out, and charted the results. The future communards were asked about their desired level of privacy, the degree of communal sharing, preferred work arrangements, criteria for membership selection, and so on (see the complete questionnaire in "Experimental Living" 61–74). Five questions dealt with specific aspects of behavior modification, that is, which reinforcers individuals would "allow to be brought under contingency control by the community for performing community duties," which behavior of individuals should be under community control, and which "methods of control" would find the respondent's approval. While these questions aimed at avoiding the misuse of behavior-modification techniques (and thus reflect a deeper concern than Skinner for the considerable power that is being placed in the hand of behavioral engineers), not one of the thirty-nine questions dealt explicitly with political attitudes, ideological preferences, or the far-ranging goals of the communards. It was not discussed whether future members wanted environmentalism to be an integral part of communal life or political activism or back-to-earth sentiments.

The results of the questionnaire, which was answered by twenty-eight people (almost none of whom ended up living at Lake Village), were duly charted in neat diagrams and revealed in scientific form that there was little unity of purpose in any area. The one clear consensus regarded which reading material on experimental communities the respondents would recommend to friends. Seventeen named Skinner, leaving all other utopian writers behind by fifteen counts. Unperturbed as to the results of the questionnaire, the group continued with its meetings. Architects were invited who quickly "became discouraged by the lack of consensus. They couldn't design if we couldn't tell them what we wanted" ("Experimental Living" 37). It seems that this lack of a common denominator as revealed by the questionnaire—not to mention the more fundamental ideological issues that were not even discussed—was not yet felt to be a major stumbling block for the successful establishment of the community.

This changed in the winter of 1971, when Rob Hren bought a snowmobile. Without giving it much thought, Hren had decided that the communal property would be ideal for riding a snowmobile, so he went out and bought one. This single act raised several fundamental issues. What was the community's attitude toward environmentalism? Did Hren have the right to buy the snowmobile without first consulting the group? Should everybody in the founding group have equal input into the decision-making process at this point, or did it make a difference that the Hrens and Jim Scherrer were the only people actually working and living on the property? What attitude would the community adopt toward property and privacy? Some of these questions had been asked in the questionnaire, but since they had merely discussed the results (that had revealed a variety of attitudes), this data left them completely unprepared for making a decision on a concrete issue that had to be settled one way or the other. Either Hren could ride the snowmobile, or he could not.

It soon became apparent that there were two factions in the snowmobile debate, those who wanted the community to adopt a nonpollution policy (and thus get rid of the snowmobile) and those who did not want to take a major reinforcer away from Hren. The environmentalists tried to convince the pro-snowmobile camp by bringing scientific studies to the meetings. The pro-snowmobile camp responded by questioning the validity of the studies. Heated debates followed, which revealed the extent of animosity among the group and the hidden power structure that Wolfe had already hinted at several months prior to the snowmobile issue. Ulrich and Wolfe sided with Hren, while the younger people grouped around Scherrer, who felt strongly about the environmental responsibility of utopian communities. In the ensuing fight, respect for scientific data was of little importance as each side struggled to push its agenda. In hindsight, Ulrich thinks that in a way they had been setting themselves up: "I myself had helped create and nurture that competitiveness. It had worked in setting up the lab and the Village. It was not working in setting up the community" ("Experimental Living" 45).

The snowmobile controversy was eventually resolved. On the surface, the anti-snowmobile people—the younger faction—won, and a nonpollution policy was adopted. However, the main person pushing for this, Scherrer, resigned his post as community chairman at the next meeting. He felt that despite the fact that they had been able to reach a decision that time, there was no clarity of purpose and too much animosity among the Lake Village people. He decided that it would be best for him to step out of the picture and let the community develop along the lines envisioned by Ulrich. Perhaps he saw the leadership by one person as the only force that would help the community survive under the circumstances. Perhaps he also realized that Ulrich was in such a position of power in terms of money and status within the context of university, preschool, and experimental community that he could—and would—single-handedly terminate the Walden Two project if he lost too much control over it: "'Marshall said yesterday and Roger has verbalized to me in the past that, if this committee put too many restrictions on him or limits on their reinforcers, that he would not hesitate to buy more land and do on it what he likes, withdrawing financial support for this project. These things cannot happen! . . . I feel very strongly that it is not fair for me to push my ideals for a non-capitalistic experimental community on you and attempt to undermine in any way the direction Roger and Marshall want to take'" (qtd. in "Experimental Living" 43–44).

Scherrer was not alone in his decision to withdraw from the Lake Village project. Several of the younger members stopped attending the meetings as well. Some of them explained their decision in writing. One person stated that he felt that the "'middle class attitude presented by people with money and control would prevail over any objections on my part, regardless of data presented by anyone for either side'" (qtd. in "Experimental Living" 44). This statement indicates that during the snowmobile debate at least some of the Lake Village people distanced themselves from the notion that science can produce values.

This assessment, that personal attitudes would be at the base of decisions at Lake Village "regardless of data presented," reflects the difficulty almost all Walden Two communities encountered with Skinner's scientific utopia: ideally, the decisions of a Walden Two community should not reflect personal preferences but be guided by science, especially by the experimental analysis of behavior. Yet when it came down to making concrete decisions in communal settings, almost all of the communities found that members were not satisfied to leave decisions to somebody else, regardless of their actual or assumed expertise. Even those groups of people who consciously set out to create Walden Twos during the heyday of communal living either questioned the motives of the supposedly neutral decision makers or simply resented the fact that they were not involved in the decision-making process, regardless of whether or not they agreed with the decisions that were being made.

At Lake Village, one of the few Walden Two communities founded by behavioral scientists who were explicitly trying to make science their guiding principle, the realization that, at least in their group, decisions were apparently not based purely on science and that it seemed impossible to base them on science alone came as a harsh disillusionment. The scientists-turned-communards were apt at backing up their position with data, but during the snowmobile controversy, they realized that *both* sides used scientific data to support their position, without a clear indication that one side misused or misunderstood the data available. This realization almost automatically led them to question the legitimacy of placing the power to make decisions for all of society in the hands of scientists. In subsequent years, Ulrich wrote extensively about the ethical dangers implied in behavior modification: "We must ask, more carefully than ever before, questions concerning who is the controller, how can we protect the rights of the controlled, who selects the goals toward which the subject will be moved, and indeed, how do we define 'rights' and 'goals' within a deterministic framework? Once I thought behavior modification could do almost anything. But the larger experiments in which I've been involved, as both subject and experimenter, have pointed out some problems in achieving the control we envisioned and in viewing the universe as we did" (Ulrich, "Some Moral" 38).

"Some of our greatest difficulties at Lake Village," writes Ulrich in another essay, "have been in the area of decision making, particularly in regard to whose goals should be adopted" ("Experimental Living II" 52). Although Ulrich had had ample opportunity in his academic career to observe behavior modification in closed settings, the experimental community differed from these other behavior-modification programs in one important respect: the attempt to be experimenter and subject at the same time.

> Behavior modification seems to work best when there is a clear definition of the role between the controller and the controlled. When one is clearly

in charge of the reinforcers and punishers the degree to which predictable behavior changes can be produced is much greater. People have criticized behavior modification as an authoritarian system and to an extent the criticism is justified. . . . If I sat down at one of our Sunday morning meetings at Lake Village and proposed a system for monitoring and differentially reinforcing everyone's social interactions, I'd be laughed out of the house. Also, I don't have a vantage point up in the sky; usually I don't have any better idea of what's going on than the other people in the community. ("Some Moral" 39–40)

The communards who had initially been eager to participate as subjects and experimenters in a behaviorist experiment soon resented the feeling of being stripped of their decision-making powers. As Ulrich had remarked, everybody had "wanted to be Frazier," and it seems that nobody had seriously considered being anybody *but* Frazier.

In hindsight, Ulrich feels that this development might have been predicted. "If you set up an experiment in which you impose a program on people who have very little to say about what happens to them," he points out, "you can't expect your results to be applicable to a situation in which no one has that kind of power" ("Some Moral" 46). "I had published a series of books on the control of human behavior and everything turned out all right in them just like in Walden II. We had study after study where people had effectively gotten other people to act in certain ways. Now, here I am, living in this commune and I can't get my kids to put away their socks. We couldn't engineer getting the dishes done. . . . The laws of behavior are out there, I'm not denying that. What I am repudiating is behaviorists who tend to paint a picture which says, 'We know,' and 'We can arrange your world so you won't have to pay the piper.' Walden II is simply not realistic" (Ulrich, Interview 15–16).

The snowmobile debate not only terminated the communards' desire to build a Walden Two, it also tore the founding group apart and left Ulrich in just the kind of position of authority that had come under attack during the debate. Ironically, the fight for greater participation in the decision-making process did not lead to a more consensus-oriented system of decision making, as it did in many other Walden Two communities. Instead, several people left the Lake Village project in disgust, making room for a group that was more willing to accept Ulrich's tendency to dominate.

In the following years, the Lake Village system of decision making was more or less undefined, with some meetings taking place that even Ulrich acknowledges were not the forum in which important decisions were actually made (Ulrich, Interview 16). Even these relatively unimportant meetings became irregular in the 1970s and have long been abandoned. "In the spirit of the times," writes Deborah Altus, "freedom was greatly valued, and, for the most part, people were able to do their own thing without getting in anyone else's way" (53). In reality, this apparently meant that people were able to do their own thing as long as they didn't get in Ulrich's way: "Ulrich freely admits that he has played a strong leadership role at Lake Village over the years. And he recognizes that, at times, he's pushed his authority a bit too far. Some members clearly resented Ulrich's influence" (54).

Ulrich maintained a position of authority in part by attracting his own students to the community, resulting in a power imbalance strongly favoring him. From 1974 until his retirement in 1998, Ulrich fulfilled his teaching obligation at WMU by declaring Lake Village his main field of research and offering two courses focusing on Lake Village. These courses mainly entailed students coming out to the community, discussing topics picked by the students, and doing manual work, like painting a barn, for academic credit.[4] This unorthodox teaching method was hailed as innovative by some students but was also bitterly opposed as exploitative and unscientific by other students and professors. In response to criticism, Ulrich often repeated the main lesson he had learned from Lake Village: "There is no experiment other than the real situation. The University is not the real situation" ("Search" 60).

Ulrich admits freely that Lake Village bore no resemblance to Walden Two after 1972, had no desire to do so, and that nobody thought about the commune's relation to a behaviorist utopia in daily life (interview with the author, June 10, 1998). Yet Ulrich continually pointed out even after 1972 that in *Walden Two*, Skinner himself had urged people to experiment with communal living arrangements and to go wherever their research might take them. As one of the future visitors of the fictional community exclaims: " 'It's a job for research, but not the kind you can do in a university, or in a laboratory anywhere. I mean you've got to experiment, and *experiment with your own life!* Not just sit back—not just sit back in an ivory tower somewhere— as if your own life weren't all mixed up in it' " (*Walden Two* 5).

Ulrich justified the use of Lake Village as his academic subject matter long after the behavioral, scientific approach had been abandoned by the communards. He was aware, however, that he could not get his papers published in behaviorist journals because his kind of experimentation, including the use of mind-altering drugs, was not what Skinner and his fellow behaviorists meant by experimentation. A scientific experiment clearly entails the use of an experimental design that can be reproduced by other scientists and the collection of data on one or more variables, all of which are requirements that Lake Village does not fulfill: "People kept asking me for data of the type that appears in the *Journal of Applied Behavior Analysis*. They asked what kind of experimental design we had for the research at Lake Village. The package I presented wasn't neat; I hadn't planned, then done, then reported" ("Experimental Living II" 48–49).

Another indication that Lake Village had clearly departed from the path of scientific experimentation favored by behavioral engineers is the fact that, according to Ulrich, Skinner, who had initially referred Walden Two enthusiasts to Lake Village, quickly stopped doing so (interview with the author, June 10, 1998).

The questionable line of argument linking Lake Village to behavioral research notwithstanding, Ulrich's university courses at Lake Village attracted a continuous flow of young students to the community, resulting in a group consisting of one professor and an ever-changing group of young students (Altus 52). Over the years, Lake Village has had several members who were surprised and bitter when they discovered that what they had taken to be a cooperative community was in fact "Roger's place" (it is even referred to as such by some former members). "I can't imagine," remarks one former member, Chris Orsolini, in an interview, "that he could go on imagining that it is a shared effort because he has managed to eliminate or alienate anybody who has tried to really get in there with him" (interview with the author, June 10, 1998). Ulrich himself admits that while he is attracted to people with a "strong will, their own ideas, who kind of like to go and do their own thing, . . . those same people are just like me. We keep our distance from one another. You need a certain amount of space. So there are ways in which you try to create an environment where it's okay to get your own way. And I like that" (interview with the author, June 10, 1998).

Ulrich's behavior after 1972, revealing his obvious inclination toward exercising power, indicates that at least part of his attraction to *Walden Two* was linked to the fact that Skinner's proposed society was run by omnipotent decision makers, and that Ulrich assumed he would be one of them. This might also explain why the majority of the people who lived at Lake Village were Ulrich's students, young teachers at the preschool he had created, or friends of his children. In other words, most of the membership of Lake Village was clearly younger than and quite often dependent on him, leaving him in a position resembling a teacher rather than an equal among equals (interview with the author, June 10, 1998).

Ulrich has managed to create an environment for himself in which he is clearly in a position of power. Thus, while the attempt to build a Walden Two failed, Ulrich did not have to let go of his notion of being an "elder," as he calls himself (interview with the author, June 10, 1998).

Yet how did the Lake Village experience affect those who were not able to establish themselves as "elders"? Chris Orsolini, who lived at Lake Village for several years with her husband, has vivid memories of the day that Ulrich and her husband had a fight and the couple realized that what they had thought was the culmination of a dream would just be a phase in their lives: "It was at that point, and it was a very heartbreaking day, that we realized that this could not be part of our lives forever. We really thought we would be there for our life. We were going to be there. And it just fell apart. And I think Roger has always had a lot of control on the farm. . . . I think there are probably other folks out there that don't have that glowing feeling about Lake Village. I was watching some of the tapes of the party out there, and yes, it's a wonderful place to go and party, but it's not an easy place to live. You'll see that a number of the people on that tape have moved off and live on the outskirts of Lake Village. Because it's hard to live in that kind of situation, it's very difficult, if not impossible" (interview with the author, June 10, 1998).

For many, it seems, living at Lake Village was a sobering experience. They came looking for life in utopia and found a temporary excursion into a not-so-perfect microsociety. The central point of disillusionment often appears to have been the leadership role played by Ulrich and the realization that a minisociety where no one is officially in power does not necessarily result in the equal distribution of power.

7    Walden Three

ONE OF THE PARTICIPANTS of the Waldenwoods conference who decided to found a Walden Two community on his own was Dr. Matt Israel, who had been Skinner's student at Harvard and had subsequently entered the field of education. While being involved in special education in Boston in the late 1960s, Israel made grand plans for an urban Walden Two community. At the same time, he was interested in establishing a residential center for handicapped children in which behavior modification would play a central role. Ideally, both goals were to be achieved in a joint project, as Israel explained in August 1969: "I'd like to propose that some of us begin to work towards the development of an experimental school based on behavioral psychology. Such a school could be one of the income-producing enterprises of an experimental community. . . . Such a school might be added to an existing Walden Two community, provided that the members of such a community wished to have such a school and its staff there. Or, the school might serve as a nucleus for a new experimental community" (*Newsletter*, August 16, 1969, 1).

In behaviorist circles, Israel was a well-known champion of *Walden Two* in the late 1950s and 1960s. He was "always talking positive reinforcement, and he was wanting to get Walden Two started," according to Roger Ulrich (interview with the author, June 10, 1998). Skinner, who was in contact with Israel, was delighted to hear that his former student "'has at times been completely dedicated to some kind of cultural design.'" As early as 1955, they went out for lunch together so that Israel could tell Skinner "'about a cooperative movement not too far from Boston'" (qtd. in Bjork 160). In the 1960s, Skinner occasionally referred Walden Two enthusiasts to his former student.[5]

In 1966, Israel founded the Association for Social Design (ASD), which was to be the basis of a future community called Walden Three. The ASD soon had chapters in Los Angeles, Albuquerque, and Washington, D.C. These chapters were primarily discussion groups that also met for social events rather than serious attempts to found a Walden Two community. The Boston chapter, in which Israel was involved, took the lead in the publication of the newsletter, social activities, and plans for cooperative ventures, as the May 1967 ASD newsletter indicates. According to this newsletter, a "spirit of fun and excited collaboration" prevailed at the ASD meetings, which were usually attended by about two dozen people (1), and a brochure published by the future communards proclaimed with boundless optimism: "Our objective is to establish a network of associated experimental communities in cities throughout the world, along the lines suggested in B. F. Skinner's *Walden Two*" (Association).

In September 1967, the first definite step toward establishing a full-fledged Walden Two was taken with the opening of the Morningside House, a miniature community of four adults and one child located in Arlington, Massachusetts (Association). This community soon folded, apparently due to "interpersonal problems," and was succeeded by the Rutland Square House, which was closed in August 1969 (Compendium).

In keeping with the step-by-step approach all of the behaviorist groups took to building a Walden Two, Israel was undeterred by the failure of these "early approximations of an experimental community," as one ASD member, J. H. Harless, called the cooperative houses (ASD Forum). Israel maintained that "a sequence of small steps can be programmed and implemented, that will lead us gradually from the mode of life that we are now living to the mode of life of an experimental community" (Association). The failure of the two cooperative houses indicated that one step, actually living together, had been taken too quickly, but not that it could not be taken at all.

Israel took great care to point out in newsletters and the brochure that he, and by extension the ASD, recommended "one particular interpretation and understanding of *Walden Two*" that potential members needed to understand and find agreeable. Rather than following the precise systems spelled out in Skinner's novel, Israel took his mentor to mean that in "designing its practices, an experimental society should make use of the science of behavior" (Association). Interested parties should therefore take a training course in "behavior technology" as a necessary prerequisite for a "full comprehension of the reasons for, and possibilities in, a Walden Two" (Association). This full comprehension focused on the role of the planners: "It is the viewpoint of the ASD that the most important aspect of *Walden Two* is its philosophy of government. Whether or not any real community will wish to adopt each of the various specific practices described in *Walden Two* cannot be determined until such a community is formed. Whether or not the practices, if tried, will prove successful is a matter for experimentation to answer" (Association).

Consequently, Israel proposed a self-selected Board of Planners for the school as well as the community part of the cooperative venture whose decisions could be overruled by two-thirds of the membership (Israel, "Proposal"). This board would also "select its own replacement for any member whose term expires, who resigns, or who cannot serve out his term for any other reason" (Israel, "'Rat Knows'" 10). Israel points out that it is important for all members of the ASD to understand the principles of *Walden Two* and to decide for themselves how radically they wish to change their lifestyle. The "principle of voluntary participation" would be maintained at all times (Association).

The young behavioral engineer stressed repeatedly the importance of experimentation, the use of the experimental analysis of behavior, and adhering to the philosophy of *Walden Two* for the success of Walden Three. While this indicated clearly that Israel advocated an elevated position for scientists in the new society, it did not clarify exactly what role he planned to play in the community himself. Several factors indicate, however, that Israel organized and wrote under the unspoken assumption that he would be the main designer of the new and improved society. It is difficult to discern which position he envisioned for his cofounders, since all his writings are kept in the plural. It is striking, however, that Israel was not only the founder of the ASD but also the only one to write at length about the envisioned community, with other ASD members only contributing comments in the form of letters published in the ASD newsletter. It appears that Israel saw himself as a future planner but was not very concerned with exchanging ideas with other potential planners; perhaps he did not think that there would be other planners on an equal footing with him.

In an article entitled "'Rat Knows Best!' or, Some Proposed Characteristics of an Experimental School Based on Behavioral Psychology," Israel shows a remarkable lack of concern for the issue of control. In his proposal, not only children but human beings in general appear to be little more than machines reacting to stimuli who are to be shaped by omnipotent "educational planners":

> For example, the educational planners may decide that a person should be able to call upon a number of hobbies and interests when he is 80 or 90 years old that do not require a great deal of physical abilities. (Stamp and coin collecting, for example.) They also might decide that it is best to develop such hobbies and interests when the individual is young, rather than to wait until he reaches an advanced age. As a result, the educational planners might program such behaviors as follows: The behaviors are to be acquired when the child is young, say between the ages of 7 and 10; the behaviors are to be maintained at some minimal level of strength throughout the individual's middle years (this is where maintenance systems come into play); then, the behaviors should be able to come into play in real strength if and when the individual reaches advanced ages. (5–6)

The educational planners not only determine which behavior is desirable and is therefore to be reinforced, they also decide whether positive reinforcement, extinction, or punishment will be most effective in shaping the desired behavior. Israel apparently does not ask himself why he should have the unrestricted power—let alone the ability—to pinpoint "appropriate and relevant behaviors," and he sees no reason why "powerful techniques" should not be employed if the alternative does not entail giving a student "free choice" but simply allowing a perpetuation of "prior conditioning" (Israel, "'Rat Knows'" 7).

In short, Israel is concerned with shaping students as effectively as possible while assuming that a detached scientific attitude will somehow reveal which behavior is objectively worthy of reinforcement and which method of shaping will be most effective. Ethical considerations apparently do not enter into his thinking, nor does he appear to have any doubt that science—and by extension, Dr. Israel the scientist—are outside the realm of human subjectivity and fallibility and therefore free of potential misuse. This attitude is highly reminiscent of Skinner's explicit recommendations for the role of behavioral scientists in a society fit for survival (*Beyond Freedom* 96–97, 166).

The impression of Israel envisioning himself as a Frazier in a real-life Walden Two community is further strengthened by the fact that he apparently possessed several character traits suggesting that he could easily have identified with Skinner's fictional protagonist. Judging from his writings during the late 1960s, it appears that Israel was at the same time a central player and a socially awkward outsider. He is mentioned again and again as the main organizer, theorizer, and writer for the nascent Walden Three community. Yet in the newsletter of the Association for Social Design, Israel announced on May 4, 1967, that he would "like to be with people for meals, supper invitations welcome" (2). Corresponding with a young couple interested in joining his Walden Two community, Marnie and Dan Parelius, Israel states that affection should be shared equally and without jealousy in the new community. He further elaborates that he is not sure whether the girlfriend will be sexually attracted to him but that this "should be the objective." After several letters between Dan Parelius and Matt Israel—in which Marnie's opinion about the proposed arrangement is not discussed—the young couple decided not to join Matt Israel in his communal efforts.[6]

Israel's mechanistic definition of happiness further suggests that the young behavioral engineer was somewhat rigid in his thinking and probably not very happy: "Happiness can be measured in a number of ways, some of which are these: Rate of Positive and Negative Indicators. . . . By identifying such positive and negative indicators for oneself, one can define an increase in one's happiness as an increase in the rates of one or more positive indicators, or as a decrease in the rates of one or more negative indicators, or as a combination of both. . . . In addition to the use of such self-recorded indicator-rates, the individual can also 'rate' the quality of his day, or of parts of his day, numerically. For example, I rate the quality of each morning, afternoon and evening, on a scale from 1 to 5" (Israel, "'Rat Knows'" 6).

Israel's happiness ratings were presumably fairly low in the summer of 1969, as the supporters of a behaviorist community–cum-school were slowly but surely beginning to distance themselves from him. At the core of the criticism brought against his brainchild, the Association for Social Design, was the secretiveness that necessarily resulted in a lack of open discussion and joint decision making. Apparently, these problems surfaced only after the two cooperative houses initiated by the Boston chapter of the ASD had failed within weeks. Donald A. Miller, one member, demanded that a list of membership be printed "so people can communicate directly, increasing the involvement between members," while another asked to hear the specific reasons why the association's first cooperative venture, the Rutland Square House, was closed (Compendium). The most scathing criticism in the summer of 1969 came from Stephen Kahn:

> The lacunae in ASD activity from November to June is very disturbing to us, and, I suspect, to many other members outside the Boston area. This is not so much because a breakdown occurred in the cooperative house (though this was a considerable shock after all the optimism and preparation described in the Newsletters) as the almost complete lack of information. This silence has been rather demoralizing and probably has reduced the willingness of many people to support the ASD a second time round. . . . The whole impression since November (particularly in contrast to the openness of the Newsletters) is one of furtiveness and secrecy, perhaps quite unintentionally so. . . . It seems to me to be desirable that you provide a more extensive analysis of what went wrong and how similar problems might be avoided in the future. I can well understand your reluctance to discuss very painful personal conflicts and to rake over dead coals. Unfortunately, what the ASD is engaged in is inevitably a kind of public trust, and those who embark on a community effort with outside support need to be willing to live under a certain amount of public scrutiny and evaluation. It should be possible to analyze these problems without getting too personal or specific. I don't think community can be built on a credibility gap. (Compendium)

Since the ASD, and especially its chapter in Boston, was very much dominated by Israel, and since he published all of the ASD material, it appears likely that the criticism was directed mainly against Israel himself. As Stephen Kahn further elaborates: "One clinical psychologist to whom I showed some ASD material said, among a number of critical comments, that it looked like the chief purpose of the ASD was having people modify each other's behavior, which didn't sound like a very interesting pastime to him. This was from an individual who had just helped set up a token economy at a school for retarded children. If our material is aversive for someone as potentially sympathetic as that, I think we need to reconsider it" (Compendium).

Kat Kinkade, a cofounder of Twin Oaks Community and a firm believer in behavioral engineering, complained with regard to Israel that she never did understand why behaviorism "attract[s] control freaks," clearly identifying the Boston behaviorist as one of them (interview with the author, April 10, 1995). The "credibility gap" arising in response to the uncooperative way in which the failure of the "cooperative" houses was handled indicates that several ASD members started to doubt the desirability of living in a Walden Two community as envisioned by Israel by the summer of 1969. A year later, after three years of planning and meeting, it was obvious that a full-fledged Walden Three community would not see the light of day, let alone "a network of associated experimental communities in cities throughout the world." Stephen Kahn remarks: "As brilliant as *Walden Two* is, I become more and more convinced that it just doesn't provide a realistic basis for a community. People just don't work the way Skinner would like them to. I imagine this is fairly obvious by now even to most of the people in the ASD, though there is still a reluctance to admit this out loud" (Compendium).

In reaction to the difficulties in setting up a Walden Two community, Israel shifted his attention to the second part of his plan: the school. Originally intended as a regular school, Israel now concentrated on building a school and treatment center for autistic children. The Association for Social Design was dissolved and replaced by the nonprofit Behavior Research Institute (BRI), with Israel as its director. Israel admits that the members "are not at this point a group living in any one building or site" but maintains that an experimental community could eventually evolve out of the treatment center.[7] After 1972, the envisioned communal aspect of the treatment center is hardly mentioned anymore. The BRI, however, opened several group homes in Providence, Rhode Island, and Boston that are still in operation today, with Israel as director.

Israel's shift from wanting to build a perfect society along the lines of Walden Two to concentrating on the field of special education is not surprising. As has been pointed out before, behaviorist procedures have found the largest measure of societal acceptance in closed settings like mental hospitals or prisons. Israel did not function well as an equal among equals. As a teacher and director among autistic and brain-damaged children he was more successful in living out his ideas. In a teacher/student situation, it is clear who reinforces whom, and even answering the question of what behavior is "appropriate and relevant" traditionally rests with the teacher, especially if the student engages in self-injurious behavior, is unable to speak, or has difficulty brushing his or her teeth.

Well into the 1970s, Israel's Behavior Research Institute had relatively free reign in its educational style for autistic children. It was only in later years that Israel's refusal to admit anything but effectiveness as a measure for educational success and his unbroken belief that he as a scientist can objectively define which behavior ought to be reinforced and which methods are to be employed was called into question. In 1978, the New York State Department of Education threatened to withdraw New York children from the BRI center in Providence,[8] initiating a long series of complaints and lawsuits against Israel.

At the center of the debate was Israel's use of physical punishment in the treatment of the autistic children put in his care.[9] Ironically, remarks Ulrich—who also strayed from the straight and narrow behaviorist path—the behaviorist most closely associated with wanting to build a society based on positive reinforcement became one of the most prominent representatives of aversive therapy, much to the embarrassment of most of his former colleagues (interview with the author, June 10, 1998). Although still controversial, Israel's treatment center remains in operation; it was renamed the Judge Rotenberg Center in 1987 in honor of the probate judge who allowed the center to continue its use of aversive therapy ("Judge to Receive").

Although the use of physical punishment is clearly not advocated in *Walden Two* or any of Skinner's writings, the line of reasoning Israel uses to advocate punishment is theoretically in keeping with Skinner's suggestions for a better society. Skinner had advocated positive reinforcement in the upbringing of the young utopians because he thought he could provide experimental proof that praise is more *effective* than punishment, but he does not apply any other measure than effectiveness. Skinner's mouthpiece, Frazier, explicitly maintains that the goals and methods of education are experimental questions. Thus, if Israel's experience proved that punishment was in fact more effective than praise, there is no safeguard that would prevent him from employing it. After all, Skinner had said in his taped message for the Waldenwoods conference that in writing *Walden Two* he had "had to assume that I knew the results of a ten-year experiment and, of course, I didn't," and that he hoped that perhaps a group of behaviorists would "try the experiment and come up with the real results." Ironically, *Walden Two* had indeed helped "to suggest some way to start" for Israel, yet his hands-on experiences with autistic children suggested that Skinner had been wrong and that aversive therapy was more effective than positive reinforcement.

Interestingly, Skinner fails to mention Israel in his rather minute account of Walden Two endeavors in his autobiography. In a similar vein, Skinner's sympathetic biographer Daniel W. Bjork mentions Israel as an enthusiastic early supporter of *Walden Two* but makes no mention of his later career as an advocate of aversive therapy (160 and 175).

After the failure of the ASD—in which adults refused to follow Israel's lead—the behavioral engineer found more fitting participants for his experimentation in autistic children who are incapable of demanding active participation in the problem-solving and decision-making process of their education. Assuming that Israel really does have the happiness of his students in mind, the setup of his residential center is actually similar to Walden Two. In a sense, Israel did indeed remain true to the Walden Two philosophy, taking Frazier's arguments to one possible conclusion.

## Notes

1. For the history of behaviorism as an academic discipline, see Bjork 143–44.

2. Rudy Nesmith to the author, March 9, 1999.

3. The author's interviews are included in the appendix. These interviews will be cited by date throughout the text.

4. Toward Experimental Living, taught from 1974 to 1993, and Introduction to Human Behavior, taught from 1980 to 1998.

5. Dan Parelius to Matt Israel, October 25, 1969, Twin Oaks Papers (no. 9840), Special Collections, University of Virginia Library.

6. Matt Israel to Dan Parelius, December 24, 1969; Dan Parelius to Matt Israel, April 20, 1970, Twin Oaks Papers (no. 9840), Special Collections, University of Virginia Library.

7. Matt Israel to unnamed friend, June 22, 1971, Twin Oaks Papers (no. 9840), Special Collections, University of Virginia Library.

8. See "New York to Remove Children from R.I. School's Care," "New York Threatens with Suit," and "Accord Reached on Autistic Children at R.I. School."

9. See "Bay States to Probe Death of Mass. Man at Providence Center," "Mother of Injured Autistic Girl Sues School for Negligence," "Judge to Receive Reports of Monitors of BRI," "Judge Allows BRI Therapy to Continue Six Months," and "Battling for the Disabled with Cesar Chavez in Mind."

# PART 3

# Twin Oaks Community and the Heyday of the Communities Movement

"The only thing we could not control," says
Kat Kinkade, cofounder of Twin Oaks, "was
the *feeling* that the average citizen had about
somebody else doing the government. They
just hated it." Although Kinkade is still a
convinced behaviorist, she has abandoned
her hopes of seeing a Walden Two in real life.
(courtesy Twin Oaks Community)

# 8    The Early Days of
       Twin Oaks Community

AMIDST THE BEHAVIORISTS excitedly drawing up proposals and gathering for discussions during the 1966 Waldenwoods conference, some of the participants decided that the step-by-step approach favored by the academics was not for them. Although the conference had been organized for the explicit purpose of setting up an experimental Walden Two community, it soon became apparent that there was little common ground between the handful of basically nonacademic, energetic, and impatient-for-change activists and the larger group of theory-oriented behavioral psychologists. The conference did, however, serve to bring together the more action-oriented Walden Two enthusiasts who were to found Twin Oaks Community. Most important among these was Kat Kinkade, the only founding member who is still—however reluctantly—a member of Twin Oaks.[1]

Kinkade recounts her reaction to the endless discussions at the conference: "[W]e wanted community and we wanted it right then, money or no money, psychologists or no psychologists, planning or no planning." The behaviorists, she felt, lacked the "necessary commitment to the ideas of community" (*Walden* 26). This realization came as a disappointment, since Kinkade had hoped to attract behavioral engineers to whatever Walden Two endeavor might take shape as a result of the conference:

> "In *Walden Two* Frazier tells his visitors that techniques of behavior-management for human society are developed and ready for use. It was years before I recognized this as part of the fiction. I thought it was literally true, and at first I was most anxious to recruit some behavioral psychologists for our leadership. My concept of their role was that of technical consultants to the planners. I didn't mean them to be officially in charge. I began to be disillusioned with psychologists even before Twin Oaks was founded.
> "The Waldenwoods conference in which I met the other people who were to become Twin Oaks founders was sponsored by just such psychologists, and

they disappointed my expectations. For one thing they planned a psychologist-king role for themselves. They conceived of an experimental community
as a group composed of selected candidates drawn from among the educated,
personally committed to the goals of the advancement of behavioral science
(and luckily possessing all the necessary work skills among them). Even in
those early days, I knew that such a group did not exist. Puzzlingly, these self-
appointed governors obviously had no talent for leadership in the ordinary
sense, and could not seem to make their training work for them even in the
elementary business of running a conference. They alienated the conferees by
their smug assumptions. Apparently not one of them had any grasp of what
would be 'reinforcing' to a group of eager idealists who had come together to
try to form a community. Any small-town politician could have done better.
Worse, they lacked the commitment even to consider starting a community
with a small group and no money. It was clear they mostly wanted to become
famous as the results of their 'experiment' got published. I despised them."
(Qtd. in Komar 10–11)

The "eager idealists" thus decided to embark on the adventure of communal
living without the support of behavioral engineers with questionable motives. This situation left a group of laypeople with very little background in
behaviorism to found what was to become the most famous of all Walden
Two communities: Twin Oaks.

As the reaction of the future Twin Oakers to the Waldenwoods conference
indicates, their understanding of *Walden Two* differed vastly from the behaviorists' interpretation. Not being behavioral engineers themselves, and
not being involved in setting up token economies among dependent populations, these readers were less likely to identify strongly with Frazier the
behavioral engineer. They were therefore less likely to plan "a psychologist-
king role for themselves," as Kinkade suspected the behaviorists of doing,
since they were not psychologists. This does not mean, however, that the
future Twin Oakers were not enamored with the concept of omnipotent
decision makers but rather that the behavioral aspect of the Skinnerian planner-manager system was of little importance to them.

Instead of approaching *Walden Two* from the point of view of behavioral
engineers, the future founders of Twin Oaks read it in a different context
and in a different way. The driving force behind the founding of Twin Oaks
was Kat Kinkade, and it is very much her personal interpretation of Skinner's
novel that is at the root of Twin Oaks. *Walden Two* is commonly described
as a badly written novel, with unconvincing, flat characters and dialogues
that are barely concealed vehicles for advocating behaviorist theories. Yet for

Kinkade, at least, reading *Walden Two* was a powerful experience: "At the time I read *Walden Two* I was thirty-four years old, divorced, raising a child, and making a living working at office jobs. I disliked office work very much, finding it boring and meaningless, and I wanted to get into an environment where I could find more interesting people to talk to. . . . *Walden Two* for me was a brilliant flash of light. I cannot exaggerate the excitement I felt when I read it. The community it depicted was everything I had ever wanted, everything I had ever believed in, everything I needed to be happy. It was impossible that there was no such place in life" (Kinkade, *Walden* 7).

The state of mind Kinkade was in when she read *Walden Two* resembles the excitement Skinner's narrator, Professor Burris, feels when he decides to join Walden Two. He, too, led a very dissatisfying life prior to discovering the secluded community of his former colleague, Frazier. A bachelor of long standing, he is no more than casually acquainted with his fellow faculty members. He does not place any value on his teaching. In fact, he has come to the conclusion that it is pointless to be in the business of proclaiming values that cannot be put into practice. All in all, he is lonely, disillusioned, cynical, and without any sense of purpose in his life. In contrast to his emotional state before coming into contact with the community, life at Walden Two appears idyllic, full of friendship, laughter, security, purpose, and esprit de corps. Remembers Kinkade: "I found a fair amount of purely novelistic material . . . that had no bearing on the basic subject matter, but for me they were lively, interesting conversations or incidents that might well happen in such a community. I loved them, just as I loved Frazier's astonishing 'proofs' of why his community worked so well" (Kinkade, "But Can He" 52).

The very features of the fictional Walden Two that were designed to give a reassuring and familiar introduction to controversial ideas caught Kinkade's interest. And to Kinkade, the "purely novelistic material" also held her interest. To her, the conversations and incidents were not introductions to something else; they were valuable in their own right.

Furthermore, Kinkade reacted strongly to the fictional Frazier, though with an interesting twist:

> To comprehend what the B. F. Skinner novel *Walden Two* meant to me in the early years, you have to understand that I was in love. Not with anyone I knew, all just flawed humans, but with Frazier. From the first time we see him, jogging on his heels down a dirt embankment, up through the last, when he shouts, "I am not a product of Walden Two" and proves it by some utterances of a rather egotistical sort, I recognized him as the man I had always wanted. There he was, mentally brilliant and emotionally warm, giving his life

to something worth doing and succeeding in bringing about a community
where I wanted to live. I wanted him for my life partner.

Of course I realized that he was only fiction and I couldn't have him. Just
the same, he was real to me in the sense that he represented my ideal. Skinner
had portrayed Frazier as very human indeed, with a sizable ego that I thought
was rather cute. Somehow I managed to dream that there would be people
attracted to his ideas who would resemble Frazier in basic ways, and I wanted
to be around people like that.

I was also in love with Frazier's creation. I longed to spend my life at Walden
Two, the community described in the book. It had everything I wanted. I
particularly wanted to join Fergy's choir and sing Bach masses, but the groups
that sat in the alcoves of the Ladder having friendly, witty conversations with
one another appealed to me, too. ("But Can He" 49)

As these sentiments indicate, Kinkade was dissatisfied not only with her job
and lack of a sense of purpose but also with her personal life. She was a
single mother who felt a strong connection to her daughter, but "not, I think,
as strong as the average mother-daughter connection." Furthermore, Kinkade had had an "alienating childhood" and decided not to have any ties to
her family as an adult—"they're just people," she once said in an interview
(Wenig and Coffman 34). Walden Two, with its communal child care and its
absence of nuclear or intergenerational families, appealed to Kinkade as a
single mother without family ties, because in a way it reflected the lifestyle
she had already chosen, yet with one important exception: it would provide
her with friendship, laughter, and a Bach choir. Kinkade admits that she
thought that if she lived in Walden Two, she would "find somebody to fall
in love with" (Wenig and Coffman 32). Incidentally, her hope to find love if
she only created a Walden Two did not turn into reality. In hindsight, she
feels that Twin Oaks "'respected me and it feared me, but it never loved me'"
(qtd. in Jones 31). In 1967, however, Kinkade was brimming with hope, and
she poured all her energy into the experiment of communal living.

Kinkade brought more than work dissatisfaction and loneliness to her
search for utopia. Being from a working-class background, she felt strongly
about equality, and equality is what she saw in *Walden Two*: "I need to say
that behaviorism was not my fundamental inspiration. I thought it was interesting, and I just assumed somehow we would attract some wonderful
psychiatrist—psychologist, I mean—who would come along, and he would
make that part of it work. And that would delight me, because I had no
objection to the theory. But what drew me was not behaviorism but what I
can only call communism. What drew me was equality. My fascination with

equality goes back to my childhood, so it's a very strong thing" (interview with the author, April 10, 1995).

Kinkade realizes that at Twin Oaks, she "took equality quite a bit further than Skinner would have taken it," and that it was this "particular emotional background, that fanatical devotion to equity" that was the "emotional spring" from which a lot of her early efforts came (interview with the author, April 10, 1995). As will be described in detail, Kinkade was also to be disappointed in her search for equality, not because she did not find it, but because she came to dislike the kind of equality she herself had helped to create at Twin Oaks.

Kinkade's cofounders came to *Walden Two* as social activists. Prior to 1966, the eight people who were to found Twin Oaks Community a year later knew each other mainly by correspondence. Reading *Walden Two* had been a powerful experience for all of them and had convinced them independently of each other that something along the lines of Skinner's utopia ought to be attempted. Most of them were dropouts from colleges and universities who had been active politically long before catching on to the idea of founding a community. When reading *Walden Two*, the features that appealed to them as social activists were those that the novel shared with Thoreau's *Walden* and Bellamy's *Looking Backward*. The fact that the founders of Twin Oaks consciously embraced their country's tradition of utopian dreaming and saw themselves as part of this tradition is reflected in the communards' practice of naming all of their buildings after previous communal experiments, like Harmony and Oneida (Komar 32–33). In trying to align himself with his country's utopian tradition—in order to make his readers accept a break with this same tradition—Skinner puts great emphasis on the nonconsumerist nature of his utopian community, pointing out that capitalistic overconsumption exploits natural resources, accepts that humanity is divided into winners and losers, and leaves the supposed winners emotionally crippled. At the same time, Skinner consciously embraces technology as a means of easing the working conditions for all, describing little inventions similar to those imagined by Bellamy. This combination of simplicity and technology attracted the future Twin Oakers, who were skeptical about the practicability and desirability of the popular back-to-the-land ideal of many other intentional communities founded around the same time. Also, Skinner described an Americanized version of small-sized socialism, which appealed not only to Kinkade but also to the other founders of Twin Oaks.

By the mid sixties, several of them started actively to search for people seriously interested in a real Walden Two. One future Twin Oaker started a mimeographed newspaper called *Walden Pool* to "get in touch with other people who might be interested in the experimental-society approach to social change" (Kinkade, *Walden* 6). Kinkade got together with some other people and founded the Walden House in Washington, D.C. Although a financial failure, it did serve as an "urban forerunner" of the rural Twin Oaks Community, and two important future Twin Oakers were attracted to the project through the Walden House newsletter (Kinkade, *Walden* 25). The Waldenwoods conference finally brought the future founders together to see whether they could agree on an approach to building a Walden Two community, and they quickly discovered that they could: they would pick from the pages of *Walden Two* what they needed for their purpose and put the rest aside, both literally and mentally. Skinner's utopia represented a lifestyle they found desirable and, perhaps more importantly, a method for achieving it.

In the tradition of utopian literature, *Walden Two* stands out for two features that are of vital importance to people who have more than an academic interest in the utopian dream. First, Skinner envisions his utopian society practically "around the corner." Second, he presents not an established world system but a fairly small, manageable community engaging in hands-on experimentation to make daily life more pleasant. The lifestyle Skinner depicts in his novel is radically different from the one adhered to by modern society, yet it is apparently quite feasible. In other words, Skinner provides a starting point for activists where most other utopian writers more obviously give mental food to dreamers (and scholars). As Skinner has remarked in his foreword to Kinkade's first book about Twin Oaks, *A Walden Two Experiment:* "Even the great Utopists showed a certain lack of confidence when they placed their better worlds in faraway places or distant times in order to make them seem plausible. Someday, somewhere, there will be a better life, but probably not here and now" (v).

It is no coincidence that the first Walden Two communities inspired by nonbehaviorists emerged at the same time Skinner played a prominent role in social reform. There were many in the protest movement of the sixties who wished for a change in the social system, and the future Twin Oakers were among them. Skinner's rejection of punitive control in education as well as in politics and his practical proposals for social reform made him part of this movement. Although there was a wide ideological gap, Skinner was at the forefront of those expressing doubts about existing societal practices and proposing ideas for change. Ingrid Komar describes the picture the early communards had of Skinner: "It is readily apparent how the promises of this new behavioral technology appealed to socially conscious Americans during the period when Twin Oaks was founded. . . . Behavior modification techniques were being applied to treat mental illness, to compensate for learning disabilities, to reinforce programmed instruction, to further certain limited forms of therapy, and to implement incentive programs. It was in this context, set in the social and political climate of the sixties, that the original members read *Walden Two*" (9–10).

Seen in this context, it is more understandable why behaviorism—which is, after all, the basic idea underlying *Walden Two*—was not all that important to those who founded Twin Oaks. For the reasons Komar recounts above, behaviorism was not a major stumbling block for the communards, yet to them, *Walden Two* presented mainly a good starting point for redesigning society, a fresh approach that held the promise of solving at least some of society's problems. Taking *Walden Two* as a manual for action, the communards' main interest lay in trying out the suggested labor-credit and planner-manager systems. Their approach to *Walden Two* was thus characterized by extracting the proposed communal structure, with the more general idea of applying behavioral principles to the design of society being secondary.

B. F. Skinner was not at all excited about having "hippies" adopt *Walden Two* as a source of inspiration. Immediately after reading his novel, Kinkade wrote to Skinner inquiring about a real-life community she could join. Skinner never replied (Jones 15). Although he recognized that young people "living in communes" were "said to be responsible for the increasing sales of *Walden Two*" in the sixties, he was not proud of the connection and maintained that he was "never one of the gurus of the sixties" (*Matter* 307). In his article "News from Nowhere, 1984," Skinner resurrects the narrator Burris from *Walden Two* to relate a fictional encounter between Frazier and Eric Arthur Blair, better known as George Orwell, in which a rather unfavorable picture is painted of the "hippie movement": "In the 1960s Frazier and Blair watched another version of anarchism—the so-called hippie movement. Young people turned against government. They broke laws, trashed, and called the police 'pigs.' . . . To Frazier's irritation, they formed 'communities' of a sort. They had their gurus: Norman O. Brown with his Freudian permissiveness and Herbert Marcuse with his mixture of Freud and Marx. Frazier may have been jealous, but when I told him that sales of *Walden Two* were soaring, he was annoyed. 'There is no connection whatsoever,' he insisted" (8).

The communards at Twin Oaks disagreed strongly with Skinner's contention that there was "no connection whatsoever" between their vision and *Walden Two*, and Skinner's attitude toward their community came as a disappointment. Kinkade in particular tried to communicate with Skinner: "I had a longing to talk to him, present him with his theory. 'This is what you thought would happen. Now let me tell you what actually happened when we tried this.' And I had a fantasy that he would be fascinated and that he would ask questions like, 'What about this angle? Whatever happened to this idea? You guys tried this, didn't you?' And somehow I was pretty badly disillusioned when nothing like that happened at all. Ever. He wasn't interested. In fact, he talked about himself, almost nonstop. . . . I am not fond of people who talk about themselves all the time. And it was a shock to me to find that Skinner was one of them. Somehow, *Walden Two* didn't make him seem like that" (interview with the author, April 10, 1995).

Kinkade recognizes that to some extent Skinner was right in not taking Twin Oaks seriously as a Walden Two experiment because of their lack of knowledge about behavioral engineering (interview with the author, April 10, 1995), yet she was bothered by the fact that Skinner did take an interest in other aspects of Twin Oaks. She remembers clearly that meeting him was disappointing to her on several levels: "I did not enjoy that. It wasn't what I expected. My problem was that I wanted Frazier, and Skinner wasn't Frazier. I thought he ought to be, and somehow he wasn't. I sort of fell in love with the character. But the man had some fussiness about him that just wasn't Frazier at all and wasn't the man I had admired in the novel. In fact, I found him rather typical of his generation. He had a kind of wistfulness about sex, about free love. . . . The fact that I was interested in *Walden Two* and in him . . . The fact that I was a woman mattered more, that I was doing a hippie commune. An I-bet-they-do-massages-in-a-hippie-commune kind of attitude" (interview with the author, April 10, 1995).

Though disappointed, the future founders of Twin Oaks were undeterred by Skinner's lack of interest. Motivated as they were, however, they did not have enough money to put their ideas into practice. Luckily for them, the otherwise disillusioning Waldenwoods conference was also attended by Bud, who had the financial means to get the community started and provided the community with a six-year lease on a farm that was to be the basis of the later Twin Oaks. His money was accepted gratefully, although Bud himself was later to cause problems because he sought to use his naturally elevated position within the community to gain political power. Thus, in the summer of 1967, the communards moved to the 120–acre farm in a rural area of Central Virginia they had bought by pooling their resources, with Bud providing the main share. Twin Oaks, as they soon decided to name their community, is within easy reach of a small town called Louisa, while two sizable urban centers, Richmond and Charlottesville, are less than an hour's drive away.

The communards' activities during the first months were directed toward little more than survival. Especially pressing was the fact that a lot of work had to be done if Twin Oaks Community was to get through its first winter. Although there were several buildings on the premises when the communards took up habitation, these had been designed for the needs of a family. They consisted of one small farmhouse, five medium-sized barns, and a few out-buildings, namely a smokehouse, woodshed, pigpen, and chicken coop (Kinkade, *Walden* 4 and 92). There were no more than four rooms, a half-cellar, and an unfinished attic to the farmhouse, which was hardly sufficient to house the rapidly growing population of the community. Very much concerned about the value of privacy, the communards' ideal was to provide a single room for every member. During the first months, however, most of the members made the various barn lofts their temporary home. Putting up a new building before winter was therefore among the communards' most urgent projects. They aptly called their first building Harmony. It was completed in 1968, just before the coldest part of the winter set in.

The communards also tried hard to keep the farm operational. Since none of them had any farming experience, this proved to be more difficult than putting up a building. Originally they had planned not only to live off the land as far as possible but also to make a profit. The communal property had originally been a tobacco farm, so the communards tried to take over the business from the prior owner. However, raising tobacco, while apparently not sparking a controversy in 1967, failed miserably as a money-making scheme.

Growing wheat, hay, corn, and beans also proved to be more difficult than they had anticipated. Due to miscalculation, 1968 saw them buried in heaps of beans and corn. They tried raising ducks and guineas and soon gave up on both. When their efforts were concentrated on putting up another building in 1969 (which was completed in 1971), the farm and garden went to pieces. Farming, the Twin Oakers discovered, is neither simple nor idyllic. It is hard and unprofitable work (Kinkade, *Walden* 59–71).

Had the community continued to rely on farming for survival beyond its first efforts, it might well have collapsed within the first two years. However, the communards admitted failure and sought other ways to sustain their community until they had worked out how to be economically independent. Only months after the founding of Twin Oaks, members started to get outside jobs on a rotating basis and continued to do so for several years. The idea was that all members should take a turn at ensuring the community's survival by getting temporary, mostly unskilled jobs in nearby towns. Since some people flatly refused to go out and get a job voluntarily, it was made compulsory. In 1971, these jobs still made up half of the community's income (Komar 33).

Much to the surprise of the Twin Oakers, an industry in which they had no prior knowledge became their main source of income: weaving hammocks. In 1967, it was no more than one of the many economic experiments the communards tried. By 1973, it made for one-third of the community's income (Kinkade, *Walden* 72), steadily rising to constituting two-thirds of the community's income. This stable source of income allowed the communards to buy adjoining land, tripling their property to more than four hundred acres.

Despite its success, Twin Oaks Hammocks is constantly under attack for two reasons. First, the hammocks are made of oil-based polypropylene and are thus at odds with the community's environmental ideals. Second, in order to sell the hammocks, the community has to partake in the capitalist market of mainstream society (Komar 157). The economic survival of Twin Oaks thus depends on a business some of the communards find unacceptable. Apart from these ideological considerations, the more practical-minded communards are concerned about the dependency of Twin Oaks on Pier One. This nationwide company buys most of the hammocks produced at Twin Oaks and has been doing so almost from the beginning of Twin Oaks Hammocks. "There are people," reports Kinkade, "who think that if Twin Oaks had not lucked into the Pier One account, the community would have folded, like so many others" (Kinkade, *Utopia* 53). Some people fear that Twin Oaks could still fold if it ever lost the Pier One account. As a preventive measure, Twin Oaks Community tries to get smaller, more diverse sales contracts for the hammocks. The fear of dependency on Pier One also continuously encourages the communards to seek new sources of income. Consequently, Twin Oaks runs a small indexing office and has recently started processing tofu. Also, the communards value self-grown food so highly that they have decided to subsidize extensive gardening. Homegrown vegetables and farm products thus make up a large percentage of the communards' diet.

Despite their stable economic situation, Twin Oaks takes advantage of free health care provided by the state for the poor. None of the Twin Oakers have health insurance (if treatment cannot be had for free the community pays for it). Those who qualify for unemployment or other aid turn over the money to the community as a whole.

Apart from these economic and housing difficulties, the early Twin Oakers were discouraged by the kind of people attracted to their community. The majority were young and neither committed to the idea of making the community work nor very responsible in any other way. Others joined enthusiastically only to drop out after a short time. The communards tried to admit only those who were committed to *Walden Two*, but since they needed everybody they could get just to survive, it was almost impossible to be selective.

Also, until 1969, prospective members had to pay an admission fee. That practice had to be dropped when the membership diminished threateningly that year. The stringent property rules Twin Oaks adhered to during its early years were suspected by some of keeping away otherwise seriously interested people. The rules were therefore amended to accommodate potential members who felt uneasy about turning over all their possessions to Twin Oaks. An agreement was reached that "any money which they might have owned before joining simply stays in the bank for their first three years," but that "Twin Oaks receives the interest on it, as well as dividends on any stocks and bonds, rents from any real property, or any continuing income of any kind" (Kinkade, *Walden* 49).

It was only when the community began to have more people interested in joining than they could accommodate, roughly five years after the founding, that a rather stringent membership admission process was instituted, although neither the admission fee nor the strict property rules were reinstituted. This new admission process provides that potential members must come for a three-week visit, pass an interview, and be accepted by the entire community as provisional members. After half a year, they obtain full membership. Even with this more selective process in place, Twin Oaks membership grew from eight in 1967 to around forty in 1973 to nearly a hundred in the 1980s, where it remains today.

Throughout these struggles for survival and then increasing stability, the communards tried to implement the economic as well as governmental structures suggested in *Walden Two*. This proved to be more difficult than originally anticipated. They soon discovered that *Walden Two* had a serious drawback as a manual: it became obvious almost from the beginning that its author had no practical experience in communal living and had not anticipated what kinds of problems the communards might run into. The founders of Twin Oaks learned the hard way that the practicability of the society described in *Walden Two* was far from being "an accomplished fact," as Skinner's mouthpiece Frazier had led them to believe (56). To get a starting point for the structure of their community, however, the Twin Oakers literally sat down with *Walden Two* in their hands and extracted from its pages the economic and governmental structure (which they found to be far less detailed than they had wished) and went about implementing the results. From there on, they had to rely on their talent for improvisation.

# 9   The Planner-Manager System

"IT SEEMED TO US when we started the Community," remembers Kinkade, "that eight people didn't need much government" (*Walden* 51). Their early, rather informal gatherings revolved around questions of what kind of decision-making process they would like for themselves and how often they should have meetings.[2] They settled for decision making by consensus, because of one person's enthusiasm for it, and had weekly meetings. Decision making by consensus, a system originally used in Quaker meetings, means that issues are not voted on but are discussed until an agreement acceptable to everybody can be reached. It seems rather surprising that decision making by consensus was even considered by the founders since it is pretty much the opposite of the idea of omnipotent planners. Also, the consensus process is by nature slow and tedious, even in a group as small as eight. Since not all Twin Oakers were committed to consensus, the less patient ones did the work they deemed necessary and made the decisions that had to be made without waiting for group consensus. Individuals with a special interest in one area of work simply took over responsibility for it, regardless of whether they were officially put into office to do so. These people came to be called managers as a matter of course. Exactly how people became managers at Twin Oaks, however, and what their duties and responsibilities were was not clear during the first few weeks of Twin Oaks life.

If the position of the managers was undefined in the beginning, planners were nonexistent. Skinner had suggested a Board of Planners to guide the community's general direction. In the early days of Twin Oaks, those who determined the general direction of the community were not officially charged with doing so. The consensus meeting, which was supposed to substitute not only for the managers but also the planners, did not fulfill this function either. Instead, Kinkade reports that "most decisions were really made by individuals who just thought of doing something and did it" (*Walden* 52). Kinkade probably speaks for herself to a large extent; she was opposed to decision making by consensus from the beginning but did not want to argue about it in order to hold the precarious communal peace. Not arguing about something, however, does not necessarily mean that one really goes along with it. Kinkade was the driving force behind the founding of Twin Oaks and held considerable power. If she was opposed to consensus, there was little chance for that form of government to survive for long.

It may still seem surprising that *Walden Two* enthusiasts would stumble along for weeks without trying to implement Skinner's idea of government. The major problem was perhaps that out of the eight people who founded Twin Oaks, only three were seriously committed to *Walden Two*. It took the resentment of one member—who wanted a managership already taken by somebody else—to formalize the community's government after it had gone almost entirely without one for five weeks. The disgruntled member's protest led to an election at Twin Oaks to establish the first Board of Planners. The board officially appointed the managers. Although decisions of a general nature were made by the Board of Planners, the actual power for most decisions lay with the managers. The community's diet, work distribution, architectural plans, and clothing, to name only a few areas, were the responsibility of the various managers. The planners were mainly charged with working out the details of the labor-credit and planner-manager systems.

It was decided that the three planners should serve staggered eighteen-month terms. By having only one new planner every six months, the communards hoped to avoid incompetence on the part of a board consisting of new planners as well as the accumulation of power in the hands of three people working together for a long stretch of time. As Skinner suggested, planners were not elected by vote but appointed by their predecessors. The main criteria were to be competence and commitment to the community. "We did not want *equal* government," says Kinkade, "we wanted *good* government" (*Utopia* 24).

As a safeguard against any possible misuse of the governmental system, the communards had the right to veto any decision. A simple majority vote was necessary to overrule a decision. To assure some kind of continuity, it was decided that the basic laws the community had given itself could be changed only by a two-thirds majority vote of the entire membership. The communards did not think it necessary to have more safeguards against the accumulation of power. They firmly believed that it was neither possible nor

Handmade hammocks are the economic backbone of Twin Oaks Community. (courtesy Twin Oaks Community)

Twin Oaks Community in its early days. (courtesy Twin Oaks Community)

desirable to hold power in an income-sharing community of free people because there was nothing to be gained from it.

Although misuse was apparently not a problem, the underlying assumptions of the Skinnerian planner-manager system began to have their effect on the community as soon as the first Board of Planners was instituted. During this time, Kinkade was one of the planners and a firm believer in professional government. Even in hindsight, she feels that the approach they tried in 1967 was a good one:

> [T]he average citizen did not trouble him- or herself with issues of government at all. They had input in the sense that somebody would say, "How do you like your life? What's wrong with it? Can you think of improvements that would make a difference to you?" And therefore you would have input. Saying, "Yeah, I don't like the lumpy oatmeal," or whatever. But you would not be asked, you know, "What do you think of the sabbatical policy?" or, "Do you think the average member works too hard?" You'd be asked, "Do you work too hard?" And that's all. So it assumed that government itself was an area of expertise and that you trained for it and you did it. If you were good at it, if you had a talent for it. . . . It wasn't supposed to be any bigger deal to be a planner than it was to be a mechanic. I liked that idea very much. And in honest truth, I still do. (interview with the author, April 10, 1995)

Kinkade clearly saw herself as one of the decision makers who would trouble themselves with thinking about lumpy oatmeal *and* the sabbatical policy. She had charged the behaviorist attendants of the Waldenwoods conference with lacking "talent for leadership in the ordinary sense" and apparently was confident that she would do better. Looking back on it, she is somewhat amazed herself "how I thought we were going to be wise enough" to make far-reaching decisions, but "I just know I felt confident that we could, and perhaps I am saying that I thought I could" (interview with the author, April 11, 1998). She admits that she is not altogether sure that professional decision makers would always make better decisions than those that are arrived upon in a democracy, yet she modifies this concession by adding, "What I had close at hand was the sure knowledge that I and some selected companions were definitely better than the little democracy of fifteen, twenty, thirty people that we had at Twin Oaks at the time. That I was sure of" (interview with the author, April 10, 1995).

Had Kinkade been the center of a group of people willing to follow her leadership, it is possible that her concept of "good government" instead of equal government could have worked out. She was part of a group of people, however, who also thought that they would make good governors in the *Walden Two* sense, and it was—once again—the fight over who would be guided gently and who would do the guiding that led to intense conflicts almost as soon as the first Board of Planners began its work. Ironically, the major person inadvertently initiating the rapid move away from the concept of the planner-manager system was someone who very much believed in it. Bud, the cofounder of independent financial means who had bought the farm and given Twin Oaks a lease on it, tried to overthrow the Board of Planners in 1968. He was dissatisfied with the slow progress the community was making. The board, he felt, was making irresponsible decisions. It especially bothered him that anybody who wanted to join the community was admitted. Most importantly, however, it bothered Bud that he had not been part of making these decisions. He strongly objected to the open-door policy, but since planner meetings were closed, he had not been able to voice his discontent with that policy when it was first decided upon. Several quarrels of a similar nature finally led Bud to insist that he be a planner, too. Much confusion and mutual accusations followed. Being a planner "wasn't supposed to be any bigger deal than it was to be a mechanic," yet Bud made it quite clear that he would not accept any other position at Twin Oaks. Since he had provided the financial means to get the community started at all, the communards were at a loss as to how to deal with the situation. The Board of Planners dissolved temporarily, thus finding a temporary compromise. Bud would not wrestle his way into a plannership, but neither would anybody else be a planner. When the other members felt that they were strong enough to oppose Bud openly, they reestablished the original Board of Planners. The embittered Bud subsequently left the community, leaving the communal property in the hands of the community as a whole because he was legally bound to do so.

Bud's criticism of the planner-manager system, motivated largely by the fact that he was not a planner but felt that he should be, stimulated a number of changes. Among other minor changes, his strong objection to closed planner meetings led to an opening of these meetings to the entire membership. However, the opening of the planner meetings to the entire membership in 1968 was only the first step toward acknowledging the fact that most Twin Oakers—even those who did not have a strong ambition to be part of the Board of Planners themselves—were not willing to leave the decision making to only three people.

Kinkade describes 1970 as an important year for Twin Oaks because the membership began to increase steadily and was somewhat more stable than during the first three years. However, the growth in membership as a result of the open admission policy had unwanted side effects. It helped Twin Oaks survive as a community, but what survived had little to do with the Walden Two community envisioned by the founders. The vast majority of the people who joined in the early seventies, when Twin Oaks was desperate for members, were simply not interested in *Walden Two*. The founders would have loved to select members on the basis of their enthusiasm for Skinner's novel, but Kinkade recounts dryly that there "just weren't any behaviorists" among the applicants (interview with the author, April 10, 1995). Predictably, says Kinkade—who did not predict it—"the original philosophy was . . . overrun" (*Utopia* 25), for it was complaints by these new, influential members that finally brought about a fundamental change in the planner-manager system.[3] While accepting a wide array of applicants ensured the survival of Twin Oaks, the community's theory of government changed radically, although this was not noticeable right away. Planners were still appointed by their predecessors. The eighteen-month staggered terms remained, as did the notion that the planners were to decide the community's general direction. The change occurred in the *conception* of the planners' decision-making process. Most of the newer members were adamant about wanting to be heard and wanting their opinions considered. Kinkade, a firm believer to this day in government "for the people, not by the people" (interview with the author, April 10, 1995), found this demand, voiced with increasing intensity by Twin Oakers, baffling: "The only thing we did not predict and could not control was the feeling that the average citizen had about somebody else doing the government. They just hated it. And even though you say to them, 'What decisions would you have wanted to be different?' They would say, 'I don't know of any decisions I would have wanted to be different, the decisions were fine. I just wanted to be part of it.' So at this point I conjecture that Skinner was wrong: the average citizen will not in fact be satisfied with such an arrangement. Then I think, maybe in some other country. Maybe in Mexico. But not in the USA. It's just not going to make it" (interview with the author, April 10, 1995).

In order to meet the demands of the dissatisfied members, the planners started spending considerable time listening to "input," a word Twin Oaks Community could not do without nowadays. The early planners had considered themselves "advocates" of ideas (Komar 94). They made decisions based on what they believed to be best for the advance of Twin Oaks towards becoming a Walden Two, even if these decisions found no majority. They considered themselves experts in government who knew best what was good for their community. The Skinnerian idea that the most competent person should be in charge was after all the main reason why planners were not elected but appointed to office according to their competence. The early Twin Oakers agreed with this, as well as with Skinner's assessment that "ordinary" members would take little interest in government. The people who joined Twin Oaks in the seventies strongly disagreed.

The conflict came to a head when a debate over expansion versus quality of life flared up among Twin Oakers (Kinkade, *Walden* 226). The expansionists were in favor of fast community growth, so that the communal lifestyle could be embraced by as many people as possible. The quality-of-life proponents wanted to see the community become a nicer, more livable place for those who were already there before expanding rapidly. The planners found themselves in the awkward position of theoretically holding the power to make a decision while receiving serious input from the membership not to make a decision going against the wishes of the general membership. The quality-of-life proponents—the majority—won. Kinkade, a fervent advocate of expansion, lost. The role of the planner shifted more and more from making long-range, independent, and undemocratic decisions to listening to membership input and trying to facilitate a compromise acceptable to everybody and representative of the majority.

Despite all of the changes that the role of the planner went through, the managerial position is still very much what it was in the beginning. People become managers if they are interested and competent in an area where there is a vacancy. Managers have no set term limits. A group of managers operating in related areas forms a council charged with making decisions of concern to those areas.

This development leaves Twin Oaks with a unique governmental system somewhere between consensus and democracy while operating on the "crumbling ruins" (Komar 99) of a strictly undemocratic, nonparticipatory, and elitist concept.

The possible misuse of power does not appear to be an important topic at Twin Oaks. The planner-manager system is quasi democratic, but without the safeguards of democracy. Skinner was reproached for legitimizing totalitarian regimes that usually claim to know what is best for the people. The Twin Oaks system, while de facto not allowing planners to make minority decisions, is still based on trust and the conviction that there is little to be gained from holding power in an income-sharing community. Seen from the outside, the Twin Oaks planner-manager system seems vulnerable to misuse, yet Kinkade is the only one to acknowledge the fact that there are serious power struggles at Twin Oaks. She sees part of the problem in most communards' hesitation to acknowledge that there even is something like power in an egalitarian community. If they do acknowledge it, they regard it as something that should be done away with. Kinkade comments on this attitude: "The only trouble is that, like sewage, power really is right there under the surface, and unless it is properly controlled, channeled, and turned to good and fertile purposes, it will pollute. Self-deception pollutes, and the more self-deception, the more pollution" ("Power" 404).

Even if the Twin Oakers do not like to think of power struggles going on within their community, perhaps these conflicts keep the system running: as long as several people struggle for power, it has not yet come to be in the hands of any one person.

Curiously enough, the biggest problem faced by Twin Oaks today in regard to its political system is not power struggles but political apathy. Komar argues that this is partly due to the fact that the decision-making process at Twin Oaks is slow, tedious, and unrewarding for those involved in it. Planners can be approached by members at any time, but the official platform for input is the Friday night meeting, which is open to everybody. After the open meeting, the planners hold a business meeting where they go through the input they received and make a decision. Komar believes that it is dissatisfying for members never to be present when a decision is actually made. They always have to wait for the planners to put up the decision on a public Opinions and Ideas board the next day (Komar 102).

Rather than showing impatience at the tediousness of the decision-making process, however, a fairly large number of members seem to be reluctant to get involved in politics in the first place. Komar suspects that the frequently heard "I trust the planners" is in fact a euphemism for "alienation, boredom, or indifference" (Komar 99). On first sight, political apathy is a strange phenomenon for an intentional community. Yet the communards' lack of interest in government may be symptomatic of the change Twin Oaks went through: New Age postulates self-discovery through spiritual means, not political activism. Although not behavioral engineers themselves, the founders of Twin Oaks had been intrigued by the idea that human behavior could be changed—via self-control and conditioning—and thereby society could be changed. The human-potential movement that excited the Twin Oakers of the early seventies, who soon made up the majority of the community's membership, did not aim at changing society but focused almost entirely on the individual, who was perceived as being intrinsically good and full of potential. "Twin Oaks," says Komar, "quickly abandoned whatever allegiance to Skinnerian behaviorism it ever had" (7). Kinkade adds: "'Behaviorism didn't stand a chance against the new philosophy. How could it? With behaviorism we concentrated on self-control. The new movement told us to express ourselves. . . . We were told, in effect, that it was now okay to give ourselves to the study of our own "needs." This gospel was strong and fresh, and it sold at Twin Oaks. . . . I think the accepted theory now is that behaviorism was one of several early religions that Twin Oaks went through, and that now that the group has matured, behaviorism is thought of as a discarded ideology'" (qtd. in Komar 191).

What Kinkade calls an "obvious New Age cultural ambience" is the result of this movement's grip on Twin Oaks (*Utopia* 202). The introduction of New Age ideas was resisted by the early members. One look at Twin Oaks today, however, shows that they lost their fight against herbal teas, Indian rituals, meditation, eastern spiritualism, feedback sessions, and sweat lodges. In 1973, while *Walden Two*—and with it, to some extent, behaviorism—was still very important to some members, including Kinkade, the community brought in facilitators to discuss openly the issues that were threatening to divide the membership. As a result, remembers Kinkade, behaviorism was "explicitly repudiated": "[T]he group rejected behaviorism at that point. They said behaviorism is one thing that a few people believe in but most of us don't. We're an eclectic group, we believe in all kinds of things, and it's been that way ever since" (interview with the author, April 11, 1998).

After the Walden Two philosophy of government was rejected, Twin Oaks has apparently managed to avoid adopting any other central philosophy or a leader figure. This was not by intention, apparently, but rather a result of a balance of power achieved by having philosophies and would-be leaders compete for the attention of a diverse membership. As Kinkade remarks, "Twin Oaks has no central theoretician. It's always been intellectually wide open. There have always been plenty of potential leaders. You know, people who come there and would love to have other people sit at their feet, but nobody is interested in sitting at their feet. It's very eclectic and very scattered. And very much in conflict all the time. All the time. Sometimes I think that's good. Most of the time, I just don't know" (interview with the author, April 10, 1995).

Although Kinkade would still prefer professional government, she has come to accept that democratic thinking prevails at Twin Oaks. She even contends that for a democracy, the community is doing quite well, "even though it's a mess" (interview with the author, April 10, 1995).

# 10 The Communal Child-Care Program

THE TWIN OAKS communal child-care program is perhaps the area in which Skinner's ideas failed most obviously to live up to the expectations of the communards. Kinkade summarized in 1994 that the community's children "are well cared for, appropriately educated, and generally happy, but very little of this can be attributed to the purely communal aspects of the [child-care] program. The fact is that the communal child rearing experiment, as originally conceived, has failed, and we are in the process of figuring out what to put in its place" (*Utopia* 146).

The one aspect of the Walden Two communal child-care program that Skinner vastly underestimated was the emotional impact it would have on parents and children. In hindsight, Kinkade—who had been strongly in favor of trying communal child rearing, and who was perhaps unaware of the emotional stumbling blocks because she herself had no close emotional ties to her family—concludes that "[p]arents want to be with the kids, they are attracted to the little things, for some reason or other. They want to raise them. They want to influence them. They want to be there. I think that is perfectly natural. And I don't think it can be interfered with much. There were things about our theories at the time, though, of early education that came directly out of Skinner. And when I say 'our,' maybe I mean 'my.' But I was completely fascinated, for example, with Skinner's notion that you would design toys to build perseverance. What an idea! Because personally I don't have much of a history of sticking to a task till it's done or overcoming small difficulties, and I see lots of people who don't" (interview with the author, April 10, 1995).

Although Twin Oaks eventually gave in to the demands of parents to be in charge of the upbringing of their own children, the early history of the community's child care marked a radical departure from the family concept. The history of child care and education at Twin Oaks can be divided into roughly three phases: during the first phase, spanning the early, more or less childless years of Twin Oaks (1967–72), a comprehensive educational program was nonexistent. An ideologically diverse, flexible, and workable child-care program prevailed for a period of twelve years (1972–84), while today the communards' ideas on child rearing and education are in flux.

The founders of Twin Oaks struggled for survival during the first several years of the community's existence.[4] Amidst economic instability, insufficient housing facilities, and high membership turnover, there was little room for theoretical discussions about children in utopia, especially since there were only one or two children, if any, living at Twin Oaks at any given point. These children came with their parents, stayed in the community for a while, and left again with their parents. Skinner's educational program, starting at birth and concentrating on the first six years of a child's life, could not possibly function because there simply were no children present from birth. Neither could a controlled, infection-free environment have been insured on a run-down farm where many of the communards had taken up temporary quarters in barn lofts. As a result of these circumstances, the community's children remained mainly their parents' responsibility. The communards did appoint a child manager, but this had little effect on the parents' authority over their children. Whenever a dispute had to be settled regarding a child, usually over safety concerns on the part of the parents, the communards gave way. It was obvious that the parents would simply leave if they did not get their wish.

The communards decided to try communal child care again as soon as children were born into the community. They hoped this would give them a reasonable chance to have a fresh start with children who would actually grow up at Twin Oaks. The mother of the first child to be born into the community in 1969, however, was reluctant to give up control over her baby. The mother had joined the community to be with her husband, an enthusiastic communard, but she was not really interested in the community's goals herself. The demand of the communards that the child be raised communally was met with fervent resistance from the mother. Living in an environment not completely of her own choosing, she was simply not willing to give up her only child. The communards, though theoretically in disagreement, were sympathetic. The fact that the child manager at the time happened to be the mother's husband complicated the community's efforts to handle the situation according to plan. The young mother finally left the community and took the baby with her. The episode convinced the communards that they were not yet ready to raise children at Twin Oaks. This insight resulted in a no-more-children rule that was enforced with exceptions until 1972.

A fairly well-organized child-care program was initiated in 1972.[5] The communards put up a children's building called Degania,[6] designed to fulfill all the children's needs from infancy to teenage years. Degania was built some distance away from the rest of the community's buildings in order to minimize haphazard interference between those who were not engaged in child care and the children. In addition to this communal setting, however, the communards recognized the need to provide a certain amount of continuity for the children's emotional attachments. They felt that depending upon child-care workers who might leave the community at any time was too precarious an arrangement. Therefore, the concept of "primaries" was established. Each child had two or more adults, or primaries, who were committed to building an emotional, long-term relationship with the child. These primaries were often the child's parents.

The children's lives at this point were centered around Degania. They slept, ate, and played there, cared for by child-care workers called "metas," a name adopted from the kibbutz term for child-care workers. The three- to five-year-olds visited a Montessori class taught by a certified teacher, a member of Twin Oaks. The older children then moved on to the Oakley Primary School in the vicinity of the community, which was run by former Twin Oakers. Since there were no older children, these two schools sufficed to meet the community's needs. A Child Board, consisting of the metas, the teachers, and the primaries, decided on broad policies and solved day-to-day problems. The weekly meetings were compulsory for metas and teachers. Going through the agenda, reports Komar, often took several hours. Since decisions were reached by consensus, all sides had to be heard and considered.

Although the system seems to have been fairly satisfactory for all involved, it was not based on any generally accepted theoretical assumptions. Ingrid Komar writes in *Living the Dream:* "My research never succeeded in unearthing a comprehensive statement of the current goals of the Child Program from either the Child Board files or the recorded notes of meta meetings. . . . The Child Board very deliberately decided on 'an eclectic approach to education.' . . . It would be completely out of character for Twin Oaks to commit itself to one educational philosophy" (212, 249).

The precariousness of the child-care program became apparent when it collapsed because one dedicated child-care worker left the community.[7] Kinkade observes: "[W]e tried to take care of our children in groups, with their age peers, but this worked only as long as we had a long-term, strong-minded, dedicated professional childcare worker in Degania. Her name was Amri, and she was with us for many years. Her theories became Twin Oaks theories. Some parents resented her dominion, but she held the program together, a fact the Community as a whole did not recognize until she left in 1984 and the program fell into serious difficulties" (*Utopia* 147).

To add to the uncertainty, the Montessori teacher left Twin Oaks as well, and Oakley Primary School had to fold in 1990 for lack of students and teachers. The communards tried home schooling. They gave up on it after a year because it cost them too many labor credits and was ineffective. Then they started sending children to public or private schools, depending on their parents' preference and the community's budget. Some parents pulled their children out of the child program completely. Others made sleeping arrangements for their children in their own quarters, sending them to Degania only irregularly. The Twin Oakers were at a loss. In 1994, Kinkade recorded in her second book that she was "writing during a period in which the child program is in flux, and we can't tell from here how anything is going to turn out" (Kinkade, *Utopia* 144).

What went wrong? It seems that, ironically, it was precisely the dedicated child-care workers initially pushing for communal child rearing who changed their minds about the desirability of the whole concept. In an interview with former Twin Oakers, several ex-members report that it was their strong attachment to their children that made them leave Twin Oaks. "When I left Twin Oaks, it was really because of Maya," remembers one person who left. "I just knew I wanted to be able to teach my kids more what I believed, and wanted to stop pretending that it wasn't important to me" ("Leaving" 20). Another ex-member agrees with this assessment and adds, "Yes, we formed the child system that we ended up leaving" (24). One ex-member, Warren, notes:

> I think that Degania being so far away was a big part of it. That was part of what made me think, "Jesus, I don't like this kind of child caring." I got into feeling strongly connected with Lauren.
>
> I remember vividly having discussions with people before we had Lauren, talking about how parents shouldn't have any special relationship with their children. 'After all, there was just this conditioning, genes and things were tossed out there, mixed together and made this other person and that was the end of that connection.' I can't believe any of it anymore. . . . I mean, it's one thing to talk about having a child, and another thing to actually do it. I didn't know what the hell I was talking about. (24)

Among the children who experienced life at Degania was Kinkade's granddaughter, Lee Ann Kinkade. Josie Kinkade, who had been part of the founding of Twin Oaks at age thirteen, gave birth to a daughter in 1974. Her mother believed very much in the concept of giving a child to the community, and Lee Ann Kinkade was raised at Degania with almost no contact with her biological parents during the first five years of her life. Lee Ann, at age twenty-five, had mixed feelings about her early upbringing:

> Metas left the community all the time. By the time I was five, all of my original caretakers had left. When someone leaves the community, and you're a child,

it's like they died. Of course in the Walden Two vision, the society would be so ideal that no one would ever leave. But I believe that, even in Walden Two, it was true that childcare was just one of many jobs one could do for a short amount of time, and then move on to, say, milking the cows or gardening. . . . Children become attached. I am still deeply attached to metas who parented me since I was five. There is a lot of pain associated with that for me. I got very used to losing people. And probably the single hardest thing for me growing up was how often I had to form new attachments. . . . Now what's also true, given the early Degania model, is that we never went without food, without clothing, without hugs, even. I was a well cared for child. If I missed a meal, it was because I hated what was being served. But in terms of attachment. . . . (47)

Lee Ann Kinkade concludes that although she benefited from the emphasis on positive reinforcement, there were "major drawbacks" in the basic assumption underlying the communal child-care system as envisioned by Skinner (46–48). "Metas are not automaton scientists, and they shouldn't be," she insists, pointing out that people's skills, experiences, and personalities differ. Yet this is "one of the things that Skinner really failed to see coming: that the individual relationship between, in this case, child and meta, superseded in some ways the structure of that relationship" (48).

In recognizing the strong emotional bond that children and parents at Twin Oaks have come to value much more than whatever benefit there might be in a Walden Two–style ethical training, the communal child-care program virtually dissolved. Nowadays, all major decisions rest with the parents, children and adults live together, and the community's children are either home schooled or enrolled in local public schools or in a Montessori school in Charlottesville. Degania, the former children's building, stands deserted.

# 11 The Labor-Credit System

THE TWIN OAKERS spent the first three weeks of their communal life together without any work system at all. They were so excited about building a community that everybody just pitched in and worked as much as they possibly could. It was when the first complaints came that they set about implementing the labor-credit system as they understood it. The initiative came from one female member who did most of the housework. She resented the fact that the other women in the community did not help out and demanded that they help her do the dishes. These other women, Kinkade and her daughter Josie, were not the least bit interested in housework and were not willing to wash dishes if the men did not do so as well. It seemed to all of them that it was time for some kind of agreement.

The communards knew they wanted to work under the kind of labor-credit system suggested by Skinner. So they studied *Walden Two* carefully to find out what they had to do next. To their dismay, they discovered that Skinner does not lay out a detailed plan of any kind. He talks about the *theory* of the labor-credit system, and portrays his communards chopping wood and liking it, but he does not elaborate on the *practical* side of such a system. Among other things, the Twin Oaks communards had trouble deciding what should be considered work. In the beginning, only dish washing was on the labor-credit system. As time progressed and the initial enthusiasm for work subsided, more and more tasks were added. "Within a month," reports Kinkade, "we were going by the concept that every kind of work that was useful to the group (except thinking, talking, reading, and research) belonged on the labor credit system" (Kinkade, *Walden* 41).

The first system they invented for the distribution of work operated without labor credits and went only by the hours that had to be spent on a job. Every week, the communards would sit in a circle and deal out a deck of cards with a work description and approximate time written on each card. Then everybody checked the cards they had been dealt and passed the card with the personally least desirable job on it to the person on their right. Whoever was satisfied with their hand and had collected the right amount of hours would stop playing. The others would continue to pass cards around. Twin Oakers kept this system for a few weeks and eventually decided to drop it. Although they enjoyed sitting in a circle and playing cards, the process of work distribution took too long and would obviously not work for more than a handful of people.

Next they experimented with various sign-up systems before finally settling for simultaneous sign-up. The simultaneous sign-up system was the first to actually employ the idea of labor credits. In this system, all the jobs that had to be done the following week were written on sheets of paper. Every communard received one of these sheets and signed up for the jobs he or she would prefer to do. The labor-credit value of a job was decided by how many people signed up for it. If a lot of people found a job desirable one week, the labor-credit value for it would go down for the next two weeks.

If a job was so unpopular that nobody signed up for it, the value went up. After everybody had ranked the jobs in order of personal preference, the collected sheets served to determine the labor-credit value of every job. Afterwards, the communards were free to sign up for any kind of work they wanted, provided they made quota. To "make quota" meant to work for however long it would take to accumulate the number of labor credits the communards had decided upon as a weekly minimum. Although this system involved a lot of clerical work, it was popular enough to be in use for two years. Especially popular were the individualized work schedules and the ability to change work areas from week to week.

In 1970, the arrival of many new members brought new ideas and yet another change to the system. Instead of giving jobs absolute labor-credit value according to the overall popularity of the job within the community, the labor-credit value of a job now differed according to how desirable the job was to the person who wanted to do it. Kinkade explains: "Our current system asks each member to take a list of all the available jobs and place them in the order of his personal preference. After that, he doesn't have to sign up at all. The labor clerical people take over and work for two days filling out everyone's schedule as close to their personal preferences as possible. These days one gets high credits for doing work which one finds *personally* disagreeable. Two people might be shoveling manure side by side, and the person who enjoys the work is getting less credit for it than the person who doesn't" (*Walden* 44).

This kind of variable credit was used for over a year until the issue of dirty dishes led to yet another change of the system. The variable credit came under attack when it became impossible to raise the credits awarded to washing dishes any higher. It was obvious that the job had to be done, and it was equally obvious that the Skinnerian labor-credit system offered no workable solution for the problem. Skinner had imagined his perfect society to be fairly affluent and thus to have a never-ceasing supply of labor credits, which Twin Oaks did not have. Labor credits had to be given out sparingly, so the most important jobs would get done. Instead of Skinner's proposed four hours a day, Twin Oakers still have regular working weeks of over forty hours. When nobody signed up for dish washing, there came a point when the labor credit for doing the job could not be raised any further without causing a major inflation on the whole credit system. "In the ensuing conflict," writes Komar, "egalitarianism won and behaviorism lost" (65). Kinkade explains the communards' dilemma:

> "To raise the credits for dishwashing required that one lower the credits for something else. Since dishwashing is a large block, a large block would have to

be lowered to keep the credit from inflating. There was no large block whose workers were willing to be so lowered. If we had done it to construction, we would have aggravated an already difficult shortage of skilled workers, who would just not have worked if so undervalued. The easy target seemed to be managers who got credit for organizing the meetings, drawing up charts and plans, and presenting things to the group in an organized fashion. Unfortunately, even lowering managerial work to .9 per hour did not offset the dishwashing, which would have had to go as high as 2.0 per hour in order to get anybody to volunteer for it. Lowering management, construction, and farming just for the sake of dishwashing was too big a pill for people to swallow. . . . The easiest solution seemed to be to have everybody do the job that would otherwise rise to astronomical figures." (Qtd. in Komar 65)

Dish washing was accordingly taken off the labor-credit system and is now a rotated duty to be performed by every member and visitor. The same applies to cleaning bathrooms.

The problem of dish washing also alerted the communards to a more severe flaw in Skinner's labor-credit system: it works only in an affluent society, if at all. In the nonaffluent Twin Oaks environment, it ultimately bred unfairness. One major problem was the difficulty of finding an objective way to determine the labor-credit value of a job. The other problem was conscious and repeated manipulation. Communards who were frankly dedicated to their jobs tended to end up with humiliatingly little credit for it, while other less dedicated communards worked shorter hours on supposedly disliked jobs. This led the communards to abandon the idea of variable credit after five years of experimentation. Nowadays one credit equals one hour, regardless of personal or overall desirability or estimated time necessary for a job's completion.

On first sight, the move away from the variable credit system seems like little more than yet another minor change. The communards still decide from week to week what they want to work on. There is still no fixed schedule. People decide for themselves when they want to do quota (unless they sign up for something that obviously needs to be done at a certain time, like cooking dinner). The flexibility the Twin Oakers value so highly is still there. Yet the concept of the labor-credit system has changed completely. In short, Skinner's system was based on the idea that *different* work should be valued *differently;* the Twin Oaks system is based on the idea that *all* work should be valued *equally.* Whereas behavioral engineering was at the root of Skinner's labor-credit system—encouraging the completion of undesirable jobs by giving them a higher labor-credit value—Twin Oaks Community has chosen egalitarianism as the principle guiding its labor-credit system.

Over the years, the strict egalitarianism prevailing at Twin Oaks was softened, enabling members to earn small amounts of private income. In the beginning, complete income sharing was an untouchable dogma. There were to be no private bank accounts, no sources of income that would not go to the community, and no monetary incentives to work. Among more idealistic reasons, the community would lose its current tax status, which is similar to that of a cloister, if it provided any financial incentives for work.[8] These days, the communards can supplement their monthly allowance nonetheless. There are three ways to do this: to work for wages off the farm in one's own vacation time, to work "overquota" in Twin Oaks production areas for minimum wage, or to receive money from relatives or friends. All of these ways of obtaining money were originally intended to enable members to travel. There is no rule against spending the money on something else, however. Members are free to purchase anything that fits into their own rooms, with the exception of items that are held to be unacceptable on community property, like televisions, pornography, microwave ovens, or air conditioners. Also, Twin Oaks provides incentive programs that benefit the whole community rather than the individual member. If a member wants to buy CDs for the hammocks shop, for example, he or she can work overquota and donate the money that would have been earned in these extra hours toward buying CDs. This process is called OPP, which stands for "Overquota Products for Projects" (Kinkade, *Utopia* 46).

Twin Oaks has developed a unique system of economic planning, the so-called Tradeoff Game. In the early days, the planners handled the budget and determined how much work had to be done in which area for the community to have a stable economy. Nowadays the planners do no more than spend the budget the way the entire membership has decided it should be spent. This is determined in the Tradeoff Game, a Twin Oaks invention. The Tradeoff Game was introduced in an effort to involve everybody in the decision-making process concerning budget spending and still have numeric results in a relatively short time: every December, the planners hold a survey in which they first present which managerial areas received how much money and labor the year before and how much money and labor the managers of the different areas have requested for the following year. Every adult member is then asked to express his or her wishes in numerical form: they can either vote to give managers less money and labor than they ask for or agree with the suggestion of the manager. To prevent people from liberally granting all work areas time and money, the overall amount of money and labor distributed by each member has to equal the amount the planners have decided can be spent the next year. The answers on the survey are then added up for each specific area and divided by the number of participants. That way the planners come as close as they can to changing the budget spending according to the wishes of the entire membership. Interestingly, though, the size of the budget is not part of the Tradeoff Game. The planners determine what the weekly quota will be for the next year (which is the basis of the total amount of hours that can be used in the Tradeoff Game) and how much money can be spent overall during the next year.

# 12 The Appeal of the Labor-Credit System for the Communities Movement; or, What Communards Meant When They Said Walden Two

THE ONE ASPECT of *Walden Two* that proved to be most successful at Twin Oaks was the labor-credit system, which was interpreted by the community as a form of egalitarianism that functioned quite well without the Skinnerian framework of behavioral engineering. In the early to mid seventies, the Twin Oaks interpretation of *Walden Two,* and more specifically the community's advocacy of structure in the form of the labor-credit system, held a considerable amount of attraction for secular communities.

"We've read that we're supposed to have a strong common religion or a powerful, inspirational leader in order to prevent disintegration as a community," writes Kinkade in her latest book. "We have neither" (*Utopia* 4). This may well be the most remarkable thing about Twin Oaks: its success cannot be explained by conventional criteria. The community seems to draw stability from its high degree of *structure,* the one feature of *Walden Two* the communards fully embraced. Acknowledging a need for structure is unusual for the utopian, secular experiments of the sixties and seventies. Kinkade, who can certainly be considered a veteran at communal living, once remarked that the "anarchistic commune may be therapeutic, but it is not serious about proposing an alternative societal structure" (*Walden* 43). The

mere fact that Twin Oaks considered structure to be essential from the beginning put it in an awkward position between "the establishment" and the
communal movement. Most of the intentional communities sought to free
themselves of any kind of structure. "The word," remarks Kinkade, "is pure
poison to nine-tenths of the commune movement" (*Walden* 22–23). The
Twin Oakers, however, sought to *improve* upon structure, which they deemed
necessary to make living together a pleasant affair for all involved. The skepticism and even antagonism towards the early Twin Oaks within the communities movement is reflected in reports by people who visited the Virginian community: "The other visitors were already up. I went downstairs,
stopping at the foot to read two typewritten pages marked 'To the attention
of visitors.' . . . We were warned not to expect personal treatment. I was not
surprised. This wasn't a hip commune, and I hadn't come here expecting to
be welcomed as a soul brother. Twin Oaks was determined to create a 'viable
alternative' to capitalism, and that was very serious business" (Houriet
297).

The early Twin Oakers were unimpressed by the sentiments of their fellow
communards and spent years refining the labor-credit system that is at the
heart of the community's structural organization. By now, the system is so
intricate that it takes some members years to understand its finer points.
However, the basic idea—one hour of work equals one labor credit—is easy
to grasp and continues to facilitate the work integration of the thousands of
people who have visited or lived at Twin Oaks in the course of its three decades of existence. Many members of Twin Oaks believe that the labor-
credit system forms the nucleus of an economic system ensuring an egalitarian and joyful society. As the Harvard-trained sociologist and former Twin
Oaker David Ruth proclaimed in 1978: "As a school of socialist living, therefore, Twin Oaks has taught many members some very important lessons. . . . In
the absence of differential material rewards, members have found that the
pride of accomplishment, concern for the group as a whole, and the need
for peer-group approval are powerful motivators" (Ruth 60).

As the Virginian community prospered, suspicion was replaced by admi-
ration in the communities movement. By the early seventies, Twin Oaks had
heavily modified the originally autocratic planner-manager system, had
proven to the communally oriented visitors' satisfaction that they were not
serious behavioral scientists designing a gigantic laboratory, and had convinced hundreds of visitors that their community was a fun place to be.
"[E]verybody who comes here is looking for love" Kinkade once said in an
interview (Wenig and Coffman 32). She thinks that it was the community's

anything-goes attitude toward sexuality—which was, of course, in stark contrast to Skinner's early-marriages solution in *Walden Two*, which the communards chose to "ignore," figuring that "Skinner would have written it differently if he had been writing in the sixties instead of the forties" (*Walden* 164)—that helped the community gain in strength and recognition: "The thing that made Twin Oaks work in those early years was a mating center. We had people who were attracted to other people, and they found boyfriends and girlfriends and love interests. And a lot of them got married, and are still married and have children. This was a major place for the major excitement of the young years" (interview with the author, April 11, 1998).

All through the "major excitement" of being "a singles community" ("Leaving" 26), Twin Oaks held on to the idea that structure is necessary. Slowly, observers from the communities scene began to agree. "'I can't say that I buy all this Skinner stuff,'" remarked one visitor in the early seventies, "'but if you're asking me if I prefer living in a community that has some kind of order or a hippie commune, the answer is order'" (qtd. in Houriet 323). This visitor equates Skinner with "some kind of order," and this was indeed how the influence of *Walden Two* on Twin Oaks was regarded in the communities movement: the advocacy of structure in the form of the planner-manager and labor-credit systems. Even Robert Houriet, who visited Twin Oaks in the early seventies and gave a rather negative report on the community, almost grudgingly admits that he found the Twin Oaks system of work distribution worthy of consideration: "Toward noon, we ran out of stained battens. Whoever had last done the job hadn't told the manager to order more lumber. It was one of the frustrating kinks in the system that inevitably results from division of labor and responsibility. My first impulse was to shrug my shoulders and moan, 'It wasn't my responsibility. . . .' But then I considered the alternative—the open-ended commune where everyone was supposedly responsible and work was typically undelegated and the cows wandered off and two women were saddled with all the cooking. . . . Though Twin Oaks' system was far more efficient and fair, it did however depress me; but this again was the reaction of a biased outsider" (306).

During the early seventies, Twin Oaks achieved a status of fame in the communities movement, which it has retained to this day. "All over the country," writes Kinkade in 1994, "when Twin Oaks' name comes up, people are likely to say, 'Oh yes, that's where they have labor credits'" (*Utopia* 29). In addition to word-of-mouth propaganda, Twin Oaks was portrayed in well-known national publications like *Time* magazine (Heyman 48–49). Also, Twin Oaks holds a yearly conference on communal living on its property that has become an important annual event in the communities scene and is still attended by hundreds of people every year. All of these factors contributed to turning Twin Oaks into a magnet for visitors, reaching a peak in 1973–74 with the publication of Kinkade's lively report about the first five years, *A Walden Two Experiment*.

Through all of this publicity, Twin Oaks continued to call itself a Walden Two community, despite the fact that it was continually moving away from its initial blueprint. Yet for all its inadequacy, the term Walden Two seemed to the communards to capture some essential aspects of their community even after the behaviorist aspects, the notion of professional government, and communal child care had been repudiated. The term Walden Two encompassed the idea of income sharing, using structure to ensure the fair distribution of work, and being secular, experimental, anticonsumerist, and environmentally conscious. Furthermore, Kinkade still fervently believed in *Walden Two* and was reluctant to let go completely of the original vision. Interestingly, Twin Oaks, following Skinner's and Bellamy's lead, by and large avoids the term "socialism" in the description of its microsociety.

As a result of Twin Oaks's continued self-description as a Walden Two community, groups that felt inspired by Twin Oaks adopted the label as well. To them, "Walden Two community" meant Twin Oaks, and Twin Oaks meant advocacy of structure in the form of the labor-credit system. Whatever Skinner may have had in mind with his utopia was of little or no consequence to this second generation of Walden Two communards, who had often not even read the novel themselves; what they knew and liked was the *interpretation* of the novel provided by Twin Oaks. Remembers Kinkade: "We had some conscious thoughts on the subject of what to call ourselves when we advertised in the early years. And so did some of the smaller communities that were offsprings. They didn't really want to say, 'We're starting another Twin Oaks. And of course we'll have our own ideas, but we're starting with Twin Oaks.' Which is what they meant. And so they'd say 'another Walden Two community,' hoping people would make the connection" (interview with the author, April 11, 1998).

People did indeed make the connection, so much so that by the mid seventies, Walden Two became a term that was closely associated with Twin Oaks in the communities movement, while the connection to Skinner was almost forgotten. For a few brief years, great hopes were attached to the Twin Oaks/Walden Two model. The labor-credit system in particular held the promise of being a recipe for success for secular communities. Most importantly, it seemed to provide a communal structure that was stable and permanent, a feature that appealed to forming and already established communities.

By the early seventies, Twin Oaks could not accommodate the many potential members that came knocking at its doors. A waiting list was established, yet this was not satisfactory to many of the eager communards-to-be, so that frequently the most active new recruits who had been attracted to the community through the communities conference or the visitor program formed their own communities instead of waiting for an opening at Twin Oaks. Also, founding their own little Twin Oaks Communities afforded the opportunity to set slightly different accents, for example, being more child-oriented during the years that Twin Oaks had a no-children policy. Among these direct offsprings from Twin Oaks with a focus on children were the North Mountain Community in Virginia, founded in 1972, Aloe Community in North Carolina, and Cedarwood in the direct vicinity of Twin Oaks, both founded in 1974. Two former Twin Oakers were involved in running a construction company at Cedarwood, which they found more satisfying than working in the more restrictive and larger work scene at Twin Oaks ("Leaving" 22).

Dandelion Community in Canada, founded in 1975, stands out among the Twin Oaks–inspired communities in having had members with an active interest in behaviorism as well as in the labor-credit and planner-manager systems. Most important among these members was Richard Graham, who has vivid memories of his introduction to *Walden Two* and communal living:

> I can still remember how exhilarated I felt reading *Walden Two*, and what a beautiful vision I thought Skinner had to offer the world in terms of solving some fundamental social problems. Toward the end of that college course, my teacher brought in a brochure about Twin Oaks, described as a Walden Two–inspired community in Virginia. "Holy Smokes!" I thought. "There are people actually building such communities. Where do I sign up?" I became so excited I dropped out of school and went exploring.
>
> My travels brought me to the 1975 Communities Conference at Twin Oaks, which turned out to be another turning point in my life. Over 400 people attended, all sharing the enthusiasm for trying something new. It felt like we were ready to change the world and nobody could stop us. (42)

After some searching, Graham joined Dandelion near Kingston, Ontario. He liked the idea of being a pioneer, "trying to figure out, 'What are we doing here?'" He recounts in an interview that they "had set up this egalitarian, behaviorist community, and we were using *Walden Two* as a model, and what we had seen happening at Twin Oaks." Graham, who is familiar with behaviorism, realizes that the egalitarianism was probably only secondary to Skinner, yet it was crucial for the income-sharing Dandelion, where "it was real important to make sure that every person was heard." Also, Graham is aware that behaviorism was not a source of excitement for all of Dandelion's members: "Most people just didn't care. So I walked around with this knowledge of behavior principles, and people didn't care." He adds: "Maybe they tolerated me. They humored me" (interview with the author, July 24, 1998).

Although behaviorism was never a major factor of life at Dandelion, it was perhaps as much a part of the Canadian community as it was of Twin Oaks. Similar to the Virginian community, the only type of behavioral engineering that found approval among the not-so-interested members were self-management programs. Modifying your own behavior was apparently deemed much more acceptable than modifying somebody else's. Remembers Graham: "I was once approached by two members asking me to help them quit smoking, and together we developed what we called the 'Outhouse Intervention.' On one column of a large poster they agreed to write down all the negative things about smoking. On the other column they wrote down all the positive effects of not smoking. Before lighting up, they had to read out loud both columns of the poster. We then put the poster up in the outhouse and agreed that that would be the only place they could smoke, which we thought added another aversive element that would discourage smoking. I remember walking past the outhouse, smiling to myself as I heard them reciting items from the poster" (43).

The one aspect of behavioral engineering that all of the members of Dandelion approved of was a positive verbal environment. Yet it seems that Graham was, once again, alone in trying to use verbal positive reinforcement as a means to an end. An attempt to have members reinforce good work habits by giving feedback on a bulletin board—for example, "I really liked the clean bathroom yesterday"—was soon turned into a bulletin board on which members made I-like-it statements of a fundamentally different kind, such as, "I really liked the sunset last night." Kinkade, at least, doubts that Dandelion made conscious use of a positive verbal environment in a Walden Two sense: "The people at Dandelion were very positive in all their verbal interactions, and they were consciously so because they were consciously trying to produce, they were consciously trying to reward. . . . No, I'm not sure what they were consciously trying to do" (interview with the author, April 11, 1998).

Despite the lack of commitment to behaviorism and professional government evident in her own community and those inspired by it, Kat Kinkade applauded the spread of the Walden Two concept and monitored its progress, as Robert Houriet reported upon his visit to Twin Oaks in the early seventies: "Kat is hopeful that in a few years Twin Oaks will serve as a training ground for other Walden Two communities around the country. Several are now in the planning stages. A group in Providence, Rhode Island, is raising money to buy a dairy farm in Massachusetts to be called Walden Three. Neverland, an urban commune in Menlo Park, California, is planning another Walden (Walden Four?) 'somewhere in the western United States.' Another has been based on a photographic industry by East Street Gallery in Grinnell, Iowa; and Community Design, Inc., a group with two communal bases, one in Montrose, Colorado, and the other in Baltimore, is looking at sites in western Texas for 'an international community' based on both Skinner and Israel's kibbutzim" (307).

Kinkade was not only an observer but also very much part of the excitement of founding more Walden Two communities. The immediate effect of the publication of *A Walden Two Experiment,* her first book on Twin Oaks, was a wave of applications for membership that lasted for several years. Rather than accepting all of these new applicants, the Twin Oakers of the seventies made the conscious decision not to expand rapidly but rather to enhance the quality of life at Twin Oaks while growing slowly. Kinkade was not satisfied with this decision, left Twin Oaks, and embarked on founding a community a second time, resulting in East Wind Community in Missouri. Kinkade remembers that at the time, she began to have doubts about the feasibility and desirability of the kind of egalitarianism she had seen in *Walden Two* and had wanted for Twin Oaks. Founding East Wind was partly an effort, apparently, to hold on to ideals she could perhaps already feel waning: "Somewhere along the line, instead of absolute equality, it was the idea of getting bigger, bringing in more people. And that felt like saving the world, saving these poor people who would otherwise have to deal with capitalism. And I would clasp them to my bosom and give them what they all really wanted, which was community and equality. And that turned out to be bullshit, but it was good while it lasted. It gave me meaning while it lasted" (interview with the author, April 10, 1995).

East Wind bears many similarities to Twin Oaks. It produces hammocks, uses the labor-credit system, has grown to about a hundred members, is dissatisfied with the planner-manager system, and has been trying to find a satisfactory substitute for it for over twenty years now. The main difference from Twin Oaks appears to be the membership makeup. Having adopted an open admission policy from the beginning, East Wind attracted a considerable amount of members who were not eager to build an alternative society but were more interested in the community as an idyllic crash pad in the Ozark Mountains of Missouri. Kinkade left the community in disappointment after only a few years and eventually returned to Twin Oaks.

Apart from the several newly founded communities inspired by Twin Oaks, several already existing communities adopted the labor-credit and sometimes even the planner-manager systems in an attempt to remedy unsatisfactory situations. The dissatisfaction seems to have been most often in the area of work distribution. A typical example is the Canadian community Headlands, which existed from 1971 until interpersonal conflicts caused the group to split up in 1975. Its cofounder, Ian Murray, reports that in the summer of 1972 there were "all kinds of issues, of course, as you would have in any group without clear leadership. I know I myself had some hard feelings because I'm a pretty good worker" (interview with the author, April 12, 1998). For personal reasons, Murray decided to take a break from his community and ended up visiting Twin Oaks: "I'd heard of Twin Oaks through a visitor who I think gave us a subscription to the *Leaves*, and that sounded pretty interesting. They were quite an old community, they were about four or five years old at that time. . . . So I came down here, to Twin Oaks, and I was very interested in the labor system. It was a very complex labor system—I think it's simplified now. Because back then, you'd sign up, and the same person might be . . . two people might be working on the same job, and one might be getting, for an hour's worth, 1.4 labor credits, and the other would be getting 1.9, depending on how they evaluated their dislike for the project" (interview with the author, April 12, 1998).

Murray liked the labor-credit system so much that he decided to suggest adopting it for Headlands as well. So he "taped an interview with Kat, went back home, and explained it" (interview with the author, April 12, 1998). Interestingly, despite his eagerness to copy the labor-credit and planner-manager systems, Murray remembers regarding Twin Oaks "with contempt" because of the Virginians' supposed attitude toward work as a necessary evil instead of a valid part of life. This impression apparently did not deter him and his fellow communards from implementing the Twin Oaks labor-credit system at their own community:

> So we sat down and went through the whole process of discussing it, and then Bill, one of our founding members, said, "I'm not going to do anything except one hour of work is worth one hour of credit, I don't care what all

this bullshit is." We tried it anyway, for one or two weeks, and after a little while we realized that Bill was right. One hour's worth of work is one credit, or it would be too much goddamn hassle otherwise. That was one of the few times I actually agreed with him. . . . Oh, and we tried the planner system as well. We did the same, we used exactly the same system as down here [at Twin Oaks]. We always said we'd copy any idea we liked. . . . The behaviorism didn't sit well at all. Alice, who was a dairy person at the commune, did work on behaviorism, and I think she used it quite well in her own life. Yeah, she practiced it but didn't preach it. (interview with the author, April 12, 1998)

The modified labor-credit system—interestingly modified in exactly the same way as Twin Oaks later did by dropping the variable credit—worked well for the communards at Headlands, effectively preventing hard workers from "getting burned out" and "letting new members know what was expected of them." The planner-manager system also worked to the communards' satisfaction, although Murray thinks that these days he would "just call it a Board of Directors and be done with the bullshit. Because that's what it was" (interview with the author, April 12, 1998).

The impetus to want more structure and perhaps some level of hierarchy was also voiced by the Woody Hill Co-op, a subgroup of the Tolstoy Peace Farm in Washington. This group reported in 1973: "A group of us are starting a Walden Two/Twin Oaks style community. Our version includes kids, a subsistence level, organic lifestyle, and maybe fifty people. We have been living together as neighbors in an anarchist, homesteading commune for three and more years, but the Walden Two scheme seems like a better way of life to us" ("Walden Group" 60).

Likewise, Fantasy Farm in British Columbia reported in 1975 that they were "building a Walden Two oriented community" ("Fantasy," *Directory* 27) by using "a labor credit system to get our work done and to distribute it as fairly as possible" ("Fantasy," *Communities* 54). Appletree Community wanted to try the "Walden Two type planner manager system" in 1974 ("Appletree" 51). Hidden Springs reported in 1975 that the "formation of a Twin Oaks type community at Hidden Springs began in the summer of '74 after the return of 2 Springers from a Twin Oaks conference" ("Hidden" 52) and called itself an egalitarian Walden Two community in the 1977 Directory of Intentional Communities (51). Julian Woods and Larchwood Community in Pennsylvania, Morningside in Alabama, Yarrow in New York, the Big Island Creek Folks in West Virginia, Community Design in Maryland, and Twin Pines in Minnesota all report being "inspired by Walden Two—Twin Oaks" ("Twin" 50), using both names almost interchangeably. Twin Oaks's fame even reached

Europe, with Crabapple Community in Wales calling itself "Walden Two based" after some of their members had visited Twin Oaks and had adopted the labor-credit system for their home community ("Crabapple" 57).

In the mid seventies, Walden Two was a widely used expression in the communities movement and coexisted peacefully with concepts that were quite in opposition to Skinner's ideas. In a letter to Kat Kinkade, Gale Harris expressed her enthusiasm for Twin Oaks as portrayed in Kinkade's *Walden Two Experiment*:

> You'll never know the inspiration your book . . . has been to me. But I'd like to tell you a little bit of it. For several years I've dreamed and read about Community life. I've not participated in anything that has been fortunate enough to be permanent. However, all of the situations were begun by others without a clear set of goals and operational principles.
>
> I began forming some of my own, and praying (yes, praying) for someone with whom to work it out. At the same time I listed my preferences (to God) in regard to what I considered a suitable place on which to begin a permanent Community. . . . Anyway, the person whom I'd prayed for to work with also appeared on the scene last week and now we're ready to begin really digging into plans. Also a third very interested person has surfaced and we're really excited about getting on with it.
>
> We have some different ideas, we believe, which we want to try to implement but we are drawing heavily on the wisdom imparted to us from our connections via print with WALDEN TWO–TWIN OAKS.[9]

Harris realized that her "own ethics based on Scriptural principles" were not "in agreement" with Twin Oaks completely, but she still felt that the Virginian community had made a contribution to developing "a community based on faith *and* works, the good life now *and* forever!" The community Nasalam in Washington was also "spiritually oriented" and inspired by Walden Two at the same time, although their spirituality probably differed from Harris's, for their main goal was to create a "gay polyfidelitous group" ("Nasalam" 41). In another interesting interpretation of *Walden Two* provided by two former East Winders who founded Jubilee Farm in Texas, David Nord describes his partner's dream as follows:

> She read *Walden Two* by B. F. Skinner.
> She visited Twin Oaks.
> She listened to Rabbi Mordecai Podet preach about Prophetic Judaism.
> She put it all together and decided (correctly, if you want my opinion) that the world needed Jewish Walden Two in Texas.

So when the time became right in her life she started the community. Unfortunately, the time wasn't right for anyone but her and me. So after a little more than 2 years of struggling the community, which didn't get properly born, died.[10]

Despite the widespread excitement of building Walden Two communities, the mid seventies were not the beginning of a movement but already represented its peak. This development was not foreseen by the people involved in building community, however. "In the middle 1970's the number of North American communities had been steadily expanding for at least 10 years," reports the long-term communard Laird Schaub. "There was no particular reason to suspect that such growth would not continue" (53). Therefore, several communards began discussing the mutual benefits of greater cooperation among communities. In 1976, Kinkade and other delegates founded the Federation of Egalitarian Communities (FEC), which encompassed an ever-changing set of about half a dozen income-sharing, secular, and egalitarian communities. Although the term Walden Two did not appear in the name of the federation, its membership consisted to a large extent of communities that called themselves Walden Two, including Twin Oaks, East Wind, Aloe, Dandelion, North Mountain, and, for a short while, Los Horcones (Schaub 54). Los Horcones dropped out because they felt that "the rest of us didn't take [behaviorism] seriously enough, and they felt estranged," according to Schaub, an FEC member. Although the federation fell somewhat short of its founders' expectations because "many [communities] faded away nearly as quickly as they came" (Schaub 43), it continues to provide joint outreach, a certain extent of social security, and the possibility of labor exchange (members from one community temporarily living and working at another community) for its member communities.

As the excitement of communal living died down in the second half of the seventies, many of the aforementioned groups folded, and the Walden Two communities still in existence began to reconsider their terminology. Walden Two, they felt, was too removed from what they were actually doing and thus gave outsiders a wrong impression. Twin Oaks in particular tired of having visitors expecting (or fearing) to find Walden Two. Consequently, the communards tried out terms such as "kibbutz-like community" ("Leaving" 20) until the expression "egalitarian community" won and firmly replaced what in the early seventies had been identified, rather inadequately, by the term "Walden Two."

# 13 Why People Leave

THE EXCITEMENT of building a whole network of Walden Two communities that Kinkade and others nurtured in the seventies has been a thing of the past for many years now. The fact that most of the communities inspired by the Twin Oaks interpretation of *Walden Two* failed to remain vibrant communities for long casts some doubt on the labor-credit system as a formula for communal success. Despite the demise of other communities, however, many members of Twin Oaks still trust that their labor-credit system is a sound basis for an income-sharing community. What are we to make of the community's confident claim to have created a viable alternative to capitalism?

At first glance, Twin Oaks indeed appears to be a communal success story. Many members of Twin Oaks find intrinsic pleasure in their work and state confidently that working for the common good is a strong motivator. Yet a closer look at the inner workings of the community reveals that the community's claim to have found a viable alternative to capitalism may have to be modified. It seems that the most central—yet often overlooked—factor in sustaining the noncompetitive economic system is the community's rate of membership turnover, which was as high as 25 percent per year during its first five years (Ruth 58). This turnover fulfills the double function of constantly providing the community with idealistic new workers while allowing disillusioned members to leave. In other words, the cooperative system of work distribution seems to work well for many Twin Oakers, but only for a while. The appearance of permanence is achieved through the fact that the community is most often discussed as if it were a stable entity rather than a constantly changing body of people. Yet the vast majority of those who were motivated to work for the common good in 1972 are not the same as those in 1983, and a member who left the community in 1987 might well have trouble finding familiar faces if he or she were to return in 1999. As Ian Murray put it in an interview: "Every time I come down here, I don't know who will still be here" (interview with the author, April 12, 1998). The crucial importance of membership turnover at Twin Oaks and its effects on work performance are perhaps best understood by focusing not on the community as a whole but on the passages of individual members through the community, including their reasons for joining as well as for leaving.

Joining Twin Oaks is perhaps best described as falling in love. To the new communard, life prior to Twin Oaks appears gray, pointless, fragmented, and dissatisfying. Then, suddenly or gradually, by reading a newspaper article or seeing a documentary or meeting a friend of a friend, Twin Oaks arrives on the horizon and offers a way to leave the rat race behind. The vast majority of recruits thus attracted to Twin Oaks are white, middle-class, well-educated, and alienated. Explains Mara Rockliff, a former member of Twin Oaks: "My world had fragmented into career, social life, recreation. I worked sixty hours a week for goals that weren't my own. I didn't know how to have fun without spending money. I looked at my boss, and my boss's boss, and his boss, and her boss, and contemplated taking their places in time. I wasn't excited. But when I thought about leaving my job, it felt like dropping my identity. If I weren't Mara Rockliff, Senior Editor, as my business cards proclaimed, who would I be? Would I be anyone?" (3).

Rockliff found an answer: she would be Mara and defragmentize her life. The excitement of leaving behind a dissatisfying situation is coupled with a boundless enthusiasm and optimism for the new lifestyle. Remembers Kinkade: "Back in 1967, when we first realized that we were really going to come to live on a farm, we were almost as excited about farming as we were about communal living and *Walden Two*. Our ignorance was boundless.... I thought we should grow every crop that would grow in our climate and construct a greenhouse to grow the things that wouldn't. I wanted a sample pair of every kind of farm animal. I grew ecstatic over ducklings and geese, delighted in feeding the pigs, grew personally acquainted with each calf. Most of the group felt somewhat the same way" (*Walden* 63).

To the new member, the community appears literally as a dream come true, a eu-topia, a good place, the culmination of all his or her hopes and dreams, and the newcomer is often determined to spend the rest of his or her life at Twin Oaks. During this first phase, which might be called enchantment, the new member tends to have a dual focus. On the one hand, there is the memory of the life left behind. On the other hand is the community, which compares favorably to the old situation. Warren, a member in the 1970s, stated: "Part of the attraction of being at Twin Oaks, after spending 6 years working in the same factory, was that we worked our own businesses. For me it was an incredible rush to work in that situation" ("Leaving" 27).

In trying to understand the origin of work motivation during this early phase, it seems important to point out that people joining always carry the memory of a different economic system with them. For better or worse, people do not come to Twin Oaks out of a void. It is understandable, therefore, that comparisons between the new and the old abound and result in a "rush to work." In fact, the high level of work motivation in new members is such a distinct phenomenon that Twin Oaks has coined a term for it: an older member can often be heard to sigh, "We could sure use some new member energy in the wood shop or kitchen."

The energy experienced by new members is efficiently channeled into work by the Twin Oaks labor-credit system. Almost as soon as they step on Twin Oaks property, visitors and new members are handed a labor sheet. This sheet is the means by which the community and the individual members keep track of work assignments and performance. Each member of Twin Oaks turns in one labor sheet every week and picks up a new one. The data is computerized by the labor manager, keeping track of the hours each member works in a specific week. Ideally, members should "do quota" every week, that is, work the number of hours that has been set as the community weekly work norm. One benefit of the labor sheet—from the point of view of the community as a whole, at least—is transparence. Members can tell quickly when they fall behind, and so can everybody else: every member's labor balance (the amount of hours a person is either above or below quota) is hung up in a public space.

Another often voiced advantage of the labor sheet is that it facilitates flexibility in the work scene. Most people at Twin Oaks choose to work in several areas, so on an average workday, a Twin Oaker might work a tofu shift in the morning, watch someone's child over lunch, do accounting in the afternoon, and wash dishes in the evening. Since the labor sheet clearly spells out one's assignments and requires people to fill in which work they actually performed, they know exactly what is expected of them as workers.

The specific working conditions of the hammocks business are another factor in facilitating the easy transition from newcomer to productive member. The easiest work involved in the production of a hammock, the weaving, can be learned within a couple of hours. The hammocks shop is the main place where even people who only spend a limited time at Twin Oaks can be a substantial addition to the community's productivity. Unlike many other communities that need to train new members before they can fully participate in the economy, the Twin Oaks hammocks business is perfectly suited for transients.

Once the new member has more or less completed the step of extricating him- or herself from mainstream society, the focus shifts from comparing Twin Oaks to the outside world to taking a close look at the internal functioning of the community. This is the phase where an affair between member Raven and visitor Pat is infinitely more interesting than an affair in the White House, and where a crash at Wall Street goes unnoticed while news about a drop in the hammocks sales figures spreads like fire. With this shift of perception, the impression of Twin Oaks as utopia begins to wear off: The partial blindness frequently accompanying enchantment is replaced by a more critical and often sharply disappointing assessment.

In regard to the motivation to work for the common good, the effect of perceiving Twin Oaks as a microcosm leads to three main complaints. First, people begin to find fault with the work performance of their fellow workers. Second, hard workers begin to feel unappreciated. And third, the question arises whether the mentality at the root of the Twin Oaks labor-credit system is really all that different from the Protestant work ethic underlying mainstream capitalist society.

Interestingly, the center of complaints about the cooperative work system is not personal lack of motivation to work but dissatisfaction with the work performance of others. During this phase of disenchantment, differences in efficiency and quality of work are perceived not as differences in ability (which are acceptable in the Twin Oaks worldview) but as differences in effort (which is harder to reconcile with a system based on voluntary cooperation). Instead of ensuring the equal distribution of labor, the not-so-recent new member may also notice that some people are adept at not exactly cheating but using the system—which is basically an honor system in which the hours a worker puts down are registered as hours worked—to their own advantage. Complaints about people spending a long time on a job that could have been performed more quickly with a little more effort are common.

Apart from the resulting unequal distribution of labor, the nonchalance with which the labor-credit system is misused by some members has fundamental implications for those who believe in the system. Although it is constantly modified to mend the loopholes, the very *need* for such intricacy is disillusioning, as one ex-member, Sara, reports: "In my strongest moments I believed that T.O. had at least the beginnings of an economic system that would slowly revolutionize the world. That this was a system that could and should work. I got discouraged at the technicalities of it, and at seeing how hard it was for the system to work for 80 people" ("Leaving" 28).

Many people join Twin Oaks in hopes of finding like-minded people. Yet the community does not only attract those who yearn to fight against fragmentation and want to take personal responsibility for their lives; it also attracts those who wish to *escape* responsibility. Twin Oaks recruiters find that the community's ideals "at times attract deeply passionate and committed people," but more often the community has to pick its new members among "loners, losers and drifters" (Jones 27). This fact may not be perceived initially but becomes apparent to many of the more work-oriented members once the first excitement of living communally is over. David Lloyd, a former member, described life before Twin Oaks in a rather different tone from Mara Rockliff's assessment: "'It just occurred to me to give up all the hassles—money, car insurance, bouncing checks, going to the bank, traffic tickets, late fees at the library'" (qtd. in Jones 27).

Kinkade, who delighted in feeding the pigs in 1967, has long since proclaimed their grand experiment in communal living a failure. The communards had discovered quickly that they could not run their community's businesses on enthusiasm alone, and they also had to refine their work system repeatedly to solve the issue of dirty dishes. By 1995, Kinkade had changed her mind about the feasibility of a cooperative work system on a more fundamental level: "Nowadays, I think you need some personal incentive in order to put out your best in the work scene. Cooperation and group reinforcement alone will just not do. . . . Castle challenged Frazier on this very point. Castle said, 'You've taken the mainspring out of the watch.' And Frazier replied, 'That is an experimental question, Mr. Castle, and you have the wrong answer.' Or something of that sort. I was absolutely delighted with this when I first read it. But at this point I'm prepared to say, 'It's an experimental question, Mr. Castle, and you're right.' We had taken the mainspring out of the watch, and we got a very mediocre response by doing so" (interview with the author, April 10, 1995).

A major part of taking out the mainspring seems to lie in the fact that efficiency and hard work are not only not rewarded but effectively punished in a system that counts only how many hours are worked regardless of how much work is accomplished during this time. Someone fully pouring his or her energy into a work project will be significantly more exhausted than someone leisurely picking up a hammer now and then. Ironically, Skinner's assertion that a behavior that is ignored will eventually cease holds true at Twin Oaks. Working hard is not reinforced by the labor-credit system, and many people apparently find it difficult to uphold work standards in the absence of some kind of feedback for hard work. However, Skinner had further maintained that it would be possible to sustain a cooperative work system without relying on personal incentives as reinforcement. This latter part of his theory has apparently not worked out at Twin Oaks.

Members finding dissatisfaction with work performance at Twin Oaks often seem to find it difficult to admit to these problems, perhaps because it is the first step toward questioning the very basis of Twin Oaks as a cooperative venture. Complaints about the work performance of others are at the center of discussion at Twin Oaks because it is basically the only way to voice dissatisfaction with the cooperative work system without admitting that one's *own* work motivation is seeping away in the face of unappreciation and punishment for working hard. To complain about lack of rewards for good work would be to question the core of the cooperative ideal. For many who join Twin Oaks, this is a taboo. Demanding that others put out their best for the common good is therefore much more acceptable than demanding rewards for one's own work efforts.

To stem the anticooperative thinking that arises in reaction to watching people's mediocre work performance, Kinkade and other long-term members of Twin Oaks have tried to consciously foster a positive attitude toward work. The resultant work mentality prevalent at Twin Oaks is arguably much closer to the Protestant work ethic that spurred along capitalism than the communards would wish. Not only is there a substantial number of members who work less than according to their ability; those who work hard seem to be driven less by intrinsic pleasure and concern for the common good than by rules, fear of negative consequences, and the need for societal validation. According to Kinkade, the only remaining founding member and the community's resident cynic, "people certainly do work in order to get labor credits. I don't mean all people all the time, but it's a consciousness that's carried at the back of our minds. Even me. I'm almost free of the labor system, I have a low quota, my work is done at my own time, my own schedule, but in the back of the mind I'm thinking, 'Do I get credit for this, do I get credit for that?' . . . It's there, it's always there. And I don't know that you would call it positive reinforcement, it's much more negative reinforcement. The absence of labor credits will make trouble" (interview with the author, April 11, 1998).

Verbal disapproval of laziness is very much a part of daily life at Twin Oaks. In Twin Oaks jargon, a "good communard" is one who works hard, whereas "loafers" and "cheaters" are met with disapproval. "Manipulation of the system," says Kinkade, "is not admired. We don't think cheating is funny" (interview with the author, April 11, 1998).

However, most noteworthy is not what specifically is said about work but the mere fact that it is talked about so much. Twin Oaks has invented its own work-related language, and there is no shortage of expressions. A new member handbook even provides a glossary explaining Twin Oaks terms and abbreviations, many of which are centered around work, such as being "in the hole," meaning one owes money or hours to the community, or "PSC," meaning one will give personal service credit to somebody else (*Living* 26–30).

Similar to capitalist thinking, perhaps, Twin Oakers are keenly aware of whether an activity is labor creditable or not. Political activism and art are among the more hotly debated candidates for labor creditability. The underlying assumption seems to be that only those activities that are on the labor system are really valued by the microsociety. Rather than finding self-fulfillment and intrinsic pleasure in work, then, Twin Oakers are still very much dependent on societal feedback. The labor credit therefore comes close to replacing the psychological function of money in capitalist society. The extent to which Twin Oakers are focused on labor credits and the intensity of the implicit understanding that making something labor creditable means to attach value to it is perhaps best illustrated by the aftermath of a suicide that shook the community to its core in 1993 (Jones 28–31). The communards succumbed to intense soul searching, questioning where and how the community had failed to be there for a member in need. However, even in the midst of this crisis, the thought of labor credits was not far from the communards' minds: "The community provided outside counseling for anyone who wanted help coping with the tragedy. There was a bitter meeting over whether labor credits should be granted for time spent in grief therapy" (29).

Exasperation at the poor work performance of fellow communards, feeling unappreciated for one's own work efforts, and questioning the source of work motivation produced by the labor-credit system are among the principal reasons for disillusionment at Twin Oaks. All of these factors lead to severe doubts about the feasibility of maintaining—on a permanent basis, at least—an economic system that hinges on the voluntary cooperation of its members.

The sobering effect of viewing Twin Oaks as a less-than-perfect microcosm necessitates yet another shift of perception. If the community is not utopia, then why stay? Does working for the common good make sense once the belief in the feasibility of cooperation as the basis of a new economic system is shaken? "Sometimes it seemed," remembers one ex-member, "as if the rules of the world were suspended at Twin Oaks" ("Leaving" 22). Yet much to the dismay of idealistic new members, the suspension does not last. During this phase of uncertainty, members go back to comparing Twin Oaks to mainstream society, but with a different twist: instead of focusing on the feeling of alienation and fragmentation, the psychological *benefits* of a competitive system are rediscovered.

Paramount among the advantages now seen in a competitive system is the monetary and social validation of effort. Rather than fundamentally questioning the fairness of a cooperative system that effectively punishes hard workers and encourages a leisurely pace of work, however, the most common initial reaction to noticing a discrepancy between ideal and reality appears to be denial. The conscientious hard worker may be upset about specific members' lack of work and may question his or her *personal* ability to find satisfaction and work motivation in a time-based cooperative system, but he or she remains hesitant to question the *ideal*. As one ex-member, Bree, put it in 1977: "I had this tendency to expect a lot from Twin Oaks. Expectations of how people ought to behave; about being unselfish and idealistic and sharing. . . . And I never really measured up. I was always trying to be consistent, to act out my ideology" ("Leaving" 27).

Since joining Twin Oaks is conceived by many as a long-term commitment, the realization that one's work motivation is steadily decreasing poses a fundamental problem. Not surprisingly, perhaps, the perceived discrepancy between wanting to "act out" one's ideals and at the same time reacting to the actual work scene with exasperation, anger, and disillusionment is at the root of many members' decisions to leave the community. Once these ex-members reenter capitalist society, their view of the Twin Oaks labor system is more openly critical. After having left Twin Oaks, Bree described her new attitude toward life: "I've been really pleased with my independence lately—really enjoying it, getting back in touch with what a selfish person I can be. Not putting myself down for it at all, but just really seeing that I like making up all the rules for myself. . . . Since I left, I've really been enjoying accepting myself not being completely the way I think I ought to be" ("Leaving" 27).

Dissatisfaction with work is among the principal reasons people state for leaving the community.[11] It is often only in hindsight that ex-members assess their communal experience in terms of fundamental skepticism about the cooperative ideal. And even though these members were disillusioned enough to leave the community, many retain respect for the ideals that Twin Oaks is trying to put into practice. The attitude I often encountered in interviews with ex-members and long-term visitors is ambivalence, a conflicting and unresolved mix of nostalgia and disappointment. Richard Graham, the enthusiastic believer in *Walden Two* who became part of Dandelion, feels in hindsight that the labor-credit system did not reinforce "mediocre work, but it didn't give people an incentive to get work done in a faster way or shorter amount of time." Yet he is not ready to proclaim it a failure: "[O]ne of the reasons that I left Dandelion, and I guess one of the reasons I decided not to join Twin Oaks, was that the older I got, the more I wanted more private space. I had my own bedroom, but I just wanted more physical space around me that I didn't have to share with people. And it was nothing against the people I was with, it was just like a maturing process or something. But that was definitely one of the reasons. But it was nothing against the ideals. I still carry those. One of the reasons I have such a hard time living in this society is that I am trying to practice an egalitarian philosophy in a nonegalitarian environment. And I'm always in conflict over that" (interview with the author, July 24, 1998).

An ex–Twin Oaker named Mary who left the community in the seventies seems to share Graham's sentiments: "Now I feel a distance from Twin Oaks. I doubt that I would ever want to go back there, although when I look at Twin Oaks, I appreciate its existence in a profound way. I learned an awful lot" ("Leaving" 27).

This deep-seated ambivalence about the cooperative system experienced by former community members appears to represent more than just the personal sentiments of a few individuals. In arguing for the perennial importance of fictional utopias, Peter Ruppert defines the value of reading utopias in a way that is strikingly similar to the value of experiencing community as perceived by ex-members: "Utopias may exist nowhere, but their critical value can be seen to exist in their capacity to defamiliarize and draw attention to real social problems. Where they may fail to convince us of the sufficiency or the finality of their sanguine solutions, they also fail to dissuade us from the need to search for social alternatives" (x).

It would, of course, be a mistake to say that nobody at Twin Oaks finds lasting satisfaction with the cooperative work system. The community does have several long-term members who remain determined to stay at Twin Oaks. Interestingly, though, most of them have chosen to specialize, often in areas that necessitate little interaction or cooperation with other workers. By doing so, they have virtually extricated themselves from the labor-credit system without leaving the community. Much of the work available at Twin Oaks is not specialized, however, so inner migration is not an option for many. In fact, the main advantage for the new member is that most work areas are easily graspable, like weaving hammocks, working in the garden, or washing dishes. The lack of specialized jobs only becomes a problem for the older and more dissatisfied member seeking ways to find fulfillment in work. There are several professions that are simply not needed at Twin Oaks, like lawyers, stock brokers, surgeons, or journalists.

While the disillusioned member is on his or her way out, new members are already knocking on the door. Until recently, Twin Oaks has had more applicants for membership than it could accommodate. The void left by disillusioned members leaving is therefore filled quickly. These new members do not usually expect to become disillusioned themselves, and it is only the seasoned member, or ex-member, who assesses the new arrivals' chances of lasting enchantment skeptically: "I feel a little sad about new people coming in all bright-eyed and bushy-tailed, because I think they're going to go through the painful process of disillusionment. . . . If I could convince myself that the process is so valuable that it doesn't make a difference whether or not it's going to be successful, I would probably choose community" ("Leaving" 28).

Since the new member is unlikely to communicate with many ex-members who have moved away—and would be unlikely to be open to seasoned arguments while in the enthusiastic stage—the points of criticism of the cooperative system are something for the new member to discover for him- or herself. In hindsight, many ex-members feel that Twin Oaks was a valuable phase in their lives; to the newcomer, it is not obvious yet that Twin Oaks will most likely be a phase, no more and no less. As an ex-member calling himself Spudly wrote in a letter to the community in 1998: "I am a 1965 graduate of Yale University and 1973 graduate of Twin Oaks. Looking back, TO played a much more significant role in my life and development than Yale, even though the TO experience was shorter and cost considerably less."

Despite the fact that membership turnover appears to be central to understanding the apparent sustainability of the Twin Oaks cooperative system, the community tends to be treated as a fixed entity. There are several reasons why the illusion of permanence is so deeply ingrained by outside observers and members of Twin Oaks. First, joining Twin Oaks is understood by many members as a long-term commitment. It is only in the course of disillusionment that leaving the community is considered. Current members will therefore state their intention to stay permanently. Second, Twin Oaks membership is so homogeneous that it is difficult to see that it is actually a constantly changing group of people. Also, the group as a whole ages roughly as it would if the original members had stayed, although it is unclear why that is (Komar 279). One popular theory at Twin Oaks is that intentional communities were attractive in the sixties and early seventies. According to this theory, communities used to attract hippies, and now they attract aging hippies. Third, the labor-credit system facilitates the integration of new workers and the replacement of old ones so efficiently that the transitory processes going on all the time are hardly noticed. However, the most important factor in creating the illusion of permanence, the illusion that we are dealing with a fixed and definable entity rather than with a fluctuating and fleeting body of people, may be that this is how we are used to perceiving communities. It is only by shifting one's attention to the passage of individuals through utopian communities that the constant inner reidealization that is apparently necessary for keeping institutionalized idealism alive at all becomes evident.

## Notes

1. Kinkade lives in a small town in the vicinity of Twin Oaks Community but is still officially a member. Her so-called personal-affairs leave enables her to return to the community at any time without having to go through the membership process and thus risk not being accepted. Kinkade's hesitancy to drop membership despite being disappointed in the current state of the community is connected with the lack of a retirement fund she could fall back on.

2. For an account of the early Twin Oaks government, see Kinkade, *Walden* 50–57 and 234–45.

3. This willingness to change, although it might involve a radical transformation of the original vision for the community, has been identified by the communal scholar Donald E. Pitzer as the main characteristic of intentional communities throughout history who have succeeded to survive for long periods of time.

4. The following account of the early phase of child care at Twin Oaks is mainly based on Kinkade, *Walden* 130–46.

5. The program is described in detail in Komar 211–57.

6. It is interesting to note that the communards chose the name of a kibbutz for the children's building, stressing the influence of the communal child-care ideas of the kibbutz movement on the Twin Oaks program.

7. The current state of affairs is described in Kinkade, *Utopia* 143–54.

8. Kinkade dedicates an entire chapter in her second book on Twin Oaks to the complicated tax status of Twin Oaks Community (*Utopia* 279–83).

9. Gale Harris to Kat Kinkade, April 26, 1974, Twin Oaks Papers (no. 9840), Special Collections, University of Virginia Library.

10. David Nord to unnamed person, n.d., Twin Oaks Papers (no. 9840), Special Collections, University of Virginia Library.

11. Other commonly stated reasons for leaving include wishing to provide a more family-oriented setting for children, moving away with a partner, or wanting to pursue careers not available in a small rural community.

# PART 4

# Comunidad Los Horcones: Utopia in the Desert

# 14 Mexican Contexts

ACCEPTING THAT ordinary members were not satisfied to leave the decision making to a select few at Twin Oaks, Kinkade concluded that Skinner had been wrong, that Walden Two was "just not going to make it." She then amended her own statement by adding, "maybe in some other country. Maybe in Mexico" (interview with the author, April 10, 1995). And indeed, the history of the Mexican community Los Horcones is strikingly different from all the other Walden Two experiments.

On first sight, Mexico seems an unlikely location for a Walden Two experiment. The prominent role Skinner played in academia and social reform in the United States of the sixties and seventies, together with the prevailing enthusiasm for the communal idea, are plausible explanations for the emergence of Walden Two groups in Skinner's home country. The conditions in Mexico in the early seventies, however, were quite different. There was no large-scale social reform Skinner's ideas could have had an impact on, and the Mexican student movement that could have inspired communal living was crushed in its infancy when government troops opened fire on demonstrating students in Mexico City in 1968. In the United States's southern neighbor, communal living was not "in the air." While Mexico's economy was only starting to gain strength, its political system, monopolized for decades by the Party of the Institutionalized Revolution (PRI), was still characterized by corruption and frequent upheavals.

While Twin Oaks and Lake Village have published ample material on the personal motivation of the people involved and the circumstances of the actual founding, Los Horcones has written next to nothing about the background and motivation of its founders, adopting instead a more academic writing style similar to Israel and the researchers at Sunflower House. This is regrettable for several reasons.

First, the very existence of Los Horcones in a country that is not known for its utopian tradition nor for its behaviorists is in no way illuminated. Second, the scarcity of information about the communards' motivation to

Comunidad Los Horcones proudly displays its philosophy of life on large signs. (photo by H. Kuhlmann)

Whitewashed buildings nestled in a green oasis separate Comunidad Los Horcones from the surrounding desert landscape. (photo by H. Kuhlmann)

found Los Horcones makes it hard to determine what events, thoughts, and feelings led to the founding of their Walden Two community and how these factors influenced the way the community developed. And third, tracing *individuals'* reactions to both the utopian novel that changed the course of their lives and to communal reality becomes next to impossible when relying on texts that studiously avoid clearly identifying individuals, thus leaving many questions unanswered.

Did the future communards have any reservations about the desirability or practicability of Skinner's utopia? Were there points of disagreement among the future founders, leading perhaps to the departure of people who had initially been interested in the project? They state, rather dryly, that they classified their community as a Walden Two community, "since the first proposal of applying behavioral technology to the design of a society was presented by the behavioral psychologist B. F. Skinner, in his novel 'Walden Two'" ("Los Horcones" 3). This does not sound like the "brilliant flash of light" Kinkade experienced upon reading *Walden Two* (*Walden* 7). The founders of Los Horcones further distance themselves from the novel and the potential effects of reading Skinner's utopian scheme by pointing out that theirs is "not a community based on Skinner's novel . . . but on the science on which that novel is based" (Los Horcones, "News" 129).

This statement already points toward the intentional nature of the community's style of writing and reflects an assumption that is at the core of Los Horcones: In the communards' view, the community and its values are the result of a science, not of a group of people. They are objective scientists engaged in redesigning society. Thus, it is only logical that they keep personal factors out of the presentation of the community. If personal experiences and the sociopolitical background somehow did not affect the development of Los Horcones, then why mention them?

To the outside observer, however, the communards' refusal to discuss these factors causes some problems. In essence, it means that all one may expect from Los Horcones is a discussion of the finer points of behavioral engineering. Even in direct interactions during a short period of participant-observation, the communards were not willing to discuss "irrelevant" topics with me. They also soon ceased corresponding, leaving my inquiries about the possibilities of a longer visit unanswered. This is in part due to the fact that Los Horcones has been and still is frequently annoyed with how they are seen by visitors. They demand the impossible, an "objective" evaluation: "Los Horcones, however, is not just what people see when they visit. To visitors, our everyday reality can be either very pleasant or very unpleasant, depending upon from which perspective they look at us. Their appreciation depends on the attitudes they take when visiting or living here. Usually, people see their social world from their own personal and emotional perspective rather than from an objective one" (Robinson 143). Anybody who fails to view Los Horcones with the eyes of a behavior analyst bent on evaluating a scientific experiment is not welcome.

Here, then, is an admittedly rather sketchy summary of the history of Los Horcones: Like their U.S. counterparts, the Mexican behaviorists were involved in applying behavior modification to a dependent population in a clearly defined setting prior to becoming interested in communal living. The seven founding members of Los Horcones (two couples, two single men, and a toddler) were originally involved in running a school for children with behavioral problems on the outskirts of Hermosillo in northern Mexico. Two of the future founders, Juan and Mireya Robinson, had studied psychology in Mexico City and had returned in 1972 to put their academic knowledge to use. The other founding members were still high school students or just beginning university. All six adult founders of Los Horcones apparently came from middle- to upper-class Mexican families living in Hermosillo. The young Mexicans' work with the children was so successful that they began to ponder whether the same techniques that helped children with behavioral problems might not be applied to improve the lives of "normal" people as well. As psychologists and laypeople who were interested in psychology, they were familiar with Skinner's writings, so when they began searching for literature that might help them in their undertaking, they read or reread *Walden Two* with interest. As far as they could tell, it was the first and most comprehensive piece of literature to suggest applying the techniques of behavior modification to building a whole new society. This is the main reason why they decided to call Los Horcones a Walden Two community. What had begun as an alternative school project thus resulted in the founding of a community only a year later. During that one year, 1972, Juan and Mireya Robinson got together frequently with several of the school's volunteers to read *Walden Two* and mentally design their own utopian community. Interestingly, Skinner never took much of an interest in this Mexican offspring of his utopian dream (author's interview with Kat Kinkade, April 10, 1995), leaving the Mexicans to try out Walden Two on their own.

Juan Robinson, at twenty-four, was the oldest of the founding group. He had graduated as a psychology major from the University of Mexico City and was an ardent behaviorist. The youngest of the future founders was Linda Armendariz, only nineteen and still in high school at the time, but very much dedicated to the idea of founding a community. The other four school volunteers who went on to found Los Horcones, including Linda's husband Ramon Armendariz, were all under twenty-two. Steve Fishman, who visited Los Horcones in 1990, imagined their nightly gatherings as follows: "At the end of the school day, Juan and Mireya hosted gatherings. Linda (La Linda), just 19, a volunteer at the school, attended; so did her husband, Ramon Armendariz, 21. Juan, old man of the group at 24, would break out his copy of *Walden Two* and read aloud. Juan's voice is high and breathy, like the sound produced by blowing air into a Coke bottle. Night after night, his audience listened to that eerie hoot go on about how, with the aid of Skinner's science, a new society could be formed" (55).

This clearly negative account of the gatherings that led to the founding of Los Horcones—while historically irrelevant, since the author was not there to witness the scene—is of interest because of the role it ascribes to Robinson. Judging from the prominent role he has nowadays at Los Horcones and taking age and state of academic education into account, Robinson was likely the main theorist of the nightly discussion group and also the driving force behind the founding of Los Horcones.

The six young teachers (together with Juan and Mireya Robinson's first child) pooled resources to buy thirty acres of land on the outskirts of Hermosillo. They named their community Los Horcones, the Spanish word for a special kind of pillar, a prominent feature of the community's architecture. The word also sums up the founders' intention: to build the pillars of a new society. The communards went about their task systematically. Instead of trying to copy Skinner's fictional utopia, the founders constructed their own community from scratch, using as a guideline the findings of the experimental analysis of behavior. This led them to formulate a new form of government they call "personocracy" (Los Horcones, "Personalized" 42–47), a work distribution system similar to the one described in *Walden Two,* and a complex system of communal behavior-modification programs. Behaviorism thus permeates Los Horcones to an extent that cannot be rivaled by even the most behaviorist phases of any of the U.S. groups.

The economic survival of Los Horcones seems never to have been threatened. The founders' fairly affluent backgrounds allowed them to buy sufficient property to house their community and to continue the school project they are engaged in to this day, and their willingness to work hard has kept them afloat ever since. All property is held communally, and money is used only when dealing with the outside world. Economic stability is guaranteed by two main sources of income: the tuition fees paid by the parents of the children with behavioral problems (the pre-founding school is still in operation) and the sale of self-processed health food (granola, yogurt, cheese, bran bread, and muffins) in nearby Hermosillo. In addition, the communards use the health food to supplement their own diet.

Most twentieth-century secular communities, including the Walden Two communities in the United States, tend to consist of young, unrelated, middle-class individuals. While Los Horcones started out with six young people as well, it has developed over the years a membership reminiscent of an extended family or small religious communities of long standing: all age groups are represented, and a majority of the members are related to one another by blood or marriage. Of the six adult founders, four still live in the community: Juan and Mireya Robinson and Ramon and Linda Armendariz. The other two founders left because their newly found wives were not interested in living the communal life. While Los Horcones often has additional members who stay for a certain amount of time, it has always had this four-member core group consisting of the two couples, with Robinson as its head. So far, the community has mainly grown through procreation and attracting relatives to the community. The Robinsons have three children, the Armendarizes four. All seven children, born between 1971 and 1986, were raised at Los Horcones and intend to stay. The oldest girl, Mireya, is married and has already given birth to two children of the third generation. Mireya's brother-in-law is also a member of the community, as is a nephew of Juan Robinson's. This means that of the community's thirty-odd current members, fourteen are related to one another, taking the Robinsons and the Armindarizes together. Perhaps the fabric of the community is linked to the communards' cultural background, since large, extended families headed by a patriarch are more typical of Mexico than the United States. What is unusual about the extended family at Los Horcones from a Mexican perspective is that it is centered around two families instead of one.

Since Los Horcones was apparently never in need of members to insure economic survival, it could afford to be more stringent in its membership selection. The core group knew it wanted only people dedicated to the behaviorist dream as defined by Los Horcones. Since they were the ones to decide whether an applicant could become a member or not, they managed to keep out those whom they felt would cause trouble later by disagreeing on basic principles. As one side effect of the decision to keep out nonbehaviorists, membership was slow to increase. Rather than growing quickly, and growing quickly into something they had not intended (as happened at Twin Oaks), they opted for gradual growth. It seems likely that the community's core group was influential in determining the development of Los Horcones at all stages, most importantly by agreeing on the criteria for membership selection. The many upheavals, power struggles, policy changes, and simple confusions springing from the diverse and ideologically heterogeneous membership of the northern communities were apparently never experienced at Los Horcones.

Los Horcones differs from its northern counterparts not only in having an extended-family membership but also in adhering to views on sexuality and monogamy that are similar to those Skinner proposed in *Walden Two*, which were simply ignored by the U.S. communities. Although Los Horcones encourages emotional commitment to one another, heterosexual monogamy is advocated and adhered to quite strictly. Early marriages are considered desirable and normal, influenced perhaps by traditional Mexican mores. Anything but heterosexuality is looked upon as slightly odd, although the community is theoretically open to people of all sexual orientations. The community's conservative views are apparently not open to debate, as Richard Graham from Dandelion Community in Canada noticed during a visit: "I remember this one guy who got up at a meeting at Los Horcones and talked about sex," he says in an interview. "I think Juan was talking about monogamous relationships in community, and some of the Americans were challenging Juan on that. Juan got real defensive, saying we shouldn't be talking about this, we should be talking about applied behavior analysis rather than talking about who sleeps with whom. I thought that was one of the cultural shifts. . . . You know, two consenting adults, and everything's okay. But I think at Los Horcones, it was more about monogamy, and I guess that comes from their culture, the Catholic background" (interview with the author, July 24, 1998).

In the late 1970s, the explosive growth of Hermosillo's population resulted in the rapid expansion of the city. Buildings, shops, and roads began to spring up all around Los Horcones. Burglaries began to be a frequent nuisance. The communards found it impossible to guard themselves against outward danger without giving up the lifestyle they wanted. They faced the choice of either moving farther away to pursue their own lifestyle or securing the community against burglars and thus robbing it of its openness. In 1980, they decided to move the community to its present location in a more isolated area of the Sonoran desert, about an hour's drive from Hermosillo. To get to the community from Hermosillo, the closest city, one has to drive about fifty minutes along the Hermosillo-Tecoripa Highway before coming to a little village called La Colorada. Shortly after leaving the village again, at kilometer post 63, a dirt road turns off the highway. This dirt road, approximately three or four kilometers long, leads directly to the community and was built by the communards themselves. Finally, two gates have to be passed, one at the beginning of the dirt road and one at the entrance to the community.

The communards found that their forced change of residence had its advantages. First, economic self-sufficiency became easier. They were able to acquire the 250–acre property at a low price and are now able to pursue a variety of work they would have found impossible to do in an urban setting, such as permaculture gardening, keeping animals, and building a cheese factory and bakery.

Over the years, the communards have put up numerous buildings on their spacious property designed for communal use, including a dining hall, a conference hall, two schools, washing facilities with an adjacent clothes-storage room, a TV room, barns, a cheese and yogurt factory, a bakery, two libraries (a general and a behaviorist one), and a number of buildings containing individual quarters for the members. The buildings are all kept clean and in good shape. Concrete footpaths, which are lit by little lamps at night, connect the buildings to each other. The communards have not only paid close attention to architecture, they have also managed to turn their patch of desert into a green oasis. They have dug a well high up in the mountains, which provides them with clean drinking water and also fills two ponds on the community's grounds. They have planted imported citrus trees, which give enough shade to allow grass to grow. A permaculture garden provides the communards with fresh vegetables, which are supplemented with products bought in Hermosillo. The communards also keep cows, pigs, and horses. Their diet is usually traditional Mexican food carefully prepared to meet semivegetarian standards. All in all, the quality of life at Los Horcones is very much above that of mainstream Mexican society and fully meets, if not surpasses, western standards.

Although geographically isolated, Los Horcones tries to maintain some contact and good relations with its neighbors. Each day, two Volkswagen vans drive into Hermosillo to sell their surplus health food and do necessary errands (such as buying groceries, going to the post office, making phone calls, and so on). The crew for these trips changes daily, giving every member a chance to go into town. Also, the communards are constantly trying to initiate lectures on behavior modification for teachers and parents in Hermosillo. However, trips to Hermosillo are not much in demand at Los Horcones. Most members have no desire to drive into town more often than necessary. All of the "salespeople" are reportedly relieved to be able to return to Los Horcones at the end of the day.

# 15 Education

THE SERIOUS BEHAVIORIST intent of Los Horcones is clearly recognizable in its educational practices. At Los Horcones, education is regarded as a process that goes on throughout one's life. Techniques of behavior modification—helping members to master communitarian behavior and academic study—are frequently employed at Los Horcones. Since all people are capable of behavioral and academic self-improvement, members of Los Horcones are expected to use this potential. As a sign at the entrance points out: "Social change is achieved when each individual makes a personal change." In the opinion of Los Horcones, this is the only way to achieve social change. Following this line of thought, the community has always given foremost importance to education. In this they are in perfect agreement with Skinner.

The educational practices of Los Horcones fall into two categories. First, the community as a whole continues to operate a school for autistic children. Second, the community places great emphasis on the education of its own children. In their treatment of autistic children, the members of Los Horcones concentrate on modifying the children's behavior. They do not try to uncover the reasons for the children's unusual behavior patterns, instead providing an environment that is as simple, predictable, and unthreatening as possible while at the same time giving the autistic child assignments of a very basic nature. Once the assignment is fulfilled, the child is reinforced by praise, hugs, sweets, or whatever other reinforcers are available. If the child does not fulfill the assignment, he or she is not punished. The undesirable behavior is simply ignored. In addition to this learning-by-reinforcement atmosphere, an autistic child living at Los Horcones must not fear being laughed at or treated disrespectfully. All this is designed to help the child gain confidence in dealing with his or her environment and learn socially acceptable behavior. The treatment somewhat resembles the "ethical training" of children in *Walden Two*.

The handful of autistic children living at Los Horcones are educated in a school building especially designed for this purpose. The children come from families living in northern Mexico and go home either on weekends or for vacations. During the week, they eat together with the other members in the communal dining room and spend a good part of the day fully integrated into communal life. They are cared for in a one-to-one teacher/student setting. Since teaching autistic children requires special skills, only a few of the members are engaged in this work, including some of its young second-generation members. The teachers usually develop a personal relationship with their charges, characterized by gentleness, patience, and respect.

Seven community children, four boys and three girls, have been raised at Los Horcones from birth. They are the children of the two founding couples. All of the children and both sets of parents still live at Los Horcones. The oldest girl has already given birth to two children. Other children have come and gone with their parents, but none of them really grew up at Los Horcones. The founders' children are at the center of the community's attention. By now, the second-generation children are fully integrated into the community as adult members. They have their own rooms, do their share of work, take part in the decision making, and enrich the community's social life. While they were growing up, they all lived together in the children's house (the first building the communards put up themselves) and were cared for by metas. As at Twin Oaks, Los Horcones has chosen the kibbutz term for their child-care workers. The behavior and education of the children was coordinated by a child manager.

The members of Los Horcones did not try to dissolve the concept of the family; instead, they extended it by supporting the concept of an open family. Their fairly small size allowed them to do this with amazing success. The children regard all the adult members who raised them as their parents, and the adults do not recognizably bestow special favors on their biological offspring or single them out in any other way. The relationship of the four founders to their children is characterized by mutual affection. This affection is strong and obvious in all their interactions. The atmosphere of love and goodwill that prevails at Los Horcones has not failed to impress many visitors.[1] One cannot say that parents at Los Horcones weaken the emotional ties to their offspring; they expand them to encompass the other community children as well. This is theoretically also what Skinner proposed with his "community love." But how can this really be practiced in a thousand-member community? With the children at Walden Two isolated in a controlled environment, parents play a marginal role in their children's lives, comparable perhaps to fathers with Sunday-afternoon visiting rights in mainstream society. By virtue of its small size, Los Horcones can afford to practice Skinner's suggestion without running into emotional difficulties. Under the specific historical circumstances of Los Horcones, the practicing of communal child care meant that the second-generation children grew up having two mothers and two fathers, and each parent had seven children.

Children at Los Horcones receive something remotely comparable to Skinner's "ethical training." They are taught communitarian behavior and also the techniques and theory involved in the process. Prominent among the behaviors reinforced is self-control. I do not have a detailed description of how this self-control is taught at Los Horcones or how much the communards are in agreement with Skinner's practical proposals. Though it would appear that the children are engaged in self-management programs similar to those of the adult members from an early age, it is not clear what else is done specifically to teach children self-control. Self-management programs are used throughout Los Horcones to tackle particular behavioral problems a member may wish to change. The behavior is first monitored for a number of days, then the person consciously tries to change the behavior in the desired direction. As a last step, the member monitors the changed behavior and its effect on him- or herself and the other members. Self-management programs are either carried out alone or with the help of the behavior manager. In a room adjacent to the communal dining hall, one can find a wall full of charts kept by members who are currently engaged in self-management programs. The charts are sometimes kept anonymously if this is what the member prefers. Children take part in these self-management programs as little experts in behaviorism: "The children who live at Los Horcones study behaviorology (behavior analysis and behaviorism) since they are very young. This helps them to better understand how and to what extent their environment influences the way in which they and other people behave, and how they can modify their environment so that it influences their behavior in the desired direction. This is not a strange thing to do for our children, because what Los Horcones is precisely trying to do is to modify the environment so that it promotes cooperative, non-possessive, egalitarian, and non-violent behaviors among its members" ("Implications" 10).

Los Horcones has refrained from establishing a controlled environment for children, perhaps because the entire community is engaged in this learning process. Besides, the relatively small size of the community may render a specially controlled children's environment impracticable. And why design forbidden bowls of soup if frustrating experiences will occur anyway and are likely to be noticed in a community as small as Los Horcones? Surrounded by loving behaviorists who secure a fairly controlled environment, children may encounter mildly frustrating experiences in their daily lives at any point, but the reinforcers necessary to overcome the frustration will almost certainly be at hand. Los Horcones has developed a system of "natural" reinforcement that makes a controlled environment almost unnecessary.[2] Rather than depending on contrived reinforcers, that is, reinforcers administered by a person or machine, the communards try to make the consequences of a desired behavior intrinsically or naturally reinforcing. For example, one can either give a child a piece of chocolate for doing the dishes (making the child's willingness to do the dishes dependent on the chocolate), or one can say, "How nice of you to do the dishes! Look how shiny the kitchen is now. I bet the cook will be very grateful for your help!" (developing a liking for clean kitchens in the child so that after a while simply looking at the results of his or her work will be reinforcing).

Contrary to what might be expected from communards determined to raise even better communards, no attempt was ever made to isolate the children from mainstream society—beyond the fact that they grow up on a remote desert property. The second-generation members go to town regularly and have friends there, they watch some television, and they listen to contemporary music. The communards consciously allow this contact with the outside society to give their children a "preparation to analyze its advantages and problems" ("Los Horcones" 9).

Academic instruction is also an important objective of education at Los Horcones. In a pamphlet designed to give an introduction to the community, one can read the following under the heading "Education":

> This cultural practice involves family, social, political, economy-related, as well as academic education. Los Horcones provides academic instruction (pre-school, elementary, and high school) within the community using the *Personalized System of Instruction*. Students obtain their legal certificates by passing standard examinations of the Mexican System of Public Education.
>
> At Los Horcones, children and adults receive communitary education in theory and practice. (*General Description* 4)

A passage in a newsletter explains the Personalized System of Instruction: "The educational system used in most of the courses is the 'personalized system of instruction,' popularly known as 'PSI.' . . . This system was designed by Fred S. Keller (1968), and has demonstrated to be very effective. Its main characteristics are the use of study material written in sequenced units that make it possible for each student to advance at [their] own pace, and having a high criterion of expertise on a subject, before proceeding to the next one. It is a system that helps the student to be more independent from the teacher and from fixed study-time schedules. This individualized system makes studying more reinforcing (pleasant) for the student" ("Los Horcones" 9).

The system seems to work well at Los Horcones. The community's children have always passed the Mexican state examinations with ease. Their technical skills are well developed. Workshops are frequently offered in carpentry, mechanics, or horseback riding. It is also the general policy of the community that whenever a child asks a member "How do you do that?" the member will stop working to explain what he or she is doing.

Kinkade once remarked that "[p]ioneers in community childcare must . . . be people who have a heavy investment in the theory" (*Walden* 145). The Los Horcones people certainly have this. Their educational system not only lives up to the one in *Walden Two,* it surpasses it in many ways. It is more humane in its parent-child relationships, it avoids some of the pitfalls of Skinner's "ethical training," and it is much more concrete regarding academic instruction.

The main difference from Skinner's "ethical training" seems to me to be the fact that Los Horcones instructs its children in the techniques of behavior modification instead of just subjecting them to a training program. Children at Los Horcones are not ignorant subjects of subtle manipulation. They are taught exactly what the community's objectives and methods are. I would assume that nobody interested in simply controlling others would tell the controlees his or her methods. Sharing the knowledge about a powerful, potentially manipulative technique ensures to a large degree that this knowledge cannot be used against a person's wishes. The way Los Horcones gives freely of its knowledge shows that its members really do seek to control themselves, not others, not even their children. Strangely enough, this attitude is apparently not perceived as a contradiction to Skinner's ideal, which clearly advocates a very minor level of awareness of behaviorist techniques and participation in decision making on the part of the ordinary members.

The members of Los Horcones have pieced together the educational ideas of Skinner, other behaviorists,[3] and the results of their own research to construct a system of child rearing and academic instruction that fits the needs of their community perfectly. Their system may not be transferable to education in mainstream society, as Donald M. Baer and Beth Sulzer-Azaroff have pointed out, but it does represent an important experiment in the possibilities of behaviorist education under ideal circumstances.

# 16 The Economic Structure

THE LOS HORCONES ECONOMY operates on the so-called labor-time system, an adaptation of the Skinnerian labor-credit system. Its main difference is that work is measured in terms of time, not a credit that varies depending on the degree of popularity of the work. Twin Oaks experimented extensively with varied credit before they, too, abandoned it. In their opinion, the system could be manipulated and misused too easily. Los Horcones simply states that the system was changed but does not give any reasons for doing so (Los Horcones, "Pilot" 26). One could speculate, however, that the varied credit was abandoned because it provides a contrived, noncommunitarian reinforcer for working. As has been pointed out before, Los Horcones puts great emphasis on creating natural (instead of contrived) and communitarian reinforcers for communitarian behavior. Skinner's labor-credit system fulfills neither of the two criteria. First, if a person is given extra credit for doing a task he or she dislikes, the fact that the person does not enjoy the task is not really changed. As soon as the extra credit is removed, the person will find the task unpleasant again. Los Horcones tries instead to modify a person's behavior in such a way that he or she will actually find the task itself agreeable, even in the absence of outward reinforcers. Second, Skinner's system reinforces good workers by giving them leisure time. The underlying assumption must be that work is to be avoided and that leisure is a desirable reward. The attitude this promotes is counterproductive for a cooperative community that depends on its members' willingness to work.

At Los Horcones, as at Twin Oaks, the flexibility of the work schedule is one of the most valued aspects of the original labor-credit system. While the work coordinator determines twice a month what work has to be done and how many hours each member will have to put in, the individual members are free to choose when they want to work, unless outward circumstances intervene (cows, for example, have to be milked in the morning), and what tasks they want to work on, as long as these tasks are on the coordinator's list of things to be done (Los Horcones, "Pilot" 26–27). Men and women have equal access to all areas of work.

The communards at Los Horcones advocate a sustainable economic system, which makes them very selective about the work habits they reinforce. "Never take anything away without replacing it" reads one of the many signs put up on the community's grounds to remind people of proper behavior. This applies not only to tools but also to the sensible use of natural resources. Thus, another sign says: "Everything can be used and reused. Little needs to be thrown out." This attitude is reflected in the work done at Los Horcones. Water is recycled, little plastic is used, work tools and other daily-life utensils are handled carefully to make them last longer, and so on. The throwaway attitude and overconsumption that prevail in capitalist societies are not acceptable at Los Horcones.

Hardly any problems with the labor-time system, past or present, are reported in the numerous articles the community has published. In fact, the community's economic basis and system of work distribution are always *mentioned* in general descriptions of the community, but they are never discussed in depth. However, it seems unlikely that there were no labor problems worth mentioning in over twenty years of community life. It is unfortunate that Los Horcones refuses to give a detailed picture of its economic system.[4] In the absence of more information, deciding whether the labor-credit system based on time but not efficiency works for Los Horcones remains pure speculation. This is all the more regrettable since Los Horcones is the only Walden Two community in which Skinner's proposals appear to function quite smoothly.

# 17   Leadership and Decision Making

SKINNER FAVORED A GOVERNMENT run by professionals or, as Kinkade put it, "by those who are good at it" (interview with the author, April 10, 1995). The ordinary citizens of Walden Two, Skinner argued, would not be interested in governmental affairs and would put their utter trust in the abilities and goodwill of the planners and managers. Safeguards against misuse of power would not be necessary because nothing could be gained by misusing power, and no member of Walden Two could be bullied into obedience anyway. The Skinnerian planner-manager system did not survive at Twin Oaks or any of the other Walden Two experiments because the "ordinary" citizens were simply not willing to give up being part of the decision-making process, no matter how much ability and goodwill the professionals displayed. Los Horcones took a different approach to the problem of governmental organization but—surprisingly—came up with very similar results.

The communards at Los Horcones did not take Skinner's governmental suggestions literally. To them, the "defining features" of a Walden Two–type government were the use of "the principles of behavior and an experimental approach to cultural analysis, design, and change" (Los Horcones, "Personalized" 42), whereas Twin Oaks took Skinner's specific planner-manager system itself for a defining feature of a Walden Two society. The way Los Horcones read and understood *Walden Two* led them to ask themselves a number of questions regarding the form of government they wished to implement: "As we started the Los Horcones community, we found ourselves confronting a number of questions concerning the system of government most suitable to a behaviorally designed community. What type of government is needed to promote cooperative and egalitarian behavior? How do we encourage pacifism and sharing? What type of government would allow our citizens to participate in all governmental functions? What type of government is needed to emphasize prevention rather than mere remediation? How do we insure that our government remains committed to our experimental approach to cultural design?" (42–43).

It is clear that Skinner's planner-manager system does not fulfill the Los Horcones requirements. Skinner does not aim at allowing citizens "to participate in all governmental functions"; quite the contrary. A later passage in the same article is even more obviously in disagreement with Skinner's benign but anti-democratic planner-manager system: "By empirically assessing the effects of different forms of government on the governors, the governed, and on the community as a whole, we should be able to determine the type of government which would be best suited to our needs. Our evaluative comparisons were based on *cooperation* (participation in the political decision-making), *equality* (equal access to political power), *non-violence* (peaceful problem solving), and *sharing* (political education)" (43).

The specifications for nonviolence and perhaps equality could be made to fit Skinner's governmental system, but "participation in the decision-making" and "political education" definitely run counter to Skinner's ideas on the subject. Despite the obvious differences between the Skinnerian planner-manager system and the approach to government taken by the Mexican community, Los Horcones very carefully avoids stating that they came to *reject* the governmental system described in *Walden Two*. Perhaps this hesitance is due to the fact that both Skinner and Los Horcones claim that their values, in regard to government and other issues, are the logical consequence of taking a scientific approach. How, then, do you explain *differences* in the realm of value judgments? Before turning to this problem in the next chapter, we shall now take a closer look at the development of decision making at Los Horcones.

In pursuit of their ideal form of government, the communards at Los Horcones tried a number of different political systems. Initially, they did implement Skinner's planner-manager system. The communards describe their experiences with it as follows: "Although the planners had final authority to make decisions for the community, they always consulted each member of the community before making any important decisions. None of the planners or managers considered that they had all the information necessary to make the best decision for the entire community. Over a period of four years, our decision-making became a progressively more cooperative effort, with the planners eventually no longer having complete authority" (Los Horcones, "Personalized" 43).

This passage—the only one dealing directly with the planner-manager system—suggests that the communards had not considered decision making to be a cooperative effort from the very beginning (as the statements quoted earlier would indicate) but rather realized by trying to live the elitist planner-manager system that it did not work for them. A 1982 article states that "Los Horcones is organized on the planner manager system described in *Walden Two*" without so much as hinting at any problems with the systems or adaptations being made (besides the reduced number of planners), while a 1989 article on government states that as early as 1977 the communards agreed to make their government "explicitly democratic" and later tried "a variety of other forms of government" before developing their own system in 1982.

The dissatisfaction with the planner-manager system, which was nominally the community's form of government from 1973 to 1977, led the communards to experiment with democracy. They made their government "explicitly democratic and chose the form of direct democracy (as opposed to a representative democracy) [because in a] direct democracy all members can participate directly in the decision-making process" ("Personalized" 43). The communards are now actively seeking a form of government that allows the highest possible involvement of all members in decision making. One year of direct democracy convinced the communards that the system actually reinforced anticommunitarian behavior, which was clearly the opposite of what they were aiming at. They discovered that any form of government employing votes almost necessarily encourages competitive behavior in all its shades:

> [W]e found that negative, competitive statements occurred frequently. Members in the minority on a vote said things like "They have made a poor decision" or "I'm sure that solution will fail." If indeed the decision of the majority turned out to be unsuccessful, we heard members in the minority say "They decided that, not me," or "That's why I was against it," or "I told them that would happen." However, when the decision of the majority turned out to be correct, the minority did not show their approval. Winning or losing the vote seemed to become more important than making a correct decision.
>
> A second problem with the democratic form of government was that it encouraged adversarial behaviors. Groups formed in opposition to one another, each promoting its own proposals. We heard competitive comments like "We'll win; there are more people to vote in favor of our proposal than theirs." We also heard discriminatory statements like "He always votes in favor of another person's proposals, so don't help him," and "They are making a mistake. We are right. They are not as interested in the community as we are." ("Personalized" 43)

The competitive atmosphere finally led to the informal establishment of "political groups" that backed one or the other of the few dominant decision makers of the group. A situation had arisen that came close to the political atmosphere of a competitive and capitalist western democracy, which the communards had hoped to avoid.

In the following three years, Los Horcones had various forms of government the communards themselves call "not-defined" but that "might be classified as totalitarian, gerontocratic, and technocratic" ("Personalized" 44). Unfortunately, only one brief paragraph is devoted to the governmental experiences of these three years. However, it seems safe to assume that the communards must have been highly dissatisfied with the way their government was, from their perspective, deteriorating. "We were still in search of a system of government that would allow every member to participate decisively in the decision-making process," ends the paragraph on the dissatisfactory forms of government between 1978 and 1982 ("Personalized" 44).

True to the experimental spirit of *Walden Two*, the communards slowly and experimentally developed their own system, the Personalized System of Government, also called "personocracy." The main characteristic of personocracy is that it "promotes the participation of all members in governmental decision[s]" while showing "the same concern for the individual members of our community as the Personalized System of Instruction shows for individual students" ("Personalized" 45). The goal of personocracy is twofold: first, to guarantee the survival of the community by teaching its members the required behavior, and second, to constantly increase the amount of reinforcement available for all (Los Horcones, "Real Life" 255). The functioning and purpose of personocracy is clearly influenced by behaviorist thinking: behavior modification is the central means—and goal—of personocracy. Specific to the Los Horcones interpretation of applying positive reinforcement to the governmental organization of a society is that participation in decision making is reinforced, skills that enable members to hold important organizational positions are taught to all, and all decision-making meetings are open to all members to avoid feelings of frustration, envy, or anger at being left out. Decisions are arrived at by consensus to ensure the support of all members.

These governmental practices are in keeping with the Los Horcones objective of creating an environment based on positive reinforcement, not punitive control. Skinner's planner-manager system was also based on positive reinforcement. What makes the Los Horcones personocracy different? It recognizes the need for communitarian behavior in all areas of community life, while Skinner thought it acceptable that a few able people "provide" a reinforcing environment in a noncommunitarian manner for the ordinary community members. For Los Horcones, it is not acceptable to let a community that is trying to promote *communitarian* behavior be governed by a structure promoting *noncommunitarian* behavior. In their opinion, equality (no planner elite), sharing (political power and skills), and cooperation (in seeking the best solution) must be integral parts of a governmental system that puts behaviorism into practice. Skinner's planner-manager system, they might argue, is sure to breed competition, dissatisfaction, frustration, and envy—the very feelings he sought to obliterate. Los Horcones is not this explicit in its criticism of the Walden Two governmental structure, but a comparison of its system with Skinner's leads logically to the assumption that Los Horcones came to *reject* Skinner's ideas on governmental organization in all major points. What the communards did not reject were Skinner's two premises for finding the best form of government: employing the findings of behaviorism and using scientific experimentation. In a way, the Los Horcones personocracy and Skinner's planner-manager system are variations on the same topic: mixing behaviorism and politics. In this they differ from Twin Oaks and Lake Village, the two surviving Walden Two experiments originally aiming at the Walden Two governmental system, who no longer seek a behaviorally sound government and have given up on the whole idea of behavior modification as the basis for the good life. Many outside observers of Los Horcones have doubted, however, whether it is really behavior modification that is at the core of the Mexican community's governmental system.

Los Horcones states blandly in one of its articles: "In this community, we have no leaders because no one reinforces the requisite behavior" ("News" 130). Similar disclaimers can be found throughout their literature.[5] "We avoid any kind of 'personality cult,'" ends an article entitled "*Walden Two* in Real Life." It goes on to claim that "[o]ur gains are always communitarian, never personal. Recognition, if any, is for all" (255). True to this attitude, all articles written by Los Horcones present the history and current state of the community in the first-person plural or using passive verb forms, making it impossible for the reader to identify and differentiate between the individual members. The theory concerning politics seems to be that a properly reinforcing form of government can make all members equally competent and decisive in decision making and that this has already happened at Los Horcones. In their article on government, the communards admit to having had problems in the past with several governmental systems that "amounted to having only a few members who were actually making the decisions for the group" ("Personalized" 44). They solved this problem, so they say, by developing their own system of government. Nowhere in their literature is there any indication that leadership by one member alone has ever played an important role in the community's development. My own impression is different, as is Kat Kinkade's: "I did not think that what made them operate so well was behaviorism. I do not think so. I think it's charisma. I think it's Juan. I think Juan's leadership is excellent" (interview with the author, April 10, 1995).

Although in designing their governmental and labor systems the communards have cut down considerably on the structural opportunity of any one person dominating over the others, Los Horcones has always been held together by a naturally charismatic leader who determines to a large extent its philosophic outlook and direction of action. Juan Robinson, the oldest of the six founders, is clearly central to the community. He is not only its chief behaviorist thinker, he is also the behavior coordinator of long standing, the coauthor (with Linda Armendariz) of most of the articles Los Horcones has published, a skilled teacher with a university degree in psychology, and the unofficial guide for visitors. He is also the father of three of the community's second generation, the grandfather of the first two third-generation children, and a husband, uncle, and father-in-law for other community members. However, similar lists could be made for at least three other members as well, namely the remaining cofounders of Los Horcones, Juan's wife Mireya and Linda and Ramon Armendariz. Juan Robinson differs from them in two important respects. He is the community's theorist, and he has charisma (for lack of a better word) combined with a knack for leadership. Robinson's leadership is quiet and unobtrusive, but it is there. It is hard to pinpoint just what makes a person charismatic and how this trait affects others. In Robinson's case, the most noticeable feature seems to be the fact that discussions in which he participated during the time of my stay were strongly reminiscent of lectures, with him talking and all the other members listening. These spontaneous or planned gatherings at which Robinson spoke did not give me the impression of partners of equal standing engaging in the exchange of ideas. Instead, I saw a dedicated teacher instructing attentive students. Also, Robinson seemed generally set apart from the other members in daily life. He appeared to me to spend a good deal of time walking from one place to another, giving a word of encouragement, squeezing someone affectionately, or giving someone a helping hand; making sure, in other words, that nothing is amiss at Los Horcones. Robinson's position at Los Horcones is reminiscent of Frazier's at Walden Two.

Walden Two is not imaginable without Frazier, just as Los Horcones is not imaginable without Robinson. In *Walden Two,* most of the talking is done by Frazier. It is not unusual in the tradition of utopian literature to have one utopian as the spokesperson for visiting outsiders. Yet Frazier does not only happen to be the guide for visitors, he is also the only member of Walden Two who could possibly fulfill the role. He is, after all, the only member of Walden Two capable of arguing behaviorism with nonbehaviorists. Similarly, Robinson is the one to discuss behaviorism with visitors. Interestingly, both Frazier and Robinson deny their leadership. Frazier "concealed his part in Walden Two as far as possible," as Skinner elaborated in his article "News from Nowhere, 1984" (6), and one could say that the Los Horcones published papers effectively do the same and may even have been designed to that end.

Despite these similarities, Los Horcones does not fall into the pattern of strong leader/weak followers. The core members of Los Horcones (the founders, their children, and the handful of long-term members) are strong personalities who do not in any way need a "leader." They are not dependent on Robinson, as is the case in many communities centered around a charismatic figure, including the fictitious Walden Two. Yet despite the Los Horcones efforts at completely egalitarian cooperation, it is Robinson's distinctive vision of the perfect society that gives shape to Los Horcones and holds the community together.[6] Kinkade, who visited Los Horcones in the 1980s and is on friendly terms with the core group, comments:

> I think . . . most of the others could be articulate on the subject [of behaviorism], [but] you would simply hear what Juan had said. They get all of their ideas about behavior theory from Juan. . . . I don't think that that kind of group attracts active theoretical minds. I think that it is very typical: they have a theoretician in the center, and most people reflect what that person thinks, and if you get two theoreticians, you'll probably end up with two communities. Like these cells that have two nuclei, they tend to stretch further and further apart until they snap in the middle. . . . I'm immensely drawn to Juan as a personality, and as a thinker. . . . But I think I would be fundamentally lonely [living at Los Horcones], because I think if I came not to agree with him—who would I talk to? (interview with the author, April 10, 1995)

Even if the decision making at Los Horcones is not as completely cooperative an affair as the communards might wish, it should be pointed out that egalitarian cooperation is still theoretically their goal. But since the communards do not acknowledge the need for leadership in a behavioral society—and in fact do their best to prove that a Walden Two does *not* hinge on a few influential behavioral engineers—they cannot very well comment on the evidence of leadership in their own community. Kinkade, however, who is very much aware of the problems of leadership (having encountered several in Twin Oaks's stormy history), reports a talk she had with Robinson in which he chided her for "losing control" over Twin Oaks affairs: "'You didn't lose control, Kat, you gave it up. You gave it over. You never should have done so. If you had insisted—you were wiser than that bunch of people—if you'd insisted, if you'd kept hold of the reins, it would be a far better community.' . . . I laughed. I didn't have the emotional stamina then to take anything of the kind, nor was my theory so autocratic as to back up any such action as that. Juan didn't have any trouble having an autocratic theory. It just didn't trouble him at all" (interview with the author, April 10, 1995).

Robinson is not troubled by an autocratic theory; Frazier does not even stop short of comparing himself to God in an emotionally charged encounter with Burris. Frazier, although apparently concealing his part in the founding of Walden Two, is obviously proud of his "creation." He explains his pride, and other "negative" emotions, by saying that he is "not a product of Walden Two" (233). It is quite possible that Robinson views himself similarly. His autocratic behavior and theory combined with his efforts at keeping himself in the background seem to point in that direction. Perhaps the majority of the members of Los Horcones have recognized Robinson's extraordinary status but believe it to be a problem that will solve itself in time, as Joseph Wood Krutch has remarked about Frazier: "Frazier himself is compelled to make a significant confession: the motives which led him to undertake his successful experiment included a certain desire to exercise power over his fellows. . . . But he insists that the danger will disappear with him because those who succeed to his authority and inherit his techniques will have enjoyed, as he did not, the advantages of a scientific conditioning process and that therefore such potentially antisocial impulses as his will no longer exist" (203).

If this is what the communards at Los Horcones hope for, their community stands on shaky ground. Who is to say if and how a void left by an absent leader can be filled? The past has shown that many communities centered around a charismatic person fall apart as soon as they lose their center. It is my guess that the stability of Los Horcones will be put to its hardest test when Robinson is not there anymore to guide the community. It may be that Los Horcones will disappear along with the "danger" of an individual's "desire to exercise power."

# 18 Behaviorism as Religion

THE COMMUNARDS AT LOS HORCONES firmly believe in the possibility of establishing objectively definable moral values. They regard themselves as scientists who have arrived at their own community's values—cooperation, pacifism, egalitarianism, and ecological consciousness—from scientific, objectively obtainable data. This leads them to believe that Los Horcones is the "product of a science," not of a "particular ideology" ("Los Horcones" 4). In the communards' opinion, this fact sets Los Horcones apart from all prior and current attempts at designing a new society:

Several ways have been proposed in the past to change these [accidental] societies to other, more planned ones. Unfortunately, these proposed changes have taken into consideration only philosophical, historical, political, economic, or religious suggestions. None of these fields has provided the objective data through which a culture can be designed to survive and produce happy people who do not harm others. Sometimes other proposals have been offered that are said to be based on "science," but the term "science" has been used in very different ways. Usually the so-called "science" is not based on scientific experimentation, which is the major requirement of a natural science. Such a "science" has nothing to contribute to cultural design. Nor can a useful contribution be made by a philosophy that is not based on a concept of man which is compatible with the image of man that scientific experimentation gives us. There is no reason to permit opinions from such a philosophy to intervene in the design of a culture. (Los Horcones, "Pilot" 25)

One is to understand that scientific experimentation alone is an eligible means of discovering and defining human values. In the opinion of Los Horcones, although "no single science is adequate for the task of designing the physical and social environments that comprise a society," nothing but natural sciences based on scientific experimentation have a "place in the process" ("Social Change" 36). The communards at Los Horcones thus fully agree with Skinner that facts can produce values.

The communards state that science can be used to design a culture that is "to survive and produce happy people who do not harm others" ("Social Change" 36). Yet by designating survival, happiness, and harmlessness as their goals, the communards are already making a moral judgment, namely that the survival of the human species is desirable, that the end product should be happy people, and that these happy people should not harm others. As we have seen, in discussing their governmental system, they started out by asking what "type of government would allow our citizens to participate in all governmental functions," without explaining how they derived at demanding a participatory system as opposed to, for example, Skinner's antiparticipatory system. They also asked themselves, "What type of government is needed to promote cooperative and egalitarian behavior?" Again, the communards treat "cooperative and egalitarian behavior"—a matter of what ought to be—as if it were a matter of fact that this is the goal of any government.

Whether the communards are ignoring the problem of deriving what "ought" to be from what "is" or are simply not aware of the highly controversial nature of their statements, the fact remains that Los Horcones is firmly convinced of having arrived at objective, scientifically "sound" moral values. Although problematic, this attitude provides the communards with a philosophy they can live by, and to their fullest satisfaction. The communards at Los Horcones believe fervently in their answers concerning the good life. Their interpretation of behaviorist data has led them to proclaim the ethical values of cooperation, pacifism, egalitarianism, and ecological consciousness as desirable, but this is their personal belief, which is beyond the reach of verification via scientific experimentation. Thus, while the members of Los Horcones consider their community the "product of a science," it must appear to all nonmembers as the product of a particular weltanschauung, to avoid the negative word "ideology." The apparently frequent refusals on the part of nonmembers to accept Los Horcones as the "product of a science" have in no way weakened the communards' own belief. On the contrary, having what they consider their formula for communal success rejected or ignored by other people seems to unify and strengthen the membership against a world of nonbelievers.

Quite similar to Skinner's suggestion in *Walden Two,* Los Horcones has also "borrowed some of the practices of organized religion" (185). There are frequent meetings with behaviorist topics, lectures by Robinson, an evening of noncompetitive games, a discussion group on the members' current reading, with emphasis on positively reinforcing reading behavior, and so on. These meetings, combined with their multiple isolation from their surrounding society, seem indeed to "inspire group loyalty," as Skinner had suggested (*Walden Two* 185).

The communards' insistence on having constructed the objectively ideal society has isolated Los Horcones from all those who do not agree with this assessment. Even outsiders sympathetic to behaviorism, like Roger Ulrich of Lake Village, have often felt that behaviorism "has almost become a religion, like with Juan (Robinson) and all the guys down in Mexico" (interview with the author, June 10, 1998). Los Horcones reports that potential members and visitors frequently complain that the Los Horcones value system is subjective. Instead of taking these critical statements seriously, however, they are viewed by the Mexican communards as willful or actual "misinterpretations" ("Los Horcones" 3): "Some new members have believed that the desirable behaviors which Los Horcones is requiring are based on a subjective criteria of the existing membership and not on an experiential investigation about these behaviors" ("Behaviorism" 50).

The frequent refusal of outside visitors to convert to the Los Horcones vision seems to strengthen the Mexicans' commitment to it. As Rosabeth

Moss Kanter has pointed out in her influential study *Commitment and Community,* most successful communities are held together by isolating themselves from the surrounding society and by their commitment to a strong, common ideology or a charismatic leader. The members of Los Horcones are bound together by all of these factors. They are also geographically and culturally isolated from their surrounding society, and they are very much committed to the community through a common ideology and the presence of a charismatic leader.

The community's fervent belief in behaviorism has also kept the community small because it has served as a powerful deterrent to potential members. Richard Graham, a member of Dandelion Community in Canada in the seventies, was excited about Los Horcones on first sight, as were some of his friends. He remembers in an interview that "Rob and Anita were talking about possibly starting a community like Los Horcones up in New York State, and then they decided, or rather, I decided, more than anyone else, that this was the place where the real pioneer behaviorists were getting together, and we should bring like an American contingent down there. Or not even that: get all the behaviorists on the planet together! We really wanted to try to start a real Walden Two community" (interview with the author, July 24, 1998).

Yet the excitement soon turned into disappointment. Marianne, a Canadian and provisional member of Los Horcones, wrote a letter to her U.S. friends whom she had met while they were visiting Los Horcones, advising them against joining the Mexican community. She talked about the Mexican communards' "commitment to behaviorism, that they already know all the answers, that they're not really experimental." Remembers Graham: "It was a real crazy time. She left under aversive conditions. There was a lot of yelling in the end, when she left. . . . I remember we were sitting at the table, and we just passed this letter around, page by page, and I read this, and I just felt my heart was breaking. And then I went for a long walk, and based on what Marianne said, I didn't have any pull for Los Horcones anymore" (interview with the author, July 24, 1998).

Los Horcones's belief in objectively definable values, combined with an almost missionary impulse, has also led to serious disputes with fellow U.S. communities. In the early 1980s, Los Horcones withdrew from the Federation of Egalitarian Communities. Kinkade recounts the reaction of the U.S. communards to Los Horcones: "Los Horcones wanted to give the Federation of Egalitarian Communities the gift of what they have learned, so that other people could use it. And the other communities dismissed them with a shrug of their shoulders and said, 'Well, maybe you Mexicans are willing to take orders, but we're not. We're doing fine as we are, we don't need your advice, and who do you think you are?' They rejected the gift, which is too bad. And so Los Horcones with injured feelings and anger quit the federation and now ignores it except to visit Twin Oaks from time to time as they're traveling for one reason or another" (interview with the author, April 10, 1995).

This episode, while relatively unimportant for both Los Horcones and the FEC, shows that the basic premises of the Los Horcones philosophy could easily lead to intolerance and arrogance. The other communities obviously objected to the way the Los Horcones people presented their beliefs—"we don't need your advice"—and were not in any way convinced that the moral values Los Horcones had arrived at were superior to or in any way more valid than their own ("who do you think you are?"). At some point in the future, when Robinson as the theoretician and main decision maker of the group falls away, the communards at Los Horcones may indeed have to ask themselves who they are, and what they believe in, and why.

## Notes

1. Reactions to Los Horcones tend to be strong. Some leave the community as convinced behaviorists, while others detect a malicious, manipulative undercurrent. Still others leave Los Horcones impressed but not convinced of behaviorism. A very negative picture of Los Horcones is drawn in Fishman, 50–60.

2. For an explanation of natural reinforcement, see Los Horcones, "Natural Reinforcement in a Walden Two Community" and "Natural Reinforcement: A Way to Improve Education."

3. For an introduction to the educational ideas used at Los Horcones, see Bijou; Keller, "Good-Bye" and *Keller Plan*.

4. The people at Los Horcones, while initially friendly and hospitable, tend to break off all communication with visitors whom they feel are hostile to behaviorist principles. This made it impossible for me in the later stages of my research to gain more insight into this fascinating community.

5. Los Horcones, "Social Change"; *General Description*, 2; "Personalized," 42–47.

6. In the handful of articles published on Los Horcones, written by people who visited the community, Robinson is almost always among the two or three communards mentioned by name or quoted. See "A Desert Group Lives by Skinner's Precepts," "Sonoran Commune Seeks Skinnerian Utopia," and "Walden Two for Real." Yaro Starak, who visited Los Horcones in the 1980s and was deeply impressed by the community, does not mention any of the communards specifically.

# *Conclusion*

THE HISTORIES OF the Walden Two communities cannot be used to "prove" anything. Just as the novel *Walden Two* is fiction and not, as Frazier argues at one point, an "accomplished fact" (56), none of the Walden Two communities were scientific experiments carried out under laboratory conditions, and it is difficult to see how an endeavor involving individuals coming together under specific historical circumstances for their own various reasons ever could be turned into a measurable and repeatable experiment. The Walden Two communities thus serve merely as examples of what *can* happen to groups trying to turn Walden Two into reality. Despite the impossibility of drawing any definite conclusions concerning *Walden Two* from the described experiments in living, however, the communities do shed new light on Skinner's utopia.

In an attempt to make his utopian vision palatable to an American audience, Skinner carefully paints a familiar and reassuring picture of his utopian community in *Walden Two*. In essence, his utopia is depicted as a pleasant summer resort reminiscent of nineteenth-century utopianism and communalism. Also, while proclaiming the individual as a free agent a myth that needs to be discarded, Skinner focuses in his novel not on portraying behaviorally engineered utopians but on the fiercely individualistic and rather eccentric founder of the fictional community, Frazier. It is only in his description of the fictional community's educational system that Skinner talks at length about behavioral engineering and why society would benefit from using its techniques.

In light of the literary techniques Skinner chose in presenting his utopian vision, it becomes more readily apparent why *Walden Two* held considerable interest not only for readers coming from a behaviorist background but also for readers who were not knowledgeable about Skinner's field of study. While *Walden Two* can be read as a blueprint for a behaviorist utopia, it can equally be read as the story of a group of people in present-day America deciding to go their own separate ways in their search for the good life, being inspired in this search by their own country's tradition of utopian dreaming. Equally, while Skinner's critics overwhelmingly tried to identify with the bulk of "ordinary" people finding happiness and mindlessness in Skinner's utopia, and therefore strongly objected, those readers who went on to found Walden Two communities by and large identified with Frazier. They did not long to be absolved from making decisions but rather felt that they, as well-intentioned and intelligent people, should be decision makers. All of them, it seems, wanted to be gentle guides, but none were willing to be guided gently. What captured their imagination was the one character in the novel who was *not* a product of Walden Two, its individualistic founder. In the ensuing struggle for power, the notion that any one of the participants of the various experiments in communal living would be accepted by the others as a psychologist-king was rapidly dropped. Although this development is not evident in all the groups, it is a strong recurrent theme.

In the wake of dropping the notion of psychologist-kings, most of these pioneering intentional communities reassessed their reading of *Walden Two*. In some cases, the fight over the Frazier position virtually ended the Walden Two experiment, as was the case at Walden Three and, to some extent, at Lake Village. Other groups, like Twin Oaks and, as far as it can be included as an intentional community at all, Sunflower House, adopted more democratic methods.

Despite the different approaches to building Walden Two, the reactions to actually trying the planner-manager system were remarkably similar among the behaviorist groups and Twin Oaks. The majority of the people involved in Lake Village, Walden Three, and Sunflower House came from a behaviorist background, which likely colored their reading of *Walden Two*. For these readers, who were involved in token economies in clearly defined settings with dependent populations, like Roger Ulrich's preschool, the benevolent paternalism of *Walden Two* was a familiar feature of their own professional lives. Rather than paying attention to the specific features of the fictional community, these readers clearly understood the novel as a call to apply behavioral engineering to the design of society and as a call to assume the position of designers. Quite in keeping with Skinner's educational ideas in general—with which they, as behaviorists, were familiar—these groups opted for a step-by-step process of adopting a communal lifestyle. Yet despite the behaviorists' careful planning, there was an almost instant emotional reaction against having somebody else make all the decisions as soon as the groups moved beyond theory.

As a result, the communards at Lake Village dropped Walden Two as a model almost before they had started living together communally. Ironically, while officially distancing itself from the notion of having psychologist-kings, the community that grew out of the initial attempt to build a Walden Two community left Roger Ulrich, the main initiator, in a clear position of power because all those who had quickly rejected the Walden Two ideal left the communal group, making room for people who were more willing to accept Ulrich's authoritarianism. The Walden Three group dissolved after the first attempts to share an apartment building and left most of the people involved disillusioned, while the main initiator, Matthew Israel, found a niche in special education without having to change his autocratic views. Sunflower House to some extent avoided having to deal with the pitfalls of the planner-manager system because the main initiators made a clear distinction between those who govern (the designers of the basic systems along which Sunflower House operates, who mostly did not live at the house) and those who are governed (the residents). Sunflower House's main claim to fame, a token economy instituted to facilitate house cleaning, is based on giving residents rent reductions for completing cleaning jobs within the house. Sunflower House's token economy therefore operates with money as an incentive and is only questionably a major step toward proving the feasibility of an income-sharing Walden Two.

The people who were involved in the founding of Twin Oaks read *Walden Two* in a different context than their behaviorist counterparts. Mostly ignorant about behaviorism, Kat Kinkade and the other cofounders read Skinner's novel as what it is: a novel. They liked Skinner's here-and-now approach, the community depicted, the pragmatic, experimental attitude, and the systems proposed for structuring the community, namely the planner-manager and labor-credit systems. In contrast to the behaviorist groups, the Twin Oakers wanted nothing to do with planning committees and gradual approximations of a more cooperative lifestyle. Instead, they pooled their money, bought a farm, and jumped into communal living head over heels.

The founders of Twin Oaks—and most importantly Kat Kinkade—shared a fundamental assumption with their behaviorist counterparts: the idea that "ordinary people" have neither the capability nor the desire to participate in decision making. However, the attempt to implement the planner-manager system soon led to resentment on the part of those members who were not planners. Responding to the discontent, the Twin Oaks planners slowly resigned their power to make decisions for the whole community, opening their meetings to the general membership, listening increasingly to input, and changing the nature of their decisions from trying to find solutions they considered best to trying to find solutions the membership as a whole would find acceptable. The function of the Twin Oaks planners thus changed from decision makers to facilitators who are in the service of a consensus-oriented society. With respect to communal child rearing, parents soon realized that very strong emotional ties bound them to their children, which they neither wished to sever nor felt capable of severing. As a result, parents reclaimed personal responsibility for rearing their children, virtually ending communal child care at Twin Oaks.

Twin Oaks has deviated far from Skinner. But by steering around the pitfalls in Skinner's governmental system, the communards have created new ones. Practical-minded Twin Oakers may argue that their system works, whatever the theoretical objections. One may ask, however, who profits from the current Twin Oaks planner-manager system. How are decisions arrived at in the absence of direct votes? Does a consensus decision really value the opinions of all members equally, or are those most influential who are persuasive, eloquent, and well respected? How can power be controlled if it is not even acknowledged? And how is it possible that political apathy is a major problem in an intentional community? Twin Oaks does not ultimately provide the answer to these questions. Furthermore, the governmental problems Twin Oaks faces today—power struggles and political apathy—seem astoundingly similar to those of the loathed society at large. The main difference seems to be that Twin Oakers justify their indifference by saying "I trust the planners," while members of society at large are more likely to say, "I don't trust politicians, anyway." This development leaves one to wonder whether the Twin Oakers of the early twenty-first century are not in fact *closer* to the members Skinner had envisioned for his utopian community than the earlier members of Twin Oaks. Is not the casual and disinterested "I trust the planners" a proclamation that could have come right out of *Walden Two?*

Overall, however, the fact remains that the explicit and intentional paternalism of *Walden Two* was rejected at all the pioneering communities, reaffirming instead the core value of the humanist tradition that Skinner had sought to discard for the sake of survival: personal responsibility.

The impact of *Walden Two* on the communities movement did not end with the intense reaction against having benevolent and omnipotent decision makers. However, the second wave of Walden Two communities was distinctly different from the pioneering communities. Instead of reading *Walden Two* directly and drawing their own conclusions, these communities felt largely inspired by the Twin Oaks interpretation of Skinner's novel. Most importantly, these newer communities were interested in the Twin Oaks labor-credit system, which functioned well without behavioral engineering as a guideline. The only major modification to the system was the shift from the variable credit to making one hour equal one labor credit, regardless of the nature of the work or individual work preferences. In the context of the communal movement of the 1970s, the most crucial aspect of the labor-credit system used at Twin Oaks was perhaps not that it provided a good system for organizing work in a secular and income-sharing society but rather that it provided a system at all. Apparently, trying to find a feasible system for distributing work in a fair way was a revolutionary concept for many of the freewheeling communards of the sixties and seventies, and Twin Oaks was initially regarded with suspicion in the communal scene precisely because of its approval of structure. Yet Twin Oaks appeared to be particularly resistant to folding, and increasingly, other intentional communities turned to Twin Oaks for advice. The Virginian community, it seemed, had found a way to make an income-sharing and secular community work—in the truest sense of the word.

Impressed by this apparent success of a work system functioning in an income-sharing community, several intentional communities adopted the Twin Oaks labor-credit system originally inspired by Skinner, who had in turn been inspired by Bellamy. Instead of calling themselves Twin Oaks communities, however, these communities opted for the label Walden Two. This resulted in the curious situation that the second wave of Walden Two communities was for the most part populated by people who often had not even *read* Skinner's novel and were only dimly aware of the novel's connection to behavioral engineering. Instead, the term "Walden Two" was used synonymously with "Twin Oaks," and "Twin Oaks" in turn was a catchword for the advocacy of structure in the form of the labor-credit system. Thus Skinner, by writing *Walden Two*, unwittingly made a notable and lasting contribution to the development of a feasible work system for secular and income-sharing communities that had no interest in behavioral engineering.

Yet even though Twin Oaks, the driving force behind this interpretive activity centered around the labor-credit system, is an impressive survivor of the communities movement, it seems highly questionable whether the resistance to folding that it has shown so far is really attributable to the fact that it has discovered a viable alternative to capitalism. For the vast majority of those who joined (and left) the community since its inception in 1967, the labor-credit system was *not* satisfactory in the long run. The excitement about building Walden Two communities in the seventies died down rather quickly, further strengthening the impression that the Virginian community has not found a "recipe" for communal success. What Twin Oaks appears to have found instead is a structure that is perfectly suited for utilizing membership turnover, thus keeping communal idealism alive within a constantly changing group of people. At the core of this communal structure is the labor-credit system, facilitating the quick integration of new workers and setting definite work standards by requiring all members to do quota. In short, the labor-credit system helps to perpetuate the communal status quo on an ideological level: individuals come with enthusiasm and leave with doubts, but the ideal of cooperation remains in place in the community, regardless of *individual* members' disillusionment. At the root of the community's vitality is therefore not sustained enthusiasm for working for the common good but new member energy and a structural setup ensuring continuity in change.

The Mexican community Los Horcones is at the same time more conventional and more astonishing than its northern siblings. It is more conventional in that its success as a community can be explained by a multitude of stabilizing factors that are absent in the U.S. communities. It is more astonishing in that the communards have succeeded in giving behavioral engineering a prominent position in their microsociety and proudly consider themselves living proof of the validity of Skinner's utopian vision as expressed in *Walden Two*. But is the community's success really based on the effectiveness of behavior modification? Is Los Horcones an exemplary Walden Two community?

The communards at Los Horcones answer both questions with a self-confident "yes." Their published writings all stress that the success of their community is the natural result of the consistent application of the techniques of behavior modification. In fact, the history of Los Horcones, as presented in the community's published papers, reads as one continuous development from good to better to almost perfect. The communards maintain that this success could be enjoyed by any group of individuals who choose to found their society on behavior analysis and modification, since their accomplishments are supposedly attributable to science and not individuals.

While all the communards' writings clearly point in that direction, my own observations lead me to disagree. I think Los Horcones *is* the achievement of a group of individuals and not primarily of a science. Behavior modification, positive reinforcement, self-management programs, natural reinforcers—the sum of these practices is not sufficient to explain the success Los Horcones enjoys. In their interpretation of *Walden Two*, it seems that several features of their Mexican background contributed to a more favorable reception of the paternalistic system Skinner proposed in his utopia. Los Horcones has the fabric of an extended family that is being guided gently yet firmly by a patriarch, Juan Robinson. The communards' Catholic background may have made them more amenable to simply substituting behaviorism for Christianity while holding on to a strong belief in something, whereas the more conservative attitudes toward sexuality kept much of the turmoil and excitement of the communities movement of the seventies away from Los Horcones, thus stabilizing the community. It is the individuals and the individual circumstances under which Los Horcones was founded that make the community what it is. Behavior modification is but one aspect of Los Horcones, and there is no knowing what effect the same behavioral techniques Los Horcones continues to apply so successfully would have under different circumstances. Los Horcones's insistence that the community is an experimental society dedicated to keeping an open mind toward all aspects of societal design, while at the same time giving the impression of a very authoritarian and closed society, is quite in keeping with *Walden Two* and validates their claim to be a living example of Skinner's utopian vision: *Walden Two* also gives itself the varnish of pseudoscientific objectivity as the final justification for all its practices. It is hard to judge just how important Robinson is for the survival of the community and how "autocratic," as Kinkade puts it, his attitude toward leadership really is. Yet Robinson's leadership is the central factor in understanding Los Horcones. What makes Los Horcones "tick"? Is it Robinson? I think it is, at least partly.

Skinner envisioned that his utopian community would "borrow" some of the techniques of organized religion to strengthen commitment. Los Horcones has done just that. Yet it seems that Skinner's fictitious society and Los Horcones have done far more than that: they have also borrowed the mindset of religious people. Behaviorism has ceased to be viewed as a science; it has instead grown into a belief system. The "ordinary" members of Walden Two had to be believers because they were intellectually incapable of grasping the concept of behaviorism. While this is not true of the members of Los Horcones, who are all quite capable of understanding behaviorism, the basic assumptions of behaviorism have long become the unshakable tenets of the Los Horcones philosophy.

Interestingly, though, Los Horcones differs in two important respects from the fictional *Walden Two*. Where Skinner advocates government *for* the people, or "professional government," Los Horcones stresses the importance of government *by* the people. In their struggle to find the best possible system, the communards developed a system they call "personocracy." Personocracy aims at educating all members about governmental questions and involving everybody as much as possible in the decision-making process. The educational process of Los Horcones is also quite different from the one described in *Walden Two*. One cannot but feel that Skinner's "ethical training" aims at conditioning rather than educating people. The adults at Los Horcones, while using Skinnerian teaching methods, treat their children— and each other—with great respect and genuine love. The toughening-up of children in *Walden Two* in a sterile, emotionless atmosphere is in stark contrast to the loving atmosphere in which Los Horcones raises its children. The children at Los Horcones are also very much aware of the techniques employed in their education; they are eloquent on the subject of behaviorism (even if reflecting mainly Robinson's opinion on behaviorist topics).

It strikes me as remarkable that Los Horcones—for all its obvious and fundamental differences with Skinner's utopian vision—has never really verbalized this dissent. The communards at Los Horcones carefully avoid describing their microsociety in terms that would set it apart from Skinner's vision in *Walden Two*. It is my guess that pointing out obvious and fundamental differences between the actual Los Horcones and the fictional Walden Two—both supposedly designed by objective criteria—would interfere unpleasantly with the communards' claim that behaviorist thinking leads automatically to one, objectively verifiable utopian vision.

What are we to conclude from the experiences of the various Walden Two communities? That Skinner's utopian vision either led to the demise of the community or had to be modified substantially to be acceptable to the participants of the communal experiments? That the only community in which Walden Two was not contested is centered around a charismatic leader strikingly similar to Frazier? While the experiences of the Walden Two communards all unearthed fundamental problems with Skinner's paternalistic vision, the experience of actually aiming at creating a Walden Two community appears to have been of lasting value to the individuals involved. Although living in an intentional community was often only an episode in people's lives, it was an important one. As Peter Ruppert puts it, "Utopias may exist nowhere, [yet where] they may fail to convince us of the sufficiency or the finality of their sanguine solutions, they also fail to dissuade us from the need to search for social alternatives" (x).

# Appendix: Interviews

## Interview with Richard Graham, July 24, 1998

Q: How did Dandelion Community compare to the fictional Walden Two when you first visited in 1976? What was your first impression?

A: I got there, and it was one building, the farmhouse. [laughs] Just one building, you know, and Walden Two was like, four hundred acres and children everywhere. My first impression was: small. But when I was there, people were so excited about what their vision was and I got along with the people so well that I thought I would fit in after the second day.

Q: While you were living at Dandelion, how did you try to apply behaviorist principles?

A: Well, there was the behavior code, the attempt to bring about changes in our behavior in a positive way.

Q: Who wrote the behavior code?

A: The original behavior code was a general one, and that was adopted from Twin Oaks. But then I went to Los Horcones to see what they were doing, and their behavior code is real specific, and after I got back, we decided to break down our behavior code into more specific items as well.

Q: And didn't you also become behavior manager after coming back from Los Horcones in 1977?

A: Yes, but it was never like a big the-behavior-manager-knows-all-and-sees-all. [laughs]

Q: Was there ever anybody else who was behavior manager at Dandelion? I sort of got the sense that it was mainly your interest, and people were okay with you trying to bring more behaviorism to Dandelion.

A: Yeah, I'd say that's true. I made myself behavior manager when I got there, and it was kind of like—not a joke, but it wasn't like a serious managership like kitchen. [pauses] You know, all we had was Skinner's book and what Twin Oaks had done. I hadn't heard of Los Horcones until I'd lived at Dandelion for a while. I mean, we were like pioneers, trying to figure out, "What are we doing here?" We wanted to do something with language, create a positive verbal environment and such. But after I came back from Los Horcones, I had a much better idea what might help the community. And I think the community was receptive, or at least open, to seeing what we could do to improve the environment.

Q: What was your vision for Dandelion in 1977, when you returned from Los Horcones, and what were the other people at Dandelion hoping for?

A: I think our vision was pretty similar—mine, Gordon's, Brian's. See, we were still pretty new. We had set up this egalitarian, behaviorist community, and we were using *Walden Two* as a model and what we had seen happening at Twin Oaks. And it was filled with a pioneering spirit. "Let's try this, see if that works. What would a behaviorist do in this situation? How do we deal with children?" There were a lot of things where we had the knowledge, but trying it in real life… [pauses] It was still experimental, I'd say. We didn't have any definite answers. I'm still not sure whether I have any answers, and I'm a rational guy.

Q: You just said you were trying to build a community that was egalitarian and behaviorist. In the communities movement, those two terms seem to go together, like Walden Two communities were about being egalitarian. Do you think that's the case?

A: Right. Yeah, that's interesting. This is a really interesting question. See, what originally brought me to community was applied behavior analysis. I wanted to see if I could change my own racist and sexist and capitalist behavior. I tried it at home with my parents, but they didn't know what I was talking about. But Dandelion was really trying to do that. The other part, the egalitarianism, I liked that, too. It wasn't for years since I left Dandelion that I realized why equality was so important to me.

Q: Do you think that equality is an important aspect of *Walden Two* the novel? Or was it mainly an important aspect of the Walden Two communities?

A: [pauses] That's a good question. [pauses] I don't have an answer to that. I think when Skinner wrote *Walden Two*, he was mainly trying to visualize how a society applying behavior analysis could work. And the equality—I think that was secondary, and it came out of the behavior analysis.

Q: I read some interesting things about the forming of the Federation of Egalitarian Communities, which Dandelion and East Wind and Twin Oaks were, of course, all part of. The people involved in this were exchanging letters and trying to come up with a good name for the federation they were about to found. Jane Dandelion wrote a letter saying, "Yeah, I really like the idea of a Federation of Walden Two Communities."

A: I never knew that.

Q: Yeah. And then a member of Walden Three said, "Well, yeah, let's have a federation of common-sense communities." And then Kat said, "How about a Federation of Egalitarian Communities?" So it seems like they were just struggling to come up with a term to describe the kind of community they were all part of. And apparently they were not necessarily trying to describe communities that were applying behavior analysis but rational and structured communities that valued egalitarianism and would neither be religious nor have a charismatic leader. And Walden Two was one of the terms under discussion for this kind of community. Does that make sense to you?

A: Yeah, that sounds valid to me. [pauses] Do you know where the term "federation" came from in what ended up being called the Federation of Egalitarian Communities? It's from "Star Trek," or so I heard. You know, Captain Kirk is part of the Federation of Planets, so we wanted to be the Federation of Egalitarian Communities! [laughs] But that's just folklore, I guess. I never verified the story. [pauses] But what you just said sounds valid.

Q: Can I ask you one more thing about *Walden Two?* It's often said about *Walden Two* that it portrays a two-class society, the modifiers and the ones who are being modified.

A: It was never like that at Dandelion. Most people just didn't care. So I walked around with this knowledge of behavior principles, and people didn't care. Maybe they tolerated me. They humored me.

Q: Did you have a planner-manager system at Dandelion? How were decisions made?

A: Well, I think originally we had a planner-manager system, but everybody was always invited to the meetings. In reality, when you have like ten people, it was real important to make sure that every person was heard. So I think in reality, it wasn't a planner-manager type thing. So, I think we switched one night from the planner-manager system to a working democracy.

Q: By "working democracy" you mean you switched to a voting system?

A: Yes. And there were only two times where we actually voted during the time that I was there. Most times we reached consensus. [pauses] You want to know what the two issues were? [laughs] They were so radical! One was this stray dog that came onto the property, and we had this thing about whether we should keep the dog or not. People got real passionate one way or the other. So we voted on that, but I think the dog died, just as we voted on him, or it left or something, and I can't remember what the vote came to. The second was when a gay person wanted to advertise our community in a gay magazine, and we thought with us being in redneck country, that might not be a real good idea. Again, I don't know what the vote was. But those are the only two times that I remember voting at Dandelion.

Q: So when did you do away with the planner-manager system?

A: Well, I think that was right after I joined, actually. But it was a process that had been slowly evolving, and in reality, if you lived at Dandelion, you could see that it was such a small group.

Q: Did you still have plannerships?

A: Oh, yeah, I think I was a planner once, but being a planner was kind of being aware if the community was going in a dangerous direction, you know. Something that you might want to bring up at a meeting or something.

Q: So outwardly you still had a planner-manager system, but it functioned differently?

A: Yeah, I think so.

Q: So pretty much the same development as at Twin Oaks, with the planners becoming facilitators?

A: I think so, yes.

Q: How did your labor-credit system work? Did you try the variable labor credit in the beginning?

A: No, I don't think so. Because when I joined, they had the same system as Twin Oaks: one hour of work was one hour of credit. But I had issues with that because I felt that it reinforced people to work in a...pace they were comfortable with. So I thought if there was a little incentive people would work a little faster and get more done. So, me and Joy, who was the assistant tinnery manager, we came up with this plan, but it would have involved inspection. What we said we were going to do was we'd sit down, both of us, and we would see how many cans we could cut in an hour in a reasonable speed. Not going in a maniac speed and not going really slow. And then we were going to say—let's say it was six cans in an hour—so we were going to say, "Okay, if you come in here and you want to work on this variable system, if you can do six cans in forty-five minutes, then you can take credit for an hour." That means people could work a little faster, get six cans done in forty-five minutes, and still get an hour's worth of credit. Then we started figuring out that if we did that, we would have to inspect those cans and make sure they were up to standard, because if people worked faster they might not be as careful. So we talked about this plan, but we never did anything with it.

Q: These days, do you believe that people can work, and work well and efficiently, even if there are no personal incentives for doing so?

A: Oh, I don't know. I wrestle with that. I mean, on a day-to-day level, in our tinnery, the labor-credit system reinforced not mediocre work, but it didn't give people an incentive to get work done in a faster way or shorter amount of time. So I don't have an answer to that, because I wrestle with it.

Q: Well, it almost seems as if whatever you can do to reward hard work almost automatically puts you on a capitalist path.

A: Right. [laughs] Well, in one sense that's true, you're right. [pauses] At Dandelion, we tried to encourage people to work hard by giving group benefits. If one person worked one hour over quota, everybody's allowance would go up ten cents, or something like that. But I think you're right about the basic problem, and I don't have an answer to that. I don't think anyone does.

Q: What kind of property and money policy did you have for joining members? Were new members expected to turn everything over?

A: We had the same policy as Twin Oaks. You can keep it, but you can't use it while you're living at the community.

Q: What were your reasons for leaving Dandelion?

A: Well, one of the reasons that I left Dandelion, and I guess one of the reasons I decided not to join Twin Oaks, was that the older I got, the more I wanted more private space. I had my own bedroom, but I just wanted more physical space around me that I didn't have to share with people. And it was nothing against the people I was with, it was just like a maturing process or something. But that was definitely one of the reasons. But it was nothing against the ideals. I still carry those. One of the reasons I have such a hard time living in this society is that I am trying to practice an egalitarian philosophy in a nonegalitarian environment. And I'm always in conflict over that.

Q: Did Skinner ever take an interest in Dandelion?

A: I invited him to come up anytime, but he was just too busy. I wanted to show him a Dandelion tape at that last convention I saw him at. He was going to see it in the morning, then in the evening he said something else had come up and he wasn't going to make it, and that was the last time I spoke to him. [pauses] He never knew what we were doing at Dandelion.

Q: Did you ever consider joining Los Horcones?

A: Well, I was planning to, but that didn't work out.

Q: Why not?

A: Well, when I visited them in 1979, I thought it was a great place. The behavior meetings and my talks with Juan. I got back to Dandelion in March of 1979 and discovered that we had lost six members during the time I was gone, so it was a low time for the community. People were kind of looking up to me to see if I could change things. And I was excited at the time, so we started all this fun craziness. And then the next year, Los Horcones had that behavior seminar, where they invited delegates from the federation. And something like twenty people went down, including me, Jane, Gordon, and Dakota. And then we had this seminar for a week, and that was really interesting. Just different aspects of community, and applied behavior analysis. I just felt that it was really talking directly to my soul, so I decided that I had to stay on, do labor exchange, or use my vacation or whatever. So the Dandelion bunch left, and I stayed on like two or three more weeks, maybe even longer.

Q: Were you the only one staying on?

A: No, but I think I stayed the longest. And then Rob and Anita were visiting. Actually, they were provisional members, they gave some of the seminars. And Bob Hewitt, and his wife and kids, from Ohio. Rob and Anita had Alpha Research up in New York State, and while I was there, Rob and Anita were talking about possibly starting a community like Los Horcones up in New York State, and then they decided, or rather, I decided, more than anyone else, that this was the place where the real pioneer behaviorists were getting together, and we should bring like an American contingent down there. Or not even that: get all the behaviorists on the planet together! We really wanted to try to start a real Walden Two community. So...[pauses] While I was down at Los Horcones, I made a decision to come back, but then when I went back to Dandelion, I felt that they were going through such a struggle. That was the period where Parrish was being born, and I felt Jane would feel less secure there if I left. So I don't know, I got back to Dandelion in late April, early May, and for four weeks, I just struggled. Finally, I put a paper up saying that I really felt that I had a pull to Los Horcones, there are behaviorists there. My plan was: I was going to work with Rob and Anita at Alpha Research over the summer, because at that point, Los Horcones had an entrance fee, something like four hundred dollars. So I thought if I worked at Alpha Research over the summer, I could make like a thousand dollars, and then when we went down to Los Horcones, I could pay the entrance fee and still have five hundred dollars to fall back on. Dandelion had a policy that for every week you lived at the community, you'd get two dollars and fifty cents if you ever left. [laughs] So I had like, I don't know, two hundred dollars when I left Dandelion. Talk about long-term payoff! [laughs] Anyway, the summer of 1980 was interesting. Bob Hewitt, Rob and Anita, and me, we were up at Alpha Research, and there was another guy there. And the plan was that we were going to sell off the land, and then we'd all go down in a caravan, back down to Los Horcones. [pauses]

Q: I suppose the caravan never left for Los Horcones?

A: No. [sighs] I think a month, or maybe two months before we wanted to leave, we got this letter from Marianne. She was a Canadian who was a behaviorist, and she was at Los Horcones while we were there, too, and she had an interesting history. I think she was a nun before, but she left that and got involved in psychology and Walden Two, and she really knew behaviorism. But anyway, she wrote us this twenty-five-page letter that just talked about what happened to her in the last couple of weeks there. And then she left, and it was sort of like something that you mentioned in your thesis, about how Los Horcones isn't really experimental? They think they have all the answers already, so they don't need to experiment? It was a real crazy time. She left under aversive conditions. There was a lot of yelling in the end, when she left. [pauses] I remember we were sitting at the table, and we just passed this letter around, page by page, and I read this, and I just felt my heart was breaking. And then I went for a long walk, and based on what Marianne said, I didn't have any pull for Los Horcones anymore.

Q: So what exactly was it that Marianne said?

Far from being a laid-back "hippie commune," Twin Oaks takes pride in its strong work ethic, while also allowing for gentle satire of its own traditions. (courtesy Jonathan Roth)

One of the biggest problems of sharing work at Twin Oaks is dealing with differences in effort, not ability. (courtesy Jonathan Roth)

Most of the Walden Two communities quickly discovered that there is no consensus on what constitutes the "good life," an assumption that had led Skinner to remain rather vague on this point. (courtesy Jonathan Roth)

A: [sighs] Well, I think it was just about their commitment to behaviorism, that they already know all the answers, that they're not really experimental, and she was saying that after the Americans left, they said a couple of derogatory things. I don't know if this should go on the tape. [pauses] The impression that we got was that we should just stay up at New York State and start our own community. [pauses] So I went for a walk after we got this letter, and I was just crying on this rock. I didn't know what I wanted to do then. I just felt totally disillusioned with Walden Two and, you know, I had two hundred dollars to my name. I didn't want to go back to Dandelion. I got disillusioned with community totally. So, anyway, I think what happened then, I just decided that after Alpha Research, I was going to visit my folks for a while, try to regroup my forces. So I visited my parents for a week or two, then went to Rochester and got a room, just to have a space to call my own, and then I stayed there from September to January, and then I went down to Aloe Community, which wasn't a community anymore, but my friend, an ex-member of Dandelion, was down there, and he said I should come on down and help with some paint jobs. And I thought that might help me, because at that point, I was really depressed. It was the only time in my life that I was really, really depressed. So I went down there, and he ended up taking off, and there weren't any paint jobs, so I got this part-time job working on a farm, which was just what I needed. It was like real heavy physical work. And then Brian and Allison from Dandelion came down to visit me in May, and Brian just talked about that I should come back to Dandelion: "People were asking about you, and they want you to come back, and I'm there, and we love you, and bla, bla." And that was a real turning point in my life. And I said, okay. So I just gave the guy I was working for three days notice, toured around a bit, and then took a bus up to Dandelion. That was in the summer of 1981.

Q: And that was the end of the Los Horcones plan?

A: Yes. [pauses] I never told them about that letter we got from Marianne. I just wrote them and said that I was doing other things now, and maybe at some point I was going to come down and visit again. And that was the last time I communicated with them. [pauses] When I read what you had to say about Los Horcones, I was depressed, because it was kind of exactly what Marianne had said. [pauses] I think there were also cultural differences that came up. I remember this one guy who got up at a meeting at Los Horcones and talked about sex. I think Juan was talking about monogamous relationships in community, and some of the Americans were challenging Juan on that. Juan got real defensive, saying we shouldn't be talking about this, we should be talking about applied behavior analysis rather than talking about who sleeps with whom. I thought that was one of the cultural shifts. [laughs] You know, two consenting adults, and everything's okay. But I think at Los Horcones, it was more about monogamy, and I guess that comes from their culture, the Catholic background.

Q: Well, Los Horcones seems to disapprove of anything but monogamy, heterosexual monogamy.

A: Right, right. That, too, I think. [pauses] Again, I wonder how much of their Mexican culture played into that. Like I remember talking to Juan about relationships, and I sort of picked up that everybody was monogamous, and behaviorism maybe was their religion. So, anyway. That's my Los Horcones story.

## Interview with Kat Kinkade, April 10, 1995

Q: What kind of governmental changes has Twin Oaks gone through since the initial planner-manager system of the founding days?

A: Skinner in *Walden Two* expressed a theory of government in which the people who governed got their information from everybody and from their experiments and their record keeping and so forth. After they got that information, they would then use it to make decisions. He proposed a Board of Planners of ten people, I think. I might have that mixed up. I know it was ten years. They were to be in office for ten years. I don't know. You can look that up. Anyway, it was a long time by early Twin Oaks standards. And there would be managers who would report to them, in theory, and the managers had their own area of governance. They made decisions about, you know, how much bran to put in the feed and so forth. And the average citizen did not trouble him- or herself with issues of government at all. They had input in the sense that somebody would say, "How do you like your life? What's wrong with it? Can you think of improvements that would make a difference to you?" And therefore you would have input. Saying, "Yeah, I don't like the lumpy oatmeal," or whatever. But you would not be asked, you know, "What do you think of the sabbatical policy?" or, "Do you think the average member works too hard?" You'd be asked, "Do you work too hard?" And that's all. So it assumed that government itself was an area of expertise and that you trained for it and you did it. If you were good at it, if you had a talent for it. Just like the people who had a talent for music would play their instruments. It wasn't supposed to be hierarchical—well, no, it was hierarchical. But it wasn't supposed to be prestigious. It wasn't supposed to be any bigger deal to be a planner than it was to be a mechanic. I liked that idea very much. And in honest truth, I still do. That is where my heart is at. Let government be done by those who are good at it. Then you'd have good government. I recognize that some controls have to be built into that, and I knew that at the beginning. And we tried to build controls into it, and they were fairly effective, as a matter of fact. The only thing we did not predict and could not control was the feeling that the average citizen had about somebody else doing the government. They just hated it. And even though you say to them, "What decisions would you have wanted to be different?" They would say, "I don't know of any decisions I would have wanted to be different, the decisions were fine. I just wanted to be part of it." So at this point I conjecture that Skinner was wrong: the average citizen will not in fact be satisfied with such an arrangement. Then I think, maybe in some other country. Maybe in Mexico. But not in the USA. It's just not going to make it.

And so, of course, I adjusted my thinking. I mean, what are you going to do? If you're going to have a successful community you can't just hang on to ideas that don't work. You've got to move with it. So the whole idea of what I call "professional government" moved into the back of my head, where it still sits. [laughs] However, in the front of my head I can present Twin Oaks's current compromises with democracy as if I fully approved of them. What I mean by doing that is that I fully approve of them under these conditions. If we can't do professional government and we have to do democracy of one kind or another, then I think Twin Oaks is doing better than anybody else has. And so I can speak of it with pride, even though it's a mess. Of course it's a mess, democracy has to be a mess. Because in any democracy you've got all kinds of influence being wielded by people who don't know what the heck they're talking about, and you're not free of interest, i.e. people wanting decisions to go a certain way because how it affects them or their families or their friends or their vacation or whatever it is. You know, like axe to grind. Any democracy is going to be absolutely chock-full of that. Skinner—and I [laughs]—were trying to get past that. We were trying to dispose of that problem by making the decision makers, oh, you know, philosopher-kings. You know, back to Plato. It was the expert in government. So anyway, I don't spend a whole lot of time sitting around thinking about what government ought to be. When I am at Twin Oaks, I deal with what government is now and how it can be improved. I concentrate entirely on improvement.

Q: In your notion of "professional government," what safeguards are there against abuse of power?

A: I think you probably want me to tell you what we did, not what I thought they should be. But what actually happened at Twin Oaks? First of all, we made an absolute prohibition against there being any material gain, better quarters, higher allowances or whatever. All that was completely prohibited. And that was completely successful. We have never had at Twin Oaks, at any time in twenty-six years, any hint of economic benefits to one class or type of service over another. So there was not a whole lot to motivate planners to abuse power. We cut down on the motivation quite a lot right there. There could, of course, be little things, e.g. they could change policy in such a way that they and their families got what they particularly wanted, but then other people would also get it. It wouldn't be just them. They would never get away with making a policy just for themselves or their class. The other thing that we did was insert this system of government into a system of checks. Not checks and balances; I can't think what balances there would be. But checks, so the whole thing works like, if a manager makes a bad decision, the decision can be appealed to the planners. If the planners back it up, that can be appealed to the people. And by a general vote, at the beginning it was a two-thirds vote, because then we were really weighing the expert opinion over the common person—common! You know what I mean. Over the ordinary citizen—but in later years the bylaws were changed, and it is now a simple majority that can overrule any planner decision. There is a great deal of detail of this kind in our bylaws. The whole thing is fixed so that nobody can do much without the consent of the group. And I have always thought that was adequate. And there is the bylaws themselves. It is so hard to change a bylaw. In fact, that's been a problem. We've made them too tight. I think I went into some detail on this in my book about that. I don't think that having checks on power is a very difficult problem. I think we managed it nicely.

Q: These days, most citizens living in the Northern Hemisphere assume as a basic right to have some kind of vote in government. How can you still hold your opinions on "professional government" in the face of this fact?

A: How can I throw out the entire twentieth century like that? Easy. [laughs] I think that the people are better served by people who want to make good government and want to serve them than they are by themselves and their peers, who can't see the broader picture. They are tunnel-visioned like crazy even at their best. And at their worst, they are perfectly awful. I have seen this develop at Twin Oaks as we have made the franchise broader and broader and passed it down to less and less capable people. Well, I make that sound like we first had real good ones, and then we had mediocre ones, and then we got worse. It's not like that. I just mean that the plannerships and managerships these days are open to people who have very little experience and nothing much beyond good intentions. And these people are now making the decisions for the group—timidly, but making them. I don't think they are as good as they could be, I don't think the decisions are of the quality they ought to be. I find that our governors of these days are seeking consensus more than they are seeking good decisions. And I went into this in my book. I don't know. I don't feel constrained by whatever current thinking there is. It doesn't seem to me to be as good as the one that came before it. It is precisely because it is so axiomatic that I look at the axiom and say, "Why? What for? What is government for?" And I say government is for the people, not by the people. They fuck it up!

Q: What you mean by "good decisions" may not be what I mean by "good decisions." Who is to decide what "good decisions" are? Isn't democracy, though flawed, the best we have come up with so far?

A: Your question is the standard one. The latter part is a logic I respect. The best we can do so far is the best we can do so far. And if democracy is it, then I would go along with it and not demand perfection of it. I understand that. The reason I prefer professional government is that it looks to the future and to the broad picture. It makes a serious attempt... [pauses] See, here's a basic question in decision making: "What will the effects be?" We've got a piece of legislation in front of us that might go this way or it might go that. Or we have a budget that has to be distributed this way or that. Or we are or are not prepared for war at any time. Or whatever, depending on what level of government we are talking about. The professional governors—in my imagination, which is the only place where they exist, as far as I know—say to themselves, What will the effects be if we do this, versus if we do this, versus if we do this? And then they think about that as broadly as they can, and then they go for that which seems to have the most good effects on the most people in the long run. A democracy does not do that, and therefore it tends to be influenced by all kinds of special interests that have nothing to do with the good of humanity or the good of the nation's citizens or the good of the environment or whatever. I don't think that the people who put through the gigantic highway system of the USA said, "Oh, and by the way, we're going to wreck the railroads and we're going to destroy or make virtually impossible the whole idea of mass transportation of people." You know, they just said, "Look at how neat it would be to have all this trucking and all this stuff," and they didn't look far enough. Well, on the one hand I say, nobody could have. We wouldn't have known who would have been the expert, who could have foreseen the future well enough, so professional government wouldn't have done any better in this case, perhaps, than democracy did. But it might have. At least it wouldn't have been battered about by selfish interests. You know, I'm not real sure of myself on this question. Because my board of professional governors are only people, they can't see the future, so it might turn out they're no better. I just somehow had the hope they were. What I had close at hand was the sure knowledge that I and some selected companions were definitely better than the little democracy of fifteen, twenty, thirty people that we had at Twin Oaks at the time. That I was sure of. I am not at all sure that if we had been three thousand whether our wisdom would have proved adequate. The amount of wisdom you get is limited by the information you have. So I am not at all sure. Maybe democracy is the best we can do. God, I hope not.

Q: How does behaviorism relate to the idea of professional government?

A: I have never been able to see the connection, to tell you the truth. The only connection I was ever able to make between behaviorism and dictatorship or whatever is that if you had a centralized government, then you'd be able to implement some of the ideas of behaviorism. You'd be able to say, "Hey, let's put together an institute that finds out whether people react in such and such a way to such and such an arrangement," and then be able to do that with the help of a few million dollars. You know, one bomber would pay for it. And then you'd be able to say, "Hey, this turned out to be a terrific idea, with only the following flaws. Let's remove these flaws with another experiment." You'd be able to get the funding, and then you'd be able to say, "Let's do this!" And so, in certain institutions all across the country, maybe the public schools, I don't know what it would be, I don't know what we're talking about here, but if you had central government, you'd be able to implement the best ideas that science can come up with. But I think that is not where the strenuous objections to behaviorism come from. They come from the notion that whoever is in control would be the ones who understood behaviorism and they would be manipulating those who don't understand it, or those who are not part of the ruling elite or something. And everybody would find themselves behaving themselves even though they didn't want to. I mean, what you really want to do is commit a murder, and you find yourself conditioned so that you don't feel like it. What a shame. [laughs]

Anyway, I don't have any sympathy with the people who think that behaviorism in and of itself is a tool of tyranny. I don't think it is.

Q: But would you agree that it can easily be turned into one?

A: It can be turned into that if you had a heavy military behind you like any other kind of power. I don't see why. Behaviorism is getting people to see their own best interests. The only place where they ever did any experimenting with behaviorism is in controlled institutions, such as prisons and mental hospitals, or occasionally kindergartens, I suppose. [laughs] We haven't been able to do it with a free people, because they haven't consented to the experiment, and so we don't and never will be able to do it, as far as I can see. I don't see why people take that mental-institute mentality and assume...You know, you can make up stories about them, but you're just making up stories. I think there are novels...I think that *Nineteen Eighty-Four* was written at the same time when this kind of thinking was going on. Huxley's novel, *Brave New World*, too, where you have all those babies crawling for the roses and getting electric shocks so that they won't like gardens. Well...[pauses] You couldn't do it. You'd have rebellion.

Q: Why?

A: Because of the innate self-preservation of the human being. You can't tyrannize over people and make them like it. Not really.

Q: But what is the difference between tyrannizing over people and making them like what is "best for them"?

A: Well, I suppose you get down to something as ordinary as teaching. Giving people the information they need in order to know what is best for them, if it is. And part of that teaching being conditioning? Yeah, why not? We are all conditioned all the time anyway. You know this argument, that we are subject to a zillion influences, all of us, all the time, being battered around all the time. To do it deliberately, as opposed to doing it accidentally. Well, for some reason or other there's supposed to be some virtue to accident, and I'm damned if I see it.

Q: Couldn't you also look at it differently? Maybe the choice is not between "accidental" and "deliberate." Once we find out how much we are controlled by our environment, wouldn't it make sense to try to reduce that influence as much as possible, rather than just controlling our and other people's environment benevolently?

A: Reduce it in favor of what? Are you postulating a human being that without influences will turn into something good?

Q: No, but perhaps there is some point in trying to reduce outward influences to give more space to whatever there is in a human being to develop from within.

A: Something intrinsic? [pauses] You are not much of a behaviorist, are you? [laughs]

Q: No. I never said I was.

A: Well, I think we are the sum of our influences. Based on that difference, I don't think there is anything to develop there other than how our particular organisms respond to particular influences. I think changing the influences so that, say, musically talented people all get a chance to develop their talent—and then we'd be overloaded with musicians, I know—but I think that would be better than a lot of other things that are happening. Things that happen by accident, and they happen all the time. [pauses] I'm not seeing that this is going anywhere.

Q: Okay. How about child education. Skinner suggests in *Walden Two* that the community's children live together in children's quarters, regarding all adult communards as their loving parents without developing a special attachment to their biological parents. Do you think that is a workable concept, or is it natural for parents to love their offspring, and vice-versa?

A: Yes, I think it is natural for parents. By "natural" I mean evolution has provided us with that tool to get the next generation raised. Parents want to be with the kids, they are attracted to the little things, for some reason or other. They want to raise them. They want to influence them. They want to be there. I think that is perfectly natural. And I don't think it can be interfered with much. There were things about our theories at the time, though, of early education that came directly out of Skinner. And when I say "our," maybe I mean "my." But I was completely fascinated, for example, with Skinner's notion that you would design toys to build perseverance. What an idea! Because personally I don't have much of a history of sticking to a task till it's done or overcoming small difficulties, and I see lots of people who don't. You know, if they run into a wall, they'll say, "I don't like this game," and they quit. Whereas other children say, "I bet there is a way around this," and keep on going. The latter children seem to be better adults. And so the idea of deliberately doing that was completely fascinating for me, and I was hoping that we'd do things like that, instead of just giving them whatever toys their mothers and grandmothers might give them. That we would have this controlled environment. But, hell, we didn't have time. Even if we had had the spirit of doing that, we were so busy trying to make a living and trying to deal with membership turnover. Just imagining having plenty of time to have people full-time engaged, or even half-time engaged, in the design of behavioral toys—it's an absurdity. To this day we don't have that kind of time. Of course, these days we don't want to anymore.

Q: How about the trade-off between sticking to the original behaviorist principles and expanding your population to anti-behaviorist people?

A: We made the latter choice, and therefore, in my opinion, we survived, as I have said in some detail in my book.

Q: Would you make the same choice again?

A: Well, I place some pretty high value on survival. I think Twin Oaks, for all its faults, is better than no Twin Oaks by a long ways. And considering that we spawned five or six other communities, each doing something somewhat different, but all doing something that they care about, and all of it as far as I know at the very least innocent—they are not doing harm. So considering all that, and that we early founders of Twin Oaks can more or less take credit for it, you know what I mean, take some credit for it, I would say, yes, we would do it again.

Q: Would you try to be slightly more selective, maybe not quite as wide open as you were for a period of time in your early history?

A: Of course, we dealt with that question back then, too. The question came down to: What would we be selective about? Some people wanted to keep out anybody who smoked pot, other people wanted to keep out anybody who were fairly rigid-minded and wanted to control people. Well, we didn't keep out either one, and so we got a balance. You can call it a balance, or you can call it a constant conflict. I don't know which you perceived when you were there. My personal opinion is that Twin Oaks sort of kept to a middle-of-the-road position in its selection, and it turned out to be a fairly good one. East Wind went too far in its openness. Acorn is being less selective than Twin Oaks, but it's hard to know what Acorn's future will be because it's so small it needs to insure its survival. It's being developed in an entirely different period of history. Nowadays, there are people in their forties who want to do community. In those days everybody was twenty-two. Except me.

Q: Why didn't you choose agreement with behaviorist thinking as a criterion for membership selection?

A: There just weren't any behaviorists. Every once in a while we'd get a student of behaviorism, or a professor, a young professor, something like that, come and visit us, and they'd immediately want to start doing something along their professional lines. And their ideas were entirely unrealistic. I remember this one naive professor who said that we could figure out a machine that would reward people for flushing the toilet. What he didn't know was that we were desperately trying to stop people from flushing the toilet because our septic system was overloaded and wouldn't take the water. That's kind of an extreme example, but I remember another one who I argued behaviorism with. I said, "Look, we're all equals. What are we going to use for reinforcers? Who is 'we,' who is 'they'? Who reinforces whom for what?" He said, "Well, you could not let them eat. You have a cafeteria line here, you could say you can't have your meal unless you have performed up to standard on certain vital community behaviors, whatever they are." And I thought, "God, why does behaviorism attract control freaks?" I certainly think I'm a behaviorist, but I just don't have any communion with the people who want to withhold meals so that other people will behave. That's not what Skinner was getting at. And I fell in love with behaviorism as seen through Skinner and through *Walden Two*. So help me God, every time I meet a behaviorist—well, not every time, but frequently—they turn out to be people...One of them used a cattle prod on autistic children, or was reputed to have done so. I think they closed him down. I never quite understood the connection. That connection doesn't really exist in my person.

Q: It doesn't go with *Walden Two* anyway, does it? Skinner is so explicitly against punitive control.

A: Exactly, that's my question. Why does behaviorism seem to hook up with desire for punitive control? Thank you for the vocabulary. I just don't think it ought to. But then I came at the field through fiction, not pure science. [sighs]

Q: Have you ever visited Los Horcones? What did you think about it?

A: I was invited to visit Los Horcones, having met some of their people, and I went down and stayed a week, just as I was leaving East Wind and going to Boston. I was extremely depressed during that period and wasn't prepared to get involved in community at that point at all. So I did not while I was there do enough work to shake a stick at. I didn't really participate in the work of the community. I was an honored guest.

I was certainly impressed. One cannot help being impressed with their level of cleanliness and order and organization, with their love for each other and their friendliness toward each other. Like Ganas, very much like Ganas. By their lack of trouble, at least at that period. I happened to be there during a period where there was no turmoil. The last batch of people who were troublesome to them had just left, and no new batch had yet formed. So I was dealing primarily with their core group. I did not think that what made them operate so well was behaviorism. And I do not think so. I think it's charisma. I think it's Juan. I think Juan's leadership is excellent, or was at that time at least. What they're teaching in the school was consistent. See, Juan was their only theorist. And they all picked up Juan's theories. They use them. They use them in the schools. They have two schools, one for the children of the community and one for the autistic. They use them both places. Their kids have grown to be exemplary. As Juan says, "We can take them anywhere." They are beautifully behaved, decent, nice, and fun, and free, and just the sort of people you want your own kids to grow up to be. And they think they did it through behaviorism. Well, good for them. And good for behaviorism. I don't care what caused it. But what I did not see there was manipulation of reinforcers. Either they were past that or they didn't need it, or what I don't know. They did have some marks of behaviorism. They had some charts where you check off if you had done such and such, and they use positive and negative information, what at Ganas we call feedback, to let people know whether the job they did of cleaning the kitchen was a good enough job or not. They weren't afraid to set standards. They did not, like any Twin Oaker or East Winder, say, "Well, who's to say how clean a kitchen should be?" They just said, "Well, this person will say. Okay? You're the manager. You set the standards, and we'll go by it." That's plenty good enough for me. So I was impressed with the level of their community life. It was there that Juan and I had the conversation—and we had a lot of conversations while I was there, we talked for hours every day—where he said, "Kat, you and I made the opposite decision at a certain point. You decided that it was more important to be a large community than it was to stick to your principles, and I decided that it was more important to stick to our principles. And so you got to be large, and we retained our ideals." [pauses] Well, okay. Yeah, that's what happened alright. Also, he said to me, "You didn't lose control, Kat, you gave it up. You gave it over. You never should have done so. If you had insisted—you were wiser than that bunch of people—if you'd insisted, if you'd kept hold of the reins, it would be a far better community." [laughs] I laughed. I didn't have the emotional stamina then to take anything of the kind, nor was my theory so autocratic as to back up any such action as that. Juan didn't have any trouble having an autocratic theory. It just didn't trouble him at all. [laughs] Anyway, I'm very fond of those people, and they of me, so that's personal. The community is another matter. Juan probably told you their side of that. Los Horcones wanted to give the Federation of Egalitarian Communities the gift of what they have learned, so that other people could use it. And the other communities dismissed them with a shrug of their shoulders and said, "Well, maybe you Mexicans are willing to take orders, but we're not. We're doing fine as we are, we don't need your advice, and who do you think you are?" They rejected the gift, which is too bad. And so Los Horcones with injured feelings and anger quit the federation and now ignores it except to visit Twin Oaks from time to time as they're traveling for one reason or another.

Q: When I was at Los Horcones, it seemed to me that it was always Juan who talked about behaviorism, while the others would talk about all kinds of practical things. They would never contribute on behaviorist theories. What was your impression? Did you hear about behaviorism from more than one angle?

A: I think if you had heard about behaviorism from any of the others, and most of the others could be articulate on the subject, you would simply hear what Juan had said. They get all of their ideas about behavior theory from Juan, and there is no reason why you would have heard anything else. This is my theory on Los Horcones: You could have someone there who would take Juan's theory and say, "Wait a minute, let me think about that, does this check with my experience?" There could be, there could have been a development in that direction, but I don't think that that kind of group attracts active theoretical minds. I think that it is very typical: they have a theoretician in the center, and most people reflect what that person thinks, and if you get two theoreticians, you'll probably end up with two communities. Like these cells that have two nuclei, they tend to stretch further and further apart until they snap in the middle. It's one of the reasons that communities are so small, most of them. Now, of course, Twin Oaks is not, but then Twin Oaks has no central theoretician. It's always been intellectually wide open. There have always been plenty of potential leaders. You know, people who come there and would love to have other people sit at their feet, but nobody is interested in sitting at their feet. It's very eclectic and very scattered. And very much in conflict all the time. All the time. Sometimes I think that's good. Most of the time, I just don't know.

Q: Could you picture living at Los Horcones?

A: Well, I have an independent mind. I'm just the sort I've been saying who would not be ... [sighs] It would be hard. I'm immensely drawn to Juan as a personality and as a thinker. And I'd be happy to be where we would be able to argue a lot. But I think I would be fundamentally lonely, because I think if I came not to agree with him, who would I talk to? I have the same problem here at Ganas. So that problem is in my mind because of current experiences. I don't know. Being fundamentally lonely also at Twin Oaks is less of a problem because it isn't such a limited society; there are so many facets of it. If I don't find one thing to do with people, I can do something else. I do music, mostly. I put most of my energy into music at Twin Oaks. And into the improvement of government. But I can't imagine being at Los Horcones and being involved in the improvement of government because it is probably good enough for the eight, ten people, or whatever they've got.

Q: They are up to twenty-five, thirty people.

A: Well, that might be interesting. It would do great things for my Spanish.

Q: Do you think cooperation is possible without personal incentives?

A: Nowadays, I think you need some personal incentive in order to put out your best in the work scene. Cooperation and group reinforcement alone will just not do. I have come to think of it that way, and I don't think that's just the way we've been conditioned. That's the absolute basic. As Frazier put it, "You've taken the mainspring out of the watch." I keep remembering that. Not Frazier! Castle. Castle challenged Frazier on this very point. Castle said, "You've taken the mainspring out of the watch." And Frazier replied, "That is an experimental question, Mr. Castle, and you have the wrong answer." Or something of that sort. I was absolutely delighted with this when I first read it. But at this point I'm prepared to say, "It's an experimental question, Mr. Castle, and you're right." We had taken the mainspring out of the watch, and we got a very mediocre response by doing so. I examined this question year by year, and it is not that you don't get a successful community by depending entirely on cooperation, it's just that you don't get as much as you would otherwise get. That's all. I would say it's something like 80 percent. Cooperation will get you 80 percent of what you would otherwise get. Cooperation and rules, you know, understanding that under these circumstances you will live here if you do quota. I think people mostly do quota. Some of them cheat a little bit. Some do more than quota. But when you add money, say, "And, if you work over quota, we will give you one dollar for every hour you work," or something like that, they'll think, "Oh, boy. Three dollars." [laughs] Whatever. But they'll work harder for it. They'll work more hours than they thought they could because they want that money. And it turned out that just extra hours didn't quite do it.

Q: Do you think Acorn Community [a newly founded community in the vicinity of Twin Oaks and subsidized by it] is working well?

A: I haven't been there for a while. I spent two months there a year ago, and I didn't think the work scene was very together, but apparently the community-feeling scene is very together. As far as I know, people like each other and are working towards that end almost every day. And they're getting by, they're not going broke. And they're getting those buildings put together little by little. So although a good attitude toward work, a good sour Protestant ethic in there could do wonders for their physical plant, I'm not prepared to say that improvements in the physical plant are more important than the psychological work they're doing with each other and the emotional connections they're making with each other. I'm kind of minding my own business on the Acorn scene. Holding my breath and hoping for them. Because they have been very much influenced by Ganas. Now of course Ganas has a terrific Protestant ethic. I mean, Ganas works its butt off. And, in addition, does all these daily meetings. And Acorn has kind of substituted the one for the other. [laughs] But as long as they get by…which we don't know yet, because they borrowed so much money from Twin Oaks for starters. We got one more year to run on that. Maybe it's mostly gone already, because what they borrowed was money to build on. They hadn't finished the buildings, but it wouldn't surprise me if they had just about finished the loan. They may be really on their own financially very soon.

Q: What was your inspiration for starting Twin Oaks?

A: I need to say that behaviorism was not my fundamental inspiration. I thought it was interesting, and I just assumed somehow we would attract some wonderful psychiatrist—psychologist, I mean—who would come along, and he would make that part of it work. And that would delight me, because I had no objection to the theory. But what drew me was not behaviorism but what I can only call communism. What drew me was equality. My fascination with equality goes back to my childhood, so it's a very strong thing, which I think I'm now through with.

Q: Because of frustration?

A: Yes. I think at this point equality will take you just so far—I think I expressed this in the book—and then you need other things. But I think I took equality quite a bit further than Skinner would have taken it. Out of my own fanaticism, almost. Here's an example: We have an area called trusterty, which means things that are intrusted to you. It's a word taken from the word "property," but instead of being your own property it's put into your trust. This includes such things as bedroom furniture. So, suppose you have a dresser, and you leave the community. Well, what everybody really wanted to do was go into your room and take that dresser. But I put a stop to that. I said, "No! That dresser is the equal property of everybody here, everybody gets an equal chance at it." And so I insisted on putting that dresser up for flips. And then that person gets the dresser, and then his or her dresser in turn goes up for flips. Equal chance, equal chance, equal chance, all along the way. Now, I couldn't maintain that after I left the first time. I came back nine years later and discovered that everybody was just walking into rooms of people who had left and taking their dressers if they felt like it. And also there were now a lot more dressers than there used to be, and the whole issue didn't have much importance. But it was the extent to which I took the idea of equality. To me, it was important. Everybody needed to get the idea that there was nobody entitled to anything that other people didn't have, except by chance, by equal chance. And the idea did not take hold. And for years I wondered, "Why does nobody see it like this?" And I guess it just has something to do with nobody happened to have that particular emotional background, that fanatical devotion to equity. And I think that was the emotional spring from which a lot of my early effort came. And when it went, it didn't leave much in its place. It left a hole in its place. And so for a long time I haven't really quite known what I was doing, or what I thought I was doing at Twin Oaks. What for! You know, what is this community for? And you know, somewhere along the line, instead of absolute equality, it was the idea of getting bigger, bringing in more people. And that felt like saving the world, saving these poor people who would otherwise have to deal with capitalism. And I would clasp them to my bosom and give them what they all really wanted, which was community and equality. And that turned out to be bullshit, but it was good while it lasted. It gave me meaning while it lasted.

Q: Why wasn't Skinner ever involved in Twin Oaks or other communal experiments?

A: Skinner did not take us seriously. At the very beginning, I think he didn't even get around to answering our letters, but then later he did, and we became friends, sort of. See, the thing is that we were definitely a hippie commune. For the reasons that I explained earlier, we had lots and lots of members who were not interested in behaviorism at all, and we were not carrying on control experiments. We were learning, and recording what we learned, but we did not have a scientific point of view, even. We lived among a nonacademic, anti-intellectual atmosphere. In some ways, it's still that way. So I couldn't write to him and say, "Dear Fred, we're doing Walden Two here, why don't you get yourself interested?" because we weren't doing Walden Two. We made some efforts. I remember this box we made and trying to get this dog interested in M&Ms so he would press this button, but the button clacked, and the dog found the clacking noise so aversive that he didn't become interested in the M&Ms, and I don't think dogs are really big on M&Ms anyway. [laughs] As I say, we got distracted with various experiments along the way, which we felt would make us sort of Walden Twoish, but really were not aimed at the accumulation of scientific data or finding out anything about humans. The only thing we ever did with humans was self-management, where we determined behavior objectives and then made charts and tried to find ways we could reward ourselves for approaching our goals. And we would sometimes stick to these for months. I was quite serious about it, and so were several other people, but it wasn't ever really community-wide. It wasn't like "We Do This"; it was interesting enough so that we might get into some article or something as an example of how Twin Oaks is interested in the science of behaviorism, but it was never really basic. What was always basic was the other side of the picture, as I said, the communist side, the equality. That was God—now don't take me literally. So when Skinner got a little bit interested was when I wrote the book. The first book. His wife loved it. She read it, and she wrote to me. She was my first fan; I loved her. She said, "I don't like behaviorism, I never did, and I didn't like *Walden Two*, but what you people have done with it is so human. I like your book much better. I like your community much better than I do the community of my husband's fiction." Anyway, she was very complimentary. Skinner himself was very complimentary. After he read the book, he said he would be delighted to write the preface. The reason that we sent it to him at all was that the publisher was counting on getting Skinner to write the preface. Skinner had just written *Beyond Freedom and Dignity,* so his name was in the press, and the publisher was figuring on getting some book sales out of that. So we had to know each other. I went and saw him in his office. I typed the manuscript—I was working for East Wind at the time—for I believe five dollars an hour. I typed the manuscript for *About Behaviorism.* [pauses] I did not enjoy that. It wasn't what I expected. My problem was that I wanted Frazier, and Skinner wasn't Frazier. I thought he ought to be, and somehow he wasn't. I sort of fell in love with the character. But the man had some fussiness about him that just wasn't Frazier at all and wasn't the man I had admired in the novel. In fact, I found him rather typical of his generation. He had a kind of wistfulness about sex, about free love, as we called it, because he was just before birth control was invented and the whole country's sexual standards blew sky high. So he never got in on the sleeping-around-and-getting-away-with-it generation. That was the young people that were doing it. And I find that men in his generation have a kind of wistful feeling that they have lost something, or missed something. They still have their hidden lusts most people have gotten rid of long ago. And I could feel them. The fact that I was interested in *Walden Two* and in him... The fact that I was a woman mattered more, that I was doing a hippie commune. An I-bet-they-do-massages-in-a-hippie-commune kind of attitude.

Q: So you believe Skinner didn't quite take you seriously because you were a woman?

A: I believe that's true. Not so much because I am a woman, but because I am not academically qualified. I had a longing to talk to him, present him with his theory. "This is what you thought would happen. Now let me tell you what actually happened when we tried this." And I had a fantasy that he would be fascinated and that he would ask questions like, "What about this angle? Whatever happened to this idea? You guys tried this, didn't you?" And somehow I was pretty badly disillusioned when nothing like that happened at all. Ever. He wasn't interested. In fact, he talked about himself, almost nonstop. [pauses] I am not fond of people who talk about themselves all the time. And it was a shock to me to find that Skinner was one of them. Somehow, *Walden Two* didn't make him seem like that. But he was more interested in telling me about this conference he was going to go to than he was in knowing what happened when we tried to imitate Walden Two. I just thought that was so discouraging and dismaying. We had a very slow, occasional correspondence over the years. He apologized for that behavior. And on paper, I liked him.

Q: Did you ever tell him what you disliked about him?

A: On paper, yes. And he more or less said, "Oh dear, I didn't mean to come across that way. I'm so sorry I came across that way. I certainly did not think you were less qualified to talk to, I didn't think anything of the kind, blah blah." But, you know, one reads behavior. I judge a man by what he does, not by what he says. Unless he's in fiction, of course. [laughs] He did come down to Twin Oaks, because they were filming him. He came down for a TV company to film him for "60 Minutes." And that was okay, he was nice to us. He gave us a video machine, which we had not had heretofore, 'cause he thought we didn't have anywhere near enough recreation. What he really thought was that we were too poor. He had never envisioned Walden Two being started by poor people. He had never thought of that. I think coming from an academic background he must have assumed funding. We had none.

Q: Well, Skinner never really talks about the actual founding of the community in *Walden Two*, does he?

A: Right, and we found that very discouraging. [laughs]

Q: So why do you think Skinner never started a community himself? He talks a little bit about not wanting to leave behind his professorship. Do you think that was the real reason?

A: He already had a good life. He was interested in what he was doing, and Walden Two was just a sideline. It was just something he thought up one summer. What if you apply this idea to a society, what could you do? And he got carried away with it to the extent of writing a book. But he never had any intention of starting a community. Other people did. Other people came to him and offered him, he says, everything except money to do it with, but he didn't think that he had the ability. And I'm inclined to think he's quite right. He didn't have the ability, and I know what it takes. It doesn't take what he had.

Q: What did he lack?

A: Leadership. Practical common sense. No, I don't know. [pauses] It takes enormous flexibility. And the ability to deal with all kinds of people. Or at least the kind that are going to join your community. Yeah, not all kinds. But that kind. He couldn't have adjusted to the hippie movement. No, he liked being where he was. He's a scientist. In his youth, I think, a good one. He's been profoundly influential on the whole field of knowledge. And he's widely used by people who don't even know that's what they're doing or don't acknowledge it. He was a great figure of the twentieth century, but he had nothing to do with starting a little commune.

Q: Has Skinner ever commented on Los Horcones to you?

A: He said somewhere, I don't know whether it was in a letter to me or somewhere else, that Los Horcones had "kept the faith." That we had drifted away from behaviorism, but Los Horcones was still with it, and he had some interest in it—I gathered, a fairly mild interest.

## Interview with Kat Kinkade, April 11, 1998

Q: Why do you think *Walden Two* was more attractive to an American audience than any other audience?

A: You know, I've never thought about this question at all. I think in an American context... [pauses] And then there are the obvious facts, that the book was published in America, by an American, and so he's appealing on some subconscious level with his countrymen, of course. But *Walden Two*, apart from all that, *Walden Two* presents a life of leisure and good feeling and good times. It's a very attractive lifestyle, at least it was to me, assuming that the manipulators of the group are of good will, or that you're going to be one of the manipulators, or something like that. Apart from the manipulation question, the Walden Two lifestyle seems very attractive. What do I know about Europeans? [pauses] Well, don't you know the answer to your question?

Q: Well, *Walden Two* was published in several languages, a lot of people knew about it, and a lot of people discussed it, and I wonder why there weren't really any groups outside of the North American continent trying to found a Walden Two.

A: Well, I guess on both sides of the Atlantic, *Walden Two* was read mostly by intelligent people, you know, intellectual types who were going to school, and were studying it, and what have you. You know, America is the only place where you could have bought that land. That you could conceive of doing this, the excitement of actually doing it. I've been told by Germans in particular that you can't just go out and buy a couple of farms. That they're either not available at all or cost more money than you could conceive of. And in England the same thing. What they do is they rent a house in the suburbs or in the city or something and try to do something cooperative there. But that's got something to do with it. The fact that you can conceive of yourself doing it, and that you can in fact do it, in this country where land is available for somebody who's got a little money. A little, not a lot.

Q: Yes, that is certainly part of it. Let me ask you something about the behaviorist interest held by the Walden Two communities in the seventies. Do you think the idea of having a positive verbal environment sprang from behaviorist thinking, or was the idea of having positive encounters part of the alternative scene anyway? I'm asking this partly because the idea of having a positive verbal environment survived much longer than the behaviorist thinking at Dandelion, Twin Oaks, and a number of other communities.

A: Did it come out of *Walden Two,* or was it just lying there in the culture, for us to soak up? [pauses] You ask questions I haven't thought about. [pauses] *Walden Two* still has an influence on us, and even though I would say three-quarters of the people in the community have not read it. And behaviorism—I still hear the traces. People will say, "Do you realize what you just reinforced?" or something like that. And that sweet talk is more effective than nastiness? No, people aren't nice to each other because it's more effective.

That's not where they're coming from. They're nice to each other because they believe in it. You do not go around thinking about effectiveness. And so, I would say behaviorism has relatively little to do with it. And in the earlier years I don't think we made a distinction, like, "We want a culture in which people speak to each other pleasantly, and therefore we will do this or that." You know? We just did. It seems very natural to me, that when somebody comes in and is very ugly in his speech, that we want to get rid of him. And so we do. Here.

Q: How about the positive verbal environment at Dandelion Community in the early years?

A: The people at Dandelion were very positive in all their verbal interactions, and they were consciously so because they were consciously trying to produce, they were consciously trying to reward…[pauses] No, I'm not sure what they were consciously trying to do.

Q: Richie Dandelion gave an example of the kind of positive verbal behavior he was trying to foster. He said he tried to have a feedback board where he would put up things like, "I really liked coming into the kitchen this morning and finding all the counters clean!" And then he said it moved away from that almost immediately, and people would put down things like, "I really liked the sunset last night!" And he could never explain what the difference between the two statements was.

A: [laughs] Yes, Richie was a behaviorist, probably still is. Very interested in the subject and kind of a true believer in behaviorism, and most people are just not interested in the subject. I used to say, behaviorism isn't reinforcing. I was with some behaviorists recently at a conference, and I realized in talking with some of them that it isn't reinforcing because it doesn't give anybody credit for anything. And everybody wants to take credit and to give blame. And behaviorism doesn't permit either one, so it's a very irritating psychology or philosophy or belief. We have a thank-you board here of the kind that Richie envisioned, and we use it fairly consciously. It's up in the office now, and it will say things like, "Wow, I really like the new bulletin board that somebody put up," or, "I really appreciate the fact that . . ." and people will be named specifically: "Olive, thank you so much for this," and, "Deborah, thank you for that," and, "Bonnie, you did my kitchen shift; I can't tell you how grateful I am." [pauses] I don't think they are trying to reinforce the behavior, that's not the object. They are trying to make the person feel appreciated. And so they are aimed at the culture in general and at the happiness of individuals. Because feeling unappreciated in this environment is a very easy thing to happen, because there are so many things to do, so many people, so many different things they've done. Somebody may feel good about doing a task until they realize that nobody noticed. So we're trying to counteract that, and I don't think that's behaviorism. I don't think there is any connection.

Q: Do you think the current Twin Oaks labor-credit system still has behaviorist traces?

A: I don't...[pauses] The obvious thing about behaviorism and the labor credit is that you get some labor credits as a reward, as cash, for the work you do, and people certainly do work in order to get labor credits. I don't mean all people all the time, but it's a consciousness that's carried at the back of our minds. Even me. I'm almost free of the labor system, I have a low quota, my work is done at my own time, my own schedule, but in the back of the mind I'm thinking, "Do I get credit for this, do I get credit for that?" That always goes on, and when I ask somebody to do me a favor, I always say, "And you can have personal service credits," or that person will ask, "Are there any personal service credits available for this work?" It's there, it's always there. And I don't know that you would call it positive reinforcement, it's much more negative reinforcement. The absence of labor credits will make trouble. And other than those handful of people who lie, most of us need them. So I think that's fundamentally behaviorist, but I'm not sure that positive reinforcement is what is being used.

Q: Would you say that the variable labor credit was more behaviorist in intent than the current system?

A: The variable credit had to do simply with the desirability of work, and evaluating a job as more or less desirable. And we are not currently using that, although some of us are thinking of using it again for certain things. But I don't think of it as positive reinforcement in particular. Just adjustment. We are talking about the same thing with variable labor credits?

Q: Well, I'm thinking about the idea that two people work next to each other but get a different amount of credit for the same work.

A: Yes, and that comes out of *Walden Two Experiment,* that was not in *Walden Two.* Skinner gave the example of somebody working in the sewer gets 1.5 because hardly anybody wants to work in the sewer, and a person working in the flower garden gets only .1 because it's so much fun. It's really their leisure activity. But Skinner hadn't thought as far as two people working on the same job might get varying credits. We went through that experiment and found it... [pauses] interesting and undesirable. It made people angry. They felt manipulated, they felt cheated.

Q: I can relate to that.

A: [laughs] Well, we had some controls on the cheating. You had to say you did like certain jobs, and you had to have a certain number of them, and so forth. But the system didn't work for emotional reasons. People feeling they were getting less reward than somebody else, and that the other person is probably lying, or is a better manipulator than they are and that the whole thing depends on manipulation, and they get angry at that because what we want here is an atmosphere where we work because the work needs doing and because we have chosen this part of it, and there is some reward in doing it, intrinsic. Because there is intrinsic pleasure in the job. And those are the good reasons. And the bad reasons are, you know, trickery. [pauses] Manipulation of the system is not admired. We don't think cheating is funny. I sometimes thought that on the outside world cheating is admired. I noticed it certainly in the history of certain cultures. The Old Testament is full of tales about how somebody fooled somebody else, African folk tales are full of it. So there's lots of cultures who think that cheating is cute, that cheating is clever, and I guess intelligence is generally admired. But here at Twin Oaks it's not admired.

Q: How about the current governmental situation at Twin Oaks? Most people seem to find it dismaying but don't know what to do about it.

A: It is as you described. Many people either think they are disenfranchised, or they're just lazy, or they're too busy with other things. They are not involved in government. They wouldn't say they were indifferent, but they act as if they were indifferent. Some of them will say, "I trust the planners." Others will say, "I don't trust the planners, but I don't want to get involved." Mostly, the honest ones will say, "The questions are too complicated for me. I don't know how to make decisions like that." And they're admitting to something that I think is, frankly, true: That some people are better at that than others. And that they're not among... [pauses] Okay, so we have a Board of Planners. And they are currently allowed to make decisions. That's what you observed, and that's an interesting observation to me because I think it's true of this particular Board of Planners, it wasn't probably true of the one before it nor necessarily of the one after it. In my opinion, we need someone who can say, "Even if people give me a hard time, I'm going to do the best I can and actually make the decision and not just put them off until yet another poll and another poll and so forth." But actually make decisions. This Board of Planners has been able to do that, and I appreciate it no end.

Q: I'm wondering whether maybe at Twin Oaks, while you were focusing on what kind of government to have, people said, "Well, I don't like being disenfranchised, it's totalitarian." And now, where people are maybe more in their natural, day-to-day routine, the planner system seems to actually work better than when you officially proclaimed it.

A: Keep in mind that these same people are also older. And people grow out of their twenties, they have children, and their focus has to change, and some of their ideas will change, too. But they are usually not willing to admit to changed ideas. But now they're older, and things that seemed important no longer do, and people you thought were dreadful didn't turn out to be. [pauses] You get in touch with the non black-and-whiteness of the universe as you get older. So people in their forties are more thoughtful than people in their twenties, there is no getting around it.

Q: But at Twin Oaks, even people in their twenties seem apathetic about the overall affairs of the community.

A: Even people in their twenties here are politically apathetic? Well. [pauses] I'm glad of it, so I don't think I have any comment to make. [laughs]

Q: Well, I was just wondering how you felt about that these days.

A: See, I'm no believer in democracy, you probably know this. It's effective as a safeguard against evil, but we don't have evil here.

Q: Okay. Let's talk about egalitarianism.

A: What about egalitarianism? Here I have opinions.

Q: Egalitarianism seems to be a key term in understanding Twin Oaks and what you were trying to do. How would you define egalitarianism, and what does egalitarianism mean to you?

A: Mean or meant? Because those are two different things. This is the basic idea about which I have changed my mind. Initially, I was enchanted by the idea of everybody having the same opportunities, even though they had different tastes and different desires, and the approach to satisfying them would all be different, nevertheless the approach—by government, as I saw it—to satisfying each individual would be of equal intensity. We would do our best for everybody, you know. That's community. I envisioned a world like that, too, but I never expected to do anything about the world, so I didn't go that far. I remember using the example of a clarinet. Just because somebody passionately needs a clarinet doesn't mean that you have to buy one for everybody. It doesn't necessarily mean that you have to spend an equal amount of money on everybody. It means that whatever that clarinet means to that individual, you try to match that degree of resources, consumption, and/or satisfaction. [pauses] I don't know. Just how I thought we were going to be wise enough to do that kind of distribution I don't know, I just know I felt confident that we could, and perhaps I'm saying that I thought I could. [pauses] I don't think so anymore. But I was younger. You know, I was in my thirties. [pauses] My impulse was the impulse away from the gross inequalities of the country in general and the fact that I come from the poorer side. I'm not middle-class, as I've probably said in some other tape, and I think I felt that I would have liked to have had some of the opportunities that other people had. I would have liked to have been able to assume that I could go to college. To know that, "Now I am going to take my summer vacation." As if it were a given. Or, "I am going to buy my school clothes." Or, "Oh, dear, my fall wardrobe is not up to snuff." These things were never part of my life. So part of my wanting equality was wanting me to have what I saw the middle class having. But that isn't what I said at the time, and it isn't the main thing, because frankly it isn't my fall wardrobe and things like that that move me. [laughs] That's not where it's at. I'm just talking about the general feeling of being deprived. But mostly it was just this glittering, shining idea that everybody had a shot at the good life. Everybody has the good life. I don't see anything wrong with that idea, as an idea, but I have changed my mind, very seriously changed my mind about the desirability of equality in any rigid sense. At this point in my life I believe that it is not a good idea. And that the founding of a community in which egalitarianism was stressed as the first principle is not something I would do again. I don't know that I would say it's a mistake. We have a nice community here, and I have a good life in it. So I'm not saying, "I wish I hadn't done Twin Oaks." But I am saying, if I were young again and were going to do a community again, it would not start with such rigid egalitarianism. [pauses] And I'll tell you why.

Q: Okay.

A: Because the aim is to make everybody feel equally served by the establishment, and that's impossible. Equal time, equal money, equal whatever. But even if we had this godlike ability to give everyone an equal amount of satisfaction in theory, there would be some who would immediately be dissatisfied, and they would be dissatisfied because they would look at what their neighbor had, and they'd say, "Well, I don't have a clarinet." And you could say to them, "But you've got a baby." [laughs] "Don't you think that baby is expensive?" And they'll say, "Oh, that doesn't count. The community is supposed to support babies." And they'll be angry, and they'll be envious of whatever anybody had. As far as I can see, envy seems to be built into the human, and I can see evolutionarily why that might be true. [pauses] But it's not only built into the human, but also into the system of equality. And I read this about people: the more they strive for equality, the more they watch to see what their neighbors have, to see if they've got something that they don't. And that trait is so ugly and destructive and hateful that I would rather give up equality than have that trait around. I would like to destroy that. I would like to have a society in which we expect some people to have more than others. Not a whole lot more, see, not gross inequalities, but some people work harder and so they get some, and other people don't work so hard so they don't get it, and some people are lucky because their parents gave them some, and other people weren't so lucky so they didn't get it. So...big deal. As long as it doesn't... [pauses] I wouldn't want anybody to be more than double, have twice as much as somebody else. But I wouldn't want anybody going around making mathematical calculations about it. And so, because I have changed my mind about this, I no longer get excited about, "Oh, this isn't equal!" I think, "Yeah, it isn't. It isn't equal, and it's not gonna be." [sighs]

Q: So when did you change your mind about equality?

A: When did I change my mind? I changed my mind little by little. [pauses] I need to think about that, because I started changing my mind about communism in general when I was at East Wind, and I saw the system being taken advantage of by unscrupulous people. I don't know if that is the same thing as this envy thing that I'm talking about. I think it was only after I returned to Twin Oaks that I saw this envy thing in operation big time because of particular personalities we have who are big on that. You know, they are just watchdogs to make sure that nobody else gets more than them. And I just loathe this trait. So little by little I thought, "This is not merely an ugly trait in a particular individual." Especially after I read this article on the kibbutz. We are creating it. And our rigid equality sanctifies envy. [pauses] You know what I said when we first started this, this community back in 1967? I wrote, "Equality in our community is that state in which no one member envies another." So in the beginning, I defined it as, if we have envy, then we haven't made it. So we should give you enough stuff or satisfactions or whatever it is so that you no longer feel envy. That was my ideal. But I had no idea at that time that that was insatiable. Because it's not insatiable in me. So I couldn't generalize from my own personality and my own character, because that particular thing isn't in me. But I found that certain people just want more and more and more. It just goes on and on, and it's sickening. And so I said, "We're creating it, here is this sickening thing, and we're making it!" And I don't like that, and that's why I changed my mind. Let's have something that doesn't, that's where I'm coming from.

Q: When we talked at Ganas, you said that after losing your passion for egalitarianism, you have had no other central core value that excites you. Is that still the case?

A: That's true. I have private concerns, just like the people we talked about earlier. I'm into music, and many of my activities have nothing to do with Twin Oaks, they have to do with my life in the local church or in my shape note groups that I go to. [pauses] In some ways it feels as if all those passions are things of youth, and as if I'm not likely at this time in my life—I'm sixty-seven now—I'm not likely to find passions that drive me. I've seen people my age who still have the passions that they had earlier, who didn't let go of them. But I have. [pauses] They proved faulty! [laughs] Feet of clay.

Q: Do you think the vision you once had of egalitarianism not only shaped Twin Oaks but also inspired people who then founded other communities?

A: You know, I don't have much way of knowing this. I have become aware over the years that many people are inspired by us and do try to do this or that or the other thing. And that there are hundreds of such people, if not thousands. But I think what they like here has to do more than anything with our mellow and friendly atmosphere, with our splitting up of the work, with our having various things we can do in the course of a day, with the labor system. I've heard the labor system very pleasantly spoken of. But I think what they're taking from Twin Oaks is not a coherent philosophy. It's a bit and piece of something they find.

Q: In the seventies, there were numerous communal groups that were inspired by Twin Oaks. More specifically, they liked the labor-credit system and the idea of egalitarianism. Do you think that those groups took their inspiration from Twin Oaks but then said, "We want to build a Walden Two community?" Twin Oaks was still calling itself a Walden Two community at this time, so do you think it's likely that those groups attached the label Walden Two to themselves without really knowing *Walden Two* beyond what Twin Oaks had done with it?

A: I think that's accurate. We had some conscious thoughts on the subject of what to call ourselves when we advertised in the early years. And so did some of the smaller communities that were offsprings. They didn't really want to say, "We're starting another Twin Oaks. And of course we'll have our own ideas, but we're starting with Twin Oaks." Which is what they meant. And so they'd say "another Walden Two community," hoping people would make the connection. Or at one point, East Wind used the term "kibbutz-like community," hoping that people would make that connection. Because, you know, Walden Two and kibbutz have a great deal in common, as far as the general organization is concerned. Although the kibbutz never thought of our labor-credit system and wouldn't have anything to do with it if they did. Neither labor system nor government is typical of kibbutz. Just the same, we have a lot in common. Because of the pooling of money and the equal splitting of resources. In recent years, we're calling that "income-sharing communities," instead of saying either Walden Two or kibbutz. That's our latest jargon.

Q: I found a letter that Jane Dandelion wrote to you regarding the founding of a federation of communities that ended up being called the Federation of Egalitarian Communities. I guess one of the original ideas was to call it the Walden Two Federation?

A: Oh, I didn't know that.

Q: Well, in her letter, Jane says, "A Walden Two Federation sounds intriguing. Yes, we definitely recognize the classification."

A: What you have there is Jane who was a behaviorist, and Dandelion, which was behaviorist-oriented. Dandelion and Los Horcones: for these people, behaviorism has meaning. In the case of Dandelion, it had. [pauses] You know, we didn't know that we were changing the term. Terms change, language changes, and it comes to mean other than what it meant before. It just happens.

Q: Yes, sure. It's just that the common use of the word "Walden Two" in the communities movement in the seventies makes it look as if there had been a lot of people excited about behaviorism in the communities movement, and I just wanted to clarify with you that that was not the case.

A: Right, in the seventies there were not a lot of people excited about behaviorism. But see, Twin Oaks was such a little thing, it didn't seem right to put Twin Oaks on a pedestal. It's just easier to take something abstract like a book.

Q: So people looked at Twin Oaks and were inspired by Twin Oaks but expressed it by saying Walden Two. And that probably came about because

Twin Oaks stressed *Walden Two* in the beginning, and that was mainly because you were into *Walden Two*. And you looked at *Walden Two* from the point of view of a very specific brand of egalitarianism. So would you say that in a way your personal interpretation of *Walden Two* was really pretty instrumental?

A: I had never thought about it, but you are probably right. [pauses] Don't think that I didn't have an interest in behaviorism as well. Our attitude toward behaviorism at the beginning—mine, at least—was that if we, who are ignorant of the science, will build the infrastructure and get the businesses going and get the buildings built, then these behaviorists who are used to a more middle-class lifestyle, some of them will come along and they'll be attracted and they'll see that there are things that they could do here and they will sit in and they will help us. And then we'll have more behavioral control in our community. That was my notion. I probably clung to that notion for at least a year after I got here. I was down to that behaviorist conference just last month, and the question that psychologist after psychologist asked me within the same question period was, "If we came, would we be welcomed, would there be things for us to do in our profession? Could you use our help at this point?" Of course I had to say, "Well, probably not. You'd probably be rejected." And since I don't really think that they know enough, they probably would be rejected. Behaviorism is still fairly primitive in terms of what can be done with human beings.

Q: Would you say, then, that behaviorism as a science never really played a role at Twin Oaks?

A: I shouldn't ignore the first several months or years of Twin Oaks experience. It's just that it's so far in the past. And it was so explicitly repudiated in 1973, when those facilitators came and the group rejected behaviorism at that point. They said behaviorism is one thing that a few people believe in but most of us don't. We're an eclectic group, we believe in all kinds of things, and it's been that way ever since. Nevertheless, before that point, I think Twin Oaks derived some of its raison d'être from *Walden Two*. [pauses] Anyway, *Walden Two* had some meaning for Twin Oaks perhaps as long as it did for Dandelion. Maybe not. But Dandelion didn't last very long. Not as a vibrant community, but it might have lasted seven, eight, or nine years.

Q: Do you have any theories about why Dandelion Community didn't work out?

A: Oh, I suppose because they were Canadian and therefore didn't have the people coming through. Because they were vegetarian and therefore put in a selector against meat eating. Because their land was not pretty at all. [pauses] The thing that made Twin Oaks work in those early years was a mating center. We had people who were attracted to other people, and they found boyfriends and girlfriends and love interests. And a lot of them got married and are still married and have children. This was a major place for the major excitement of the young years. And Dandelion was the same kind of place, but it didn't have the population base to start with. And so there were very few of them there, and if people went through, they would see whether there was anybody for them or not. [pauses] See, this is my theory. I don't know how much validity there is to it. One might say Dandelion would have worked if Twin Oaks hadn't been here, but if you had your choice between living at Dandelion and living at Twin Oaks, you were likely to choose Twin Oaks, so Dandelion got only a few Canadians and an American here and there. Somebody who fell in love with Jane or Gordon or something like that. It did attract some people. Who are now here. [laughs]

Q: So you think it was mainly outside circumstances that worked to the detriment of Dandelion?

A: Yes. I think Dandelion was essentially a good community in its beginnings, and if it hadn't been for things beyond their control, they would have made it. But they were beyond their control, and they were big.

## Interview with Ian Murray, April 12, 1998

Q: What's the occasion for your current visit to Twin Oaks?

A: Oh, visiting friends. Mainly, I'm accompanying my son who's connecting with other musicians here.

Q: Sounds good. So let's talk about Headlands Community. Who was involved in the founding of your community in Canada in the 1970s, and what's your connection to Twin Oaks?

A: There were five of us, and we bought the communal property on Amherst Island in Canada in 1971 and started living there as a group in 1972. We tried organic farming and raising cattle. And I'll say this about farming: it's an immense labor and capital sink. And very few people who want to live in communes are prepared to work hard enough or dedicate themselves enough to be successful at it. It was a huge mistake that we made. So the summer of 1972, there were all kinds of issues, of course, as you would have in any group without clear leadership. I know I myself had some hard feelings because

I'm a pretty good worker. Actually, all five of us were quite work-oriented. And if you didn't want to work you didn't stay. That was always the way it was.

The attempt at a labor system was fairly crude. I forget exactly how we did it, but we reached some agreement whereby a person would do a certain amount of work, and then that was a great thing for me because it reduced my resentment considerably.

Q: When was this happening?

A: That would be during the summer of 1972.

Q: Who was instrumental in introducing the labor-credit system at Headlands?

A: It wasn't even a credit system. It was very crude, and I'd have to go back to the records and try to piece that together. My daughter has been after me for five years to do that, but it's still… [pauses] It's like a mirage that went sour, it's a hard thing to revisit, and I'm still not ready to do that, even though this is now twenty years later. We had quite a bit of fun, quite a bit of heartache. My wife and I had already been having considerable problems, and we just put it off. But we always had a strong commitment to our daughter and continued to have it.

The fall of 1972, I was fairly unhappy. I certainly had the desire to leave. I wanted a break, and I'd heard of Twin Oaks through a visitor who I think gave us a subscription to the *Leaves,* and that sounded pretty interesting. They were quite an old community, they were about four or five years old at that time. [laughs] And I was also interested in alternative sources of energy or something like that, and there was something about that in their newsletter. So I wrote them and found out that they were putting the newest newsletter together down near New York State, which was just on my way down to Florida. So I made up my mind, took the old VW, and went down there, and helped to put together issue X of *Alternative Sources of Energy.* Then I drove to Florida, and I spent about a month in Florida with friends who I had met through draft dodging. Stayed about a month, worked underground, and in January I made my way back up to Twin Oaks. Of course, the place is very different now from what it was back then. The pool we're looking at wasn't here, among other things. Anyway, that first time I got here, it was during a really cold spell, it was like below zero, and I'm getting up the first morning and wandering out, and there were two women milking over where the volleyball court is now, and I asked if I could help, and they were pretty glad. [laughs] I was a pretty good milker, and of course it was all hand milking.

So I came down here, to Twin Oaks, and I was very interested in the labor system. It was a very complex labor system—I think it's simplified now. Because back then, you'd sign up, and the same person might be...two people might be working on the same job, and one might be getting, for an hour's worth, 1.4 labor credits, and the other would be getting 1.9, depending on how they evaluated their dislike for the project.

I hung around for a week, ten days, two weeks, I forget. Very intense period. It was the period in which Kat and Velma and Gerri and Jessie went up to somewhere in Vermont to found what eventually became East Wind. And it was the time that their construction company started. So I came down here, sucked up information from Kat, and watched the beginning of what they later called Glorious Mud.

I taped an interview with Kat, went back home, and explained it. So we sat down and went through the whole process of discussing it, and then Bill, one of our founding members, said, "I'm not going to do anything except one hour of work is worth one hour of credit, I don't care what all this bullshit is." We tried it anyway, for one or two weeks, and after a little while we realized that Bill was right. One hour's worth of work is one credit, or it would be too much goddamn hassle otherwise. That was one of the few times I actually agreed with him. [pauses] Oh, and we tried the planner system as well. We did the same, we used exactly the same system as down here. We always said we'd copy any idea we liked. [laughs] The behaviorism didn't sit well at all. Alice, who was a dairy person at the commune, did work on behaviorism, and I think she used it quite well in her own life. Yeah, she practiced it but didn't preach it.

Q: Back in the seventies, were there any other ways in which Headlands was influenced by Twin Oaks besides the labor-credit system?

A: Yes. We very seriously thought of doing hammocks. Allison and my wife Wendy and David came down to Twin Oaks in maybe March of 1973, or something like that, to learn how to do hammocks. There has always been an antihammocks faction down here, probably still is, and they very much preferred the antihammocks faction. So they came back and said, "We think they're a great thing, but we ain't doing them. Anybody else wants to do them can go down and learn about them." [laughs] I think that was a big mistake, quite frankly. And I, myself, didn't want to do hammocks, but I thought having an industry like that would be a good idea. But we wanted to do productive work, like farming. So we did a lot of outside labor. [pauses] In Canada at the time it was very easy to get unemployment insurance. Like, you work for maybe three months, and then you could draw unemployment for maybe ten months. It was ludicrously easy and very corrupting. And I don't remember when we started that, whether we did that in 1972 or started in 1973, because here at Twin Oaks there was very much of an outside-work-rotating thing going on, and I don't know how many years that went on. So we started that. But anyway, we used the Twin Oaks model of three months outside work, which worked very well, because in three months you could get yourself quit, laid off, or whatever, and come back, and you would still have that income coming in. And we had a lot of money coming in. Like myself, I quit my job in August of 1972, I think, and I had a good severance package, plus I could draw unemployment insurance. And actually for the whole life of the commune, we did very well on that corrupting—and it is a corrupting thing—"outside work for three months, come back in and still draw a lesser paycheck" system. But several men picked up construction skills, which served them well when they went off on their own.

Q: How did the labor system evolve at Headlands?

A: As I said, we quickly went away from the .5, .9, 1.4, and whatnot, and the system we came up with—and I don't remember the evolution, although I was very much part of it and was labor manager—was that we had blocks of time. The planners would lay out blocks of time, which shifted with seasons, but basically we had a house A.M., who would clear up from breakfast, clean the house, and make lunch. The house A.M. person would help clear up after lunch and help with the dishes, and then the house A.M. person was done, and the house P.M. did whatever needed to be done in the afternoon, which wasn't that much, but then would have to do supper. Which was interesting in that miniscule kitchen, preparing meals for up to twenty-five people. [pauses] It was a large sheet that was laid out, it was like wrap paper, and it would be blocked out with the weeks, and our week started on a Friday or something like that. It was laid out, and there were blocks, like house A.M., house P.M., children A.M., children P.M., children evening, the housework was all blocked out, and other things that needed to be done, like shopping and laundry, were separate things.

Q: So people signed up?

A: Yes, it was all laid out, and people signed up. And below that, you knew how much labor you had, you know, depending on how many people there were, and you multiplied that times, like probably forty-nine or fifty hours a week, I forget. [pauses] People would presign up to a certain extent. [pauses] I know how it was: the sheet would be preprepared, and then we'd all sit around the table, everybody who wasn't on outside work, and I don't know whether we drew lots for it, or what, but we'd just go around the table, and you signed up for up to four hours at a time, and you knew that you had to do one or two blocks of housework, or whatever it was at the time.

Q: Was that the only mandatory job?

A: Yes, that was the only thing that was required. And then there'd be the regular things like milking and going into town and such. Going into town always involved two people and a couple of kids. I know my daughter always went because she loved going to town. So there'd be the shopping person and the laundry person and the kids. And then there'd be all the extra work, like the garden manager would have a certain block of hours. [pauses] There was a certain amount of gamesmanship to it. Like Allison and I liked to do dishes together because we were both orderly people. We'd always try to do dishes together. So anyway, we had the one master plan, and then everybody had a labor sheet. And the master plan was hung up, so you could look and see what was going on. And you had the labor sheet, which was roughly patterned after Twin Oaks. [pauses] I haven't looked at one of those for over twenty years, but I can look it up. I've got all the archives, and I'd like to write it up someday.

Q: For how long did you use the labor-credit and planner-manager systems?

A: The system was probably in place sometime in 1973, and it stayed that way, the way I just described it, until June 30, 1975, when we officially broke up.

Q: Why did you break up?

A: That was over interpersonal issues. It had nothing to do with the labor-credit or planner-manager system.

Q: What is on the property that used to be Headlands these days?

A: Well, it's called Topsy Farm Limited. It's a fairly large sheep farm and a consumer cooperative.

Q: During the period that you were living communally, so until 1975, how did the planner system work?

A: It worked pretty well. We had a lot of really competent—well, we had maybe fifteen members, tops—but we had very competent people. I would have no hesitation, even today with still not liking some of the people, I would have no hesitation to lend any of them money. I would lend any of them money, and I would know that I would get it back. I would trust any one of them with my life. Easily. Even the ones I didn't like, there is still a real fundamental trust. [pauses] In terms of the work, we came from really different premises than Twin Oaks.

Q: In what way?

A: We assumed that working was a valid part of our life. It wasn't something like, "Jeez, I got my 38.9 credits this week, that's it. Fuck off." It wasn't that way with us. If we started a project, and you had to work later, we'd do it. I suspect that most people's philosophy is pretty similar. It's the right livelihood thing that I have never seen here. Like, I see people with that here, but I see them get burned out. Every time I come down here, I don't know who will still be here. I hear Gordon is getting burned out, Gordon could leave yesterday. Sandy used to live here, and Mary Krantz, and Rob Jones, people that were really good. They're excellent workers. But the bar is too low here. You know, as in high jumping? The bar is too low here. Here, work is a necessary evil. That's the norm, that work is a necessary evil. And that bothers me. I mean, I like most of the people here, but...hard workers do not receive respect for their efforts here. Do you see that yourself?

Q: Yeah. I just talked about that with Kat last night.

A: There is nobody in the world I respect more than Kat.

Q: And she got burned out, too.

A: Yeah! And she accepted it, maybe she had to. [laughs]

Q: Who would you say is attracted to living in a community?

A: People who are disenfranchised with their present lifestyle. Which is good, I mean, this is good. And I said the same thing to Kat last night. Why aren't there a hundred, two hundred, three hundred Twin Oakses? I don't understand it, I still don't understand it. To me it's a fine way of living.

Q: Who joined your community, Headlands? What was their aim? Did you have any common goals that you propagated?

A: We never had a shared ideology. I think the fairest thing I could say is that people thought that Headlands for that time and that place was the best thing for them, and when it wasn't, they moved on.

Q: How about the planner system? Did you ever have problems with that, complaints from people who wanted to be more involved?

A: It wasn't a particular issue. [pauses] If I was to do it again, I would just call it Board of Directors and be done with the bullshit. Because that's what it is.

Q: How was Twin Oaks regarded by you back then? Was it sort of a model community?

A: No, we regarded it with contempt.

Q: Why?

A: Because there were a few good people here, and they were getting the short end of the stick. How I saw Twin Oaks, quite bluntly, was that if we could have evolved toward…I look at this as a breeding ground. I would have mined this place. I would have said, Donna, look at what we're doing, come on and visit. Sandy, McCune, come up and visit, and see what we're doing.

Q: So despite this view of Twin Oaks, you chose to adopt the labor-credit system?

A: Oh, I thought it was very sound. I just thought the basic tenet, or a basic tenet here, was work is evil. I'll do my 45.6 credits—and fuck you! Or I'll do fifty so I can go off somewhere.

Q: Couldn't that be related to each other, the labor-credit system and the work attitude?

A: No, we did the labor-credit system mainly because we wanted to keep track of things. It wasn't, among the older, more influential members, it was never an end in itself. Here it was an end in itself.

Q: Why?

A: Here it was an end in itself because Kat and some of the early members believed it was the only way to get work out of people. That was not how we…We wanted to allocate things better. Work was never considered an evil, and people who came visiting felt that, and some would never come back, others would never come in the first place.

Q: But if you didn't have problems with people not doing their share, why did you need to keep track of labor?

A: It was perceived as fair, and it was probably seen as a way to prevent people like myself getting burned out. And it was also a way of letting new members know what was expected of them, it was a way of dealing with vacation, and deciding who got the marbles when the game broke up. [pauses] I am certain that everybody at some time would have said, "Jeez, I've got to work two more hours to make my labor credit." That probably happened to everybody, if you're burned out or unhappy. But by and large, it was a record-keeping system rather than a, "This is how we will get a certain amount of work out of people."

Q: Over the years, what do you think helped Twin Oaks survive when so many other communities folded?

A: It survived because it had people like Kat and McCune here for the long haul. Mainly, it accumulated capital. You came here, you worked for eight years, you leave with how much?

Q: Fifty Dollars, I think.

A: Yeah, and all the soybeans you can take with you. If you had been at our place, you would have left with…Anytime a person left, we paid them back. And that's difficult, very difficult to do, and maybe impossible to do, as Kat said. She said you can't do it, and maybe she is right. But what built this place up was the accumulation over time of the capital. And I know that if they gave people any more, they would lose their monastery status. And that's a very valid reason. [pauses] But how many Negroes do you see here as members? How many blue-collar guys are members here? I don't see too many. And if you were raised poor, and you didn't see the immense benefits you would get…[pauses] People can get a wonderful education here, but you don't see that. You can't see that, you think, "Jeez! Everybody here, or at least most people here, have a return ticket!" They can go back and say, "Mom and Dad, I made a mistake, do you think you could help me get through college, finish my college?"

Q: And they would probably be happy to do so.

A: Yes! And I know that bothers Kat a lot. But that's the way it is. It is very difficult for a person from a blue-collar background to work an unknown amount of labor here and come out with fifty dollars.

## Interview with Chris Orsolini, June 10, 1998

Q: Lake Village was started as an experiment in communal living. Was it your sense that it was a shared effort? And how central a figure was Roger Ul-rich?

A: It was a hard way to live in a lot of ways. But we were willing to do big changes and found that it was rather hard to instigate those things. We found ourselves coming into conflict with Roger. [pauses] I feel that it's his farm in a lot of ways. He calls the shots. And that was very difficult. We also started to see that a lot of the animals were dying. We came back from the Farm in Tennessee to our land and found that our pigs had been slaughtered and put in the freezer and were going to be somebody's dinner. That was upsetting, but, you know, it was done. But it started to get to me, about the animals dying. It just seemed like something wasn't being managed properly. We had seen some other ways to approach things living at the Farm. When we finally approached Roger, he basically just...[pauses] I don't know, it was a horrible scene. He pretty much told us off, you know, "What farm had we ever lived on?" And it's like, where have we been living? Haven't we been living on a farm? Aren't we part of this? And Roger just seemed to blow it off. It was at that point, and it was a very heartbreaking day, that we realized that this could not be part of our lives forever. We really thought we would be there for our life. We were going to be there. And it just fell apart. And I think Roger has always had a lot of control on the farm. I think if it were a true family feeling there, some of the conflicts could have been resolved perhaps, and worked through, but it just seemed that it was never going to happen. [pauses] I think there are probably other folks out there that don't have that glowing feeling about Lake Village. I was watching some of the tapes of the party out there, and yes, it's a wonderful place to go and party, but it's not an easy place to live. You'll see that a number of the people on that tape have moved off and live on the outskirts of Lake Village. Because it's hard to live in that kind of situation, it's very difficult, if not impossible. And I just credit anybody that can hang in there.

Q: Why, do you think, were there animals dying at Lake Village?

A: I think they were being mismanaged, you know. [pauses] I don't know. There may have been some kind of disease that was going around.

Q: Was your husband one of Roger Ulrich's students?

A: Yes, my husband was a behavior student of Roger. [pauses] He quit grad school, he got real disillusioned with the whole behaviorist thing.

Q: What's he doing now?

A: He's just now getting back to teaching elementary school. He loves kids, and he's going to be a really great teacher. But I know that leaving Lake Village really hurt him. I mean, after a year he was getting a little better, and it got to the point where I wanted to talk about it because it was like a big cloud. We had lived at Lake Village I think for seven years. We had a long history there, he had been Roger's farmhand for a while. [pauses] They used to have Work Sundays, maybe Roger talked about that, where the people were supposed to help with the farm work. By the time I got there, a lot of that kind of utopian, ideal stuff was starting to wash away. We did get a group of us together to cook communal meals three or for times a week, which was great. It was wonderful. At that time, there were all these young folks kind of living in all the little dwellings. It really felt like a little village, a group of people that were there that you could hang with, or not.

Q: In how far do you think is Lake Village actually a farm?

A: [laughs] I don't think you could really call it a farm unless somebody was really farming it, really doing it, whether it be for profit or to feed people or whatever.

Q: How was the work distributed at Lake Village? How was it worked out how much your fair share of work was?

A: I think that's partly why the Work Sunday thing maybe devolved. I think that they charged people more for the apartment to cover paying someone to do a lot of the farm chores. For a while, my husband was Roger's farm boy. So I don't know. I think if we had wanted any improvements... [pauses] And he was charging pretty much what you would pay all over town, you know. [pauses] This is another interesting thing. Lake Village was bought by the corporation which had come out of the behavior-modification program. Well, who is the corporation now? Who really owns it? When it's been divided, it was divided with Roger's daughters, each a share of the land. [pauses] I would have loved to have a piece of that land. You know, my husband and I lived in a cabin in the woods, and we would have loved to build our own little place there. It's kind of a joke. Now I see that she's doing what we would have loved to be able to do. But it's kind of like, she's his daughter, so she gets to do that. Outside of Roger's family, nobody has been able to buy land. Paulette and Howard, they bought a piece, but other than that . . .

Q: How were decisions made at Lake Village? What was the formal setup and how were they really made?

A: Well, they would have meetings, I think, like Monday afternoon, or whatever, and everybody would bring their blights or their agenda to the meeting, and there would be a discussion. But then—and I heard this more than once—Roger would say, "Well, I have the ultimate responsibility, so I will make the call."

Q: Why did Roger feel that he had the ultimate responsibility?

A: Partly because nothing was done unless he approved it, basically. Like, one of the things we were pushing for was to add on to the community kitchen and have a warm place. I mean, here I was with a newborn baby, and I'm cooking in a freezing-cold kitchen.

Q: Do you think that in Lake Village's history, all the people who opposed Roger ended up leaving?

A: I think so. I think it was always the old thing, you know: when push comes to shove... [pauses] And there wasn't anybody else to answer to. And if you asked him, "Who owns this place?"...[pauses] And that's the thing about paying a share, I think that term "share" was kind of a joke. If you invest in something by giving a share, aren't you part owner then? And when you leave and get nothing for that, when you have some kind of equity in it? [pauses] I can get kind of bitter about him, too. About how he's managed the thing.

Q: Do you think it is also Roger Ulrich's sense that he is the person who ultimately owns Lake Village, or do you think he really feels that it is a shared effort?

A: I can't imagine that he could go on imagining that it is a shared effort because he has managed to eliminate or alienate anybody who has tried to really get in there with him. There was a large group of people that lived there at one time, and now it's what, five people?

Q: But there was also the bust in 1995 for not having building permits that could account for that.

A: Yeah, right. And that was something...[pauses] Whenever we would complain too much about our conditions, it was explained to us that, "If you complain too much, we could get busted." You know, "Don't complain to the authorities. After all, this is our home." So it's kind of like, "Okay, we'll let it go, and we won't push things too much because we could end up ruining the situation." But ...

Q: Of the people who lived at Lake Village, were most of them students of Roger Ulrich?

A: Oh, yeah. I think a lot of people came and went because they'd been introduced to the place as students.

Q: Isn't there a power imbalance right there?

A: Yeah, I would think so. Or they were like friends of his kids, really young, you know. There's the story of how they raised their own kids, but that's a whole other thing. [laughs] Yeah, you're right, that really threw off the balance. And he really did have that kind of attitude. Well, I'm the teacher, and you're just a student. [laughs]

Q: How important do you think was behaviorist thinking at Lake Village?

A: Well, the whole concept of behaviorism is out of fashion, now. To be a behaviorist means you want to manipulate people. Which is exactly what he does, you know. [laughs] When you have arguments with Roger, he'll get you so mad by saying, "That's just the way it is, sorry," that you blow up. He gets people to blow up at him. He gets people so angry that they just want to get away, and he's not going anywhere.

Q: Have you ever seen Roger take something back, saying, "I was wrong," or, "I will reconsider"?

A: Well, when my husband and he had their big fallout, I think my husband sent him a letter, saying, "This is why you made me so angry." And Roger sent him a letter back and basically would not apologize. I mean, my husband really just wanted an honest apology. "I'm sorry I insulted you." And he just really wouldn't spell it out that way, at least not to my husband's satisfaction. He quoted, you know, some Indian chief, kind of justifying why he said what he did. But not really thinking that he did anything wrong. Thinking that he had a justification for why he did it. So I think that his ego is pretty strong. [laughs] And he's not going to abandon it.

## Interview with Roger Ulrich, June 10, 1998

Q: If somebody who is totally unfamiliar with your community asked you, "So what's Lake Village all about?" what would you answer?

A: [pauses] It would be very difficult for me, from my perspective, to be able to encapsulate an answer to that question. So I'd probably say, "I have no way in the world to tell you what Lake Village is all about." [laughs]

Q: What did you find inspiring about *Walden Two,* and how has that changed?

A: What I found inspiring about *Walden Two* is that I liked Skinner. I tend to personalize things, and I liked Skinner. At that time in history I liked the idea of exploring and researching, I was getting more into that mode from a clinical psychology mode. I saw many problems in our society. So what attracted me to *Walden Two* was its social conscience. That for better or for worse, we should be doing some things with children early, and things like that. And all of the researchers and all of the other people that I knew in the Skinnerian movement drew me to reading *Walden Two.* And then I got very much taken by the thing that he had Rogers say to him in the opening pages of the book. "It's a job for research, but not the kind you do in a university. You have to experiment with your own life. Teaching is alright to turn people on, but in terms of finding things out, you've got to experiment, and experiment with your own life." So that was, and still is, very important to me.

Q: Would you say that the passage about having to experiment with your own life was probably what attracted you most to *Walden Two?*

A: Absolutely. [pauses] There is so much theory in the book. It's a theory that has almost become a religion, like with Juan and all the guys down in Mexico and so forth. Which is alright, but that's data. And they did experiment with their own lives, and experiments, they show what they show. So what they're doing down there is beautiful, what they're doing at Twin Oaks is beautiful, and all the others. It's just what's happening. Again, there is no experiment other than a real situation, which comes kind of from Rolling Thunder. So that very much governs my outlook on a lot of things.

Q: When did you begin to be influenced by the medicine man Rolling Thunder and other spiritual experiences? And when did your Amish-Mennonite background begin to resurface in your thinking?

A: The Amish-Mennonite ethic was instilled in me in my mother's milk, and there were times when that got to be a bit oppressive, particularly when the Christianity side of it excluded other forms of spirituality. That very early on became a stumbling block for me, and so I started arguing with my Sunday school teacher. So there were a whole bunch of years of arguing with the Amish-Mennonite teachers and so forth. But you never escaped the love and the caring and the family that was around you, and even though people disagreed with you they still loved you and cared for you. [pauses] The question again was?

Q: When did these various spiritual influences resurface in your thinking?

A: They resurfaced again out here, after coming back to the land with a more scientific, nonspiritual approach to things. Out here, the land almost demanded of me that I start to look at that which is, the great mystery which is the Sioux Indian characterization of God, the Great Spirit and so forth. And so I was drawn into and became a part of the right place at the right time. And the spiritual side of, "We don't control the world, we are a part of it, look at it, and try to flow with it as comfortably as you can, and do the right thing."

Q: How important do you think were your hands-on experiences with drugs in making you realize that behavior is less predictable than behaviorism had led you to think?

A: I'd say that for many Americans, LSD, taking the pill, was an instant enlightenment in some ways. I mean, for a moment there... [pauses] It's a typical American-European way of doing things. We are not going to sit in a cave for thirty years. Boom! We need it now! And it brought an awareness to myself and others of the sorts that was very, very important and did, for me, provide data that I followed as opposed to sticking with the laboratory experiments of shocking animals and all that kind of stuff. That became silly.

Q: Let's get back to *Walden Two* for a moment. As a novel, would you say it presents a completely positive utopia, or do you see potential dangers in what Skinner proposes?

A: Again, life is made up of contradictions. Utopia is nowhere, so perfection is in the eye of the beholder, depending on who is calling the shots. From my perspective, it's a book to assign students in introductory psychology, which they're not even all that interested in reading and find it boring upside of Ishmael and *The Message Down Under* and Rolling Thunder and a whole bunch of things. It's not even a particularly well-written novel. [pauses] That's how I see it now. When I read it the first time...[pauses] Are there dangers in a system in which we're presumptuous enough to say that there is no such thing as freedom, but we're free enough to arrange controls around children, adults, everybody? Of course. It's very, very potentially the same kind of thing that keeps reoccurring over and over again. It's just so much simpler to make a decision like that and not have anybody argue with you. As you go down that path, there is a lot of travesty that can occur with someone getting lots of control. I think Skinner was sensitive to trying to set up a situation in which there was a lot of faith by a lot of people and so forth. [pauses] Are there dangers in *Walden Two?* There are so many more monumental dangers out there than what Skinner said in that book that it's probably fairly inconsequential.

Q: What are the more monumental dangers?

A: Oh, a quarter of a million new people being added to us every day. And the fact that we have become so addicted to the abstraction of money in the First World countries that we have forgotten what wealth really entails anymore. So we're hooked on secondary reinforcers, and we'll kill to get them. We're worried about children being shot in our schools, and we're wondering why that's happening, not noting that they're watching television in which we're going over and bombing the crap out of Baghdad because they're supposed to have used gas on somebody. [pauses] The problems that are in the world today have the function of the human being evolving into a life form that reacts very quickly to reinforcers that follow their behavior. It has taken us off on a whole variety of tangents that are just very detrimental to the survival of all life forms. And we're proud of our "progress." *Walden Two?* You can't even find it in a bookstore anymore.

Q: Let's get back to Lake Village. Was there ever in the beginning or later on the idea that you would create an alternative society? Was it ever the plan that Lake Village would be something like a microsociety?

A: I think in the very beginning, after having read *Walden Two* and being somewhat enamoured with the power of positive reinforcement and all that kind of stuff and the realization that things needed changing, there was the hope that we could do things that would bring about positive social changes. [laughs] Then we realized that we were our own problem. That there was not much hope in us saving the world or certainly me not saving it while I had all these problems myself. I had enough trouble modifying my own lifestyle and behaviors that defined at times a fairly sick person. In terms of just looking in the mirror. [laughs] It's like, "Oh, why should I be the one that helps solve the world's problems?" I mean, good lord, look at our own! So it didn't last very long. It was just sort of an initial flash in the pan, an arrogant bit of self-righteous thinking that flashes back every once in a while but hopefully doesn't last through the night.

Q: So would you say *Walden Two* was only influential at Lake Village for the first few months of its existence?

A: I don't know. I mean, I'm sure that on any given day, I have a self-righteous let's-go-save-the-world-you-can-do-it thought. But it doesn't last very long. Hopefully, you get older and wiser.

Q: So in the very early days, when you were still thinking you could do something grand, how did you envision Lake Village to be, in terms of membership, size, structure, child rearing?

A: I didn't tend to do that much. I had done acid by the time I came out here, and I'd had a lot of nonordinary-reality-type exposures. I had already gotten in touch with Carlos Castaneda, with a number of indigenous folks, so it was very much, remember to be here now. So again, what do you mean? This place is barely able to make it through the week, it's going to be a model? Why should Twin Oaks and Los Horcones think that they had anything whatsoever new to offer to a world that had the Amish Anabaptist movement and all the other movements? I mean, there is nothing new under the sun. That's just—those are theses. Those are just what Harvard and Stanford and Michigan and all these places force people into. "Ah, we got to write something down, so we write stuff down." It has very little to do with . . . [pauses] It's trivial pursuit.

Q: If you are fairly sure that at least for you, Lake Village was not a grand plan to save the earth, what do you think attracted other people to Lake Village?

A: It varies pretty much with everybody who came. Someone trying to get out of their home because they're scared that they are going to get busted for pot, or someone else is just out of prison, somebody got a divorce and needed a place to live. Each person came here for such differing reasons, usually because it was a cheaper place to crash than a lot of others, and they didn't maybe have to clean up as much. You have 251 different reasons for why people came out here, you have to talk to each one of them.

Q: So largely it was personal, practical reasons that made people come out here? Do you think there were many people with utopian ideas, in the sense that they thought about how society should be and tried to actually do that at Lake Village?

A: While people were high or low or going through a divorce or whatever they also had ethics and had feelings about how life should be, and they had a spirituality about them, in varying degrees. Everybody deserves respect, and everybody that came here had concerns about life forms in varying degrees, their fellow human beings, the animals. So, yes, everybody was also utopian. A utopian thinker. Some people win Pulitzer Prizes writing about utopia and making movies, and others carry water and chop wood.

Q: Did you ever have people who came to Lake Village because they thought you were "doing" Walden Two? Was your connection to Walden Two anything that was important to the people who came, or that they even knew about?

A: Very little. [pauses] Most of the people who had any incentive of that sort were in the original group that came out. They were part of the Learning Village, from 1965 to 1970, and they were part of the Racine Conference. So early on, maybe our first six months or so. And then very quickly the reality that was really in *Walden Two*—"You've got to experiment with your own life!"—took over, and we went in a hundred and one different directions. And I was not theologically imbued with, "It's got to stay a particular way." [laughs] I didn't support that, and the other elders that were around supported it even less. My wife Carole didn't give a damn whether it was Walden Two; she wanted a good goat herd. Skinnerians were always putting down abstract theories anyway, yet that's basically what Skinner put down in *Walden Two*.

Q: Why do you think Skinner was never interested in living in a community? He has said himself that it was because his wife wouldn't like it and that being a professor at Harvard was just too reinforcing. Why do you think he was really not interested in living communally?

A: His wife wouldn't like it and Harvard was very reinforcing, and going to conferences and talking about it was much more reinforcing. It's a pain in the ass to go and do what the kids at Twin Oaks did and what Los Horcones did. It's work. It's the same reason that early on in my life I said, "Well, I think I'll go to college instead of putting the hay up." It's a lot of work, so Skinner was just being pretty honest. Life is work.

Q: Why did Skinner refer Walden Two enthusiasts to Twin Oaks rather than Los Horcones or Lake Village?

A: Kat Kinkade visited with Skinnerians, and it was very much a case where it was going to be a Walden Two experiment. Skinner did early on send people to us. I don't know whether it appeared in any of his writings or not, but I know that he did, and he came out here and talked to people and so forth. But then, after a while, we didn't reinforce that behavior in him. I mean, they were coming back and sort of saying, "Roger isn't a believer!" [laughs] So it wasn't reinforcing with Skinner. Because Skinner became a convert to his own religion, and he started to believe what he wrote.

Q: Was *Walden Two* ever talked about at Lake Village? Was it anything that you ever went back to and said, "Well, what are the suggestions in *Walden Two?*" Was it ever in your mind at all that that was the original impulse?

A: It was in my mind when somebody was asking me questions like you are asking and when interviews occurred and so forth. On the day-to-day basis this is irrelevant. For the most part, literally irrelevant. [laughs] We were much more benefited by things like having the people from my Amish church coming up here and helping us build a barn and telling us what they knew and stuff like that. And they knew something. It wasn't a bunch of, in a sense, literary bullshit. *Walden Two* was essentially irrelevant to our system, other than some of the getting us started, getting us thinking about it.

Q: So do you think it would be accurate to say that for Lake Village, *Walden Two* was the impulse but also the point of instant departure?

A: I wouldn't even say *Walden Two* was the impulse. I would say that Vietnam, the civil rights movement, my brothers on the north side of town getting busted on the head, and the kinds of things that we were going through in the early sixties. That was much more important than *Walden Two* in why we came here. We came out here as social activists, no kidding about it. I mean, we weren't just playing around.

Q: So do you think it probably wouldn't make much sense to look at your child rearing or decision making and compare that to *Walden Two* because that wasn't the plan anyway?

A: Certainly we used reinforcing strategies, and used a lot of behavior-mod strategies early on, with my children Tom and Traci and the other kids. We ran the Kalamazoo Learning Village, we have films that we made where we're using tokens and are charting and all of that. But if you watched over the years, that became less and less critical, because we were charting the things we were getting done and not noticing that we were listening to what people told us, and what they were saying they were doing they weren't doing anyhow.

Q: Did you use behavior modification mainly with the children?

A: In a sense, we're doing it right now. The way I look and the smile, back and forth, we are in a control–counter control situation, where I modify what you hand over to me and then I speak, and that goes on all the time. Are we using b-mod? In a purist sense, you cannot help but use behavior-modification strategies.

Q: Let me modify my question, then. Were you consciously and in a planned way using behavior modification at Lake Village with the explicit intent of having planned, conscious, scientific social interactions?

A: Okay, again, back to earlier in the interview, when we were talking about when we came out here. I had already been through the Learning Village experience. We came out here, it was about the same time that I damn near killed myself shooting up cocaine and dropping acid. So a whole bunch of things were modified as a function of the fact... [pauses] Some of the textbook things that said this is how you should run things didn't matter anymore. We were under the umbrella of a lot larger power than scientists wanted to acknowledge. There is a power around us that is the great spirit, is the part of Mother Earth telling us how to live, and very early on I acknowledged that consciously or unconsciously and started to go along with that. I was not religious about, "We're going to follow what we were talking about in the psych department."

Q: Why was the preschool called the Learning Village? Why a "village"?

A: That was just a name. Eve Segal came up with the idea of a living and learning village. And we thought that sounded like a good name, so we called that the Learning Village, and when we came out here we called it Lake Village. No rhyme or reason. You'd be surprised how little thought went into everything that's around you. [laughs] Maybe not, if you visit with us longer.

Q: How would you describe the role that you have played at Lake Village over the years?

A: Everything from a confused junkie to an absolute dictator. My role as I see it—again, in an idealized form—is to be a child of God, a child of nature, an ethical being, and to do the right thing, as Spike Lee says in his movie, and so forth. And my more perfect description of where I'm coming from is: I want to get rid of poverty, I want to see to it that we're not polluting the environment, all of these things. There's the other side of me that jumps in my van, gases it up, takes gas and oil from Kuwait, adding to part of the world's problems. I still strive to get my reinforcers, like you and like anybody else. How I'm behaving on a particular day varies from a spoiled child having a tantrum to someone who looks like a calmer elder who's sixty-six.

Q: Kat Kinkade once theorized that if a group has a fairly strong person in their midst, it is unlikely that there will be another strong person within that same group, because there is a high likelihood that those two people would clash. At Lake Village, have you seen many people coming through who you experienced as your equals?

A: I would disagree with Kat in terms of what she defines as strength. It's not clear that always getting one's way or seemingly getting one's way defines strength. That might define fear, cowardice, not allowing somebody else to have a shot at running the show.

Q: Okay, so I'll modify the word "strength." How about power? A person who holds a lot of power in a community, for whatever reasons, and regardless of whether that's good or bad, the person is wise or foolish. How does that affect the community, and how does it affect who is attracted to the community?

A: Well, we need to get down to power again, and a lot of times that is defined by who has a lot of money. There are a lot of people in this country who have a lot more bucks than I do. Whether they have more power than I do, I have no idea. And as far as bucks go, maybe I have more bucks than Rolling Thunder, but I sure wouldn't equate that with power. So what do you mean by power?

Q: I mean power within a certain group to move that group in a certain direction. Being influential in the decision-making process, and being more influential overall than the other people.

A: Well, I have always been attracted to people who have a strong will, their own ideas, who kind of like to go and do their own thing, even though I get into arguments with them. Those are the ones I'm attracted to.

Q: Have those same people been attracted to living at Lake Village?

A: A lot of those same people are just like me. We keep our distance from one another. You need a certain amount of space. So there are ways in which you try to create an environment where it's okay to get your own way. And I like that.

Q: But doesn't that point in Kat's direction? That someone who has very strong ideas about what they want is likely to have a radius of not having another person with strong ideas around them?

A: Could be, could be.

Q: Would you say that Lake Village strove to be democratic in its communal days?

A: Well, again, I'm really not hung up on words and abstractions. Democracy? What's that supposed to be? We use that term "free society" as we go around the world crushing certain forms of freedom. [pauses] We follow to a certain degree the laws of Pavilion Township, of Kalamazoo County, State of Michigan, and so forth. And when I go out that driveway, I stop at stoplights sometimes. So, if you call that a democracy, then the answer is yes. We never tried to fool ourselves that we are somehow outside the boundaries of man-made laws, human-made laws, or natural laws.

Q: I didn't actually mean how you relate to the society around you, but rather internally. While interacting with each other, did you use democratic methods, like votes? Or consensus? What did you think of the idea of "professional government," Kat's term for the Walden Two idea of placing decision making in the hands of those who know most about it?

A: But Kat was defining who knows most about it.

Q: But between those two poles, consensus and professional government, where would you say that you stand in your thinking?

A: Probably in the middle. Because those are words, and it depends on what issue is being discussed. There's a whole bunch of things that I don't even want to be part of making a decision on. You know, where to put the pins in a boy's diaper. And other things are very important to me. And if something becomes very important to me, I can become a mean ass, I suppose, to some people. Not that I mean to be. It's just that I have my beliefs in certain things that I'd rather see happening.

Q: And how were those issues resolved that were personally important to you?

A: Well, a lot of them went unresolved. And others... [pauses] Some days I'd get my way, some days I wouldn't. Some days someone else would get their way, and some days they wouldn't. We bent, I thought, way over backwards to allow some people who I admired for their anarchy. Up to a point. But I was being somewhat anarchistic myself.

Q: Do you think people who drift in and out of communities tend to have a slight problem with taking on responsibility?

A: I think that's a growing Euro-American problem, particularly in this country. Not feeling responsible for your actions. And it's not unrelated to determinism and some of the things that Skinner was talking about. There is a reason for everything, so that we can always look and say, "Well, it's not me." [laughs] I wasn't breastfed long enough, or this, that, or the other thing. Yes. A lot of people simply turn and point their finger at somebody else and say, "It wasn't my fault." And certainly a lot of people that drift in and out of communities don't have to worry about the taxes being paid. A lot of the realities that keep a place like this going: they don't know they're there! [pauses] You've got a good point there. Responsibility is something that a lot of people skirt, in my opinion. And it takes one to know one: I sure skirted a lot of responsibilities in my life. [laughs]

Q: What is the legal status of Lake Village? And what exactly was the financial arrangement? How did new people join, and what happened to their money?

A: Okay. It started out that there already was a corporate bylaws in place, and we were a 501 c3 corporation running the Learning Village. And when the land became available, we purchased this land under the umbrella of that corporation. So we were legally bound by the laws of the United States, the State of Michigan, and so forth, to follow the rules set up for corporate entities, which means you needed a Board of Directors, members, and so forth. In less legalistic times, it's been a tribe. So that group was the one legally responsible for the land. So that answers that part of the question. And that's still how it works today.

Q: How about new members' money?

A: Nothing happened whatsoever to new members' money. You are still your own person. You cut a deal, like, here's a spot to stay, and in return for it you wash some windows. And we'll see where things go tomorrow.

Q: Did people pay rent from the beginning?

A: From the beginning, people insisted on calling it rent. From the beginning we said, no, everybody here puts in a specified share, and "share" had a real meaning. It was trying to say, "You're a part of it, you're sharing in the thing, and you're not paying rent for another entity." In our culture, that was almost impossible to get across, and it still is almost impossible to get across. Because that is not the way we've been trained to think from the time that we were born. We weren't born in Indian tribes.

Q: So members paid a monthly share to the corporation?

A: Yes.

Q: Was there a defined amount of time that people were supposed to work, and could they either pay more money or work?

A: That was determined by where you lived. So if you lived in this place or that place, we had prices attached to how much space you had. And over the years, those kinds of things varied, depending on the economy of the greater Kalamazoo area.

Q: So not everybody paid the same share.

A: No, not everybody paid the same share.

Q: Who actually worked on the farm, and how was that organized?

A: Those expectations varied day to day based on one's ability that day to do things. Carole is pretty much on the farm all the time, so she has a whole bunch of things that she does to see to it that the farm runs. Tony is here most of the time; he has a whole bunch of things that over six or seven years he has learned to do.

Q: It's fairly clear to me how it works now, but I'm wondering how things were done in the early days. Who ran the farm?

A: In the earlier days you were required to do even less. [pauses] Also, in the early days we had Work Sundays. So in addition to the share, you worked for two hours every Sunday.

Q: But who performed the many daily tasks required on a farm?

A: You know, it's almost hard for me to remember, given all the years, who was here during what time doing things. Because people came and went. For a long time Leon was here and pretty much did what Tony is doing now.

Q: I'm still not clear on that point. How did you keep track of where people worked and for how long? Did you have a labor manager or something like that?

A: Basically, I can understand where you're coming from. Because again, what happened to us, we became more like an Amish-Mennonite farm, where none of that stuff is specified. People got up at five in the morning and knew what they had to do, and they went and did stuff. And over the years we have moved further along that path. That's probably difficult to understand.

Q: Okay. Here's a different question. What do you know about Matt Israel?

A: Matt Israel [pauses] was very, very strongly motivated, highly motivated by *Walden Two*. He was Skinner's student at Harvard, he was always talking positive reinforcement, and he was wanting to get Walden Two started. And in the Boston area he, a number of times, got groups together in apartment buildings and started mini Walden Twos.

Q: What happened then?

A: Oh, Matt, pretty much after the Racine conference, went back out to the Boston area, and then he, out of his interest in Walden Two, and funding it and so forth, got involved with group-care homes for autistic kids. And then over the years his... [laughs] his positive reinforcement thing went so that they were slapping kids around and really using heavy aversives to get autistic kids to behave. And he got a lot of notoriety and was having a lot of success—you know, this is off the top of my head—in that area, and then started to run into civil rights groups and people sort of saying you shouldn't be hitting... you shouldn't be treating... you shouldn't be using aversive control like that. So Matt, who was closely identified with and was always talking positive reinforcement, ended up heavily using aversives, 'cause it kind of worked.

## Interview with Ted Millich and Kristen Dakota, December 9, 1998

Q: In how far would you say was Sunflower House a community?

Dakota: It was a community of students. Like, I think in *Communities* magazine, I see that their definition of "community" is really broad. Like cohousing is a community. So in that context, I think that Sunflower House was a community. But it was not a community like Twin Oaks.

Millich: It's frequently referred to as a co-op.

Q: In your conception of what was important, if somebody had asked you what you were doing, would you have mentioned the fact that you lived at Sunflower House?

Millich: Probably not.

Q: So it was more sort of just the place where you lived?

Millich: Yeah.

Q: These days, one of the first things you would tell people who were asking what you were doing with your life would probably be that you live at Twin Oaks, right?

Millich: At Sunflower House, we had meetings every Monday and about four hours of work a week. So we spent a lot more time in class than even working or meeting at Sunflower House.

Dakota: I thought it was a really great place. When I moved there, I didn't know where else to live. And then I lived there, and I really liked living with other people. But it wasn't really a fundamental lifestyle change. Getting kicked out of Sunflower House would mean you get another place to stay. Getting kicked out of Twin Oaks would mean you have to move, get a job, get health insurance, get a car.

Q: Did you get the sense that the systems that were in place at Sunflower House, like the house cleaning, were actually what the people living there as a group wanted to do, or did you ever get the sense that they were just there, for you to follow?

Dakota: Yeah, well, in every bathroom there was a list of what you had to do to clean the bathroom, and then after you cleaned the bathroom, somebody would come and check, to make sure you really had done the right thing. So yeah, it very much felt like, you know, "I'm living here, and I'm doing these things so I can live here."

Q: How did people feel about the fact that their work performance was being checked?

Dakota: It was hated at Sunflower House. I think we all had to take turns doing that inspector job because everyone...It was, you know, a certain police, sort of the clean police.

Millich: Yeah, I never did it. But I think it was necessary at Sunflower House. It was never very clean, anyway.

Q: Were there systems that you really liked?

Dakota: Maybe the meeting thing. I thought that was a neat idea. I still think that's a good idea. That little problem-solving groups would go off, solve the problem. [pauses] You know, here would be a way to have a whole new way of doing Twin Oaks meetings. Where we would actually decide things, vote on things.

Millich: The main difference to Twin Oaks is that at Sunflower House, there were all irresponsible students, so you needed very rigid instructions. At Sunflower House, the three systems were cleaning, cooking, repairing. Here, we have a kitchen manager, somebody who will kind of take care of that area, and there'll be a building maintenance person, and so on. [pauses] There used to be a process at Sunflower House that trained people to facilitate, and when I first got to Twin Oaks and went to meetings, I remember thinking that I could do better than them, because I'd had that training. I don't know, I'm very interested in facilitator stuff, and I frequently think that meetings could be better here.

Dakota: At Sunflower House, because it was rotated, it wasn't this big ego thing, and here sometimes I think it's an ego thing.

Q: How many people lived at the Sunflower House?

Millich: About thirty people, in two houses.

Q: How often did you have dinner together?

Millich: I think it was five dinners a week, and sometimes a Saturday dinner.

Dakota: The Sunflower House was very dependent on the supermarket. We didn't grow our own food, like here. And the rotating meals are sort of an appealing idea, but the cooks hated it. Once I copied out all the menus for use at Twin Oaks, and it was just too explicit, it was like, "Open this can, pour it into this bowl, etc." It works very, very well for students who aren't cooks, but you know, for people here? Also, at Sunflower House we didn't take into account seasonal variety.

Q: How about the people who conducted the behavioral research project at Sunflower House, like Deborah Altus. Did they tend to be very active in the house?

Dakota: No. When I lived there, Deborah didn't even live at Sunflower House, and she didn't come to the meetings. She came to a couple of them, and she videotaped some of them for her research. But, yeah... [pauses] I was surprised to find out after I had lived there for a few months that there were graduate students studying the Sunflower House.

Q: Oh, really?

Dakota: Yeah. There wasn't anybody living there that was studying it.

Q: I thought the idea was that it would be graduate students who also live at the Sunflower House?

Dakota: No.

Millich: Well, they did at some point, but after you've lived there for a while, you're likely to want to move out.

Dakota: Well, and your life changes. You know, you want to live with your boyfriend, or get married.

Q: I once heard Deborah mention something about Sunflower House, where she said that there was this strong, undercurrent feeling that behaviorism was sort of a drag. That the people who lived there didn't really want to be part of any research and had a "Fuck the Behaviorists" party.

Dakota: Oh, cool. [laughs] I don't think people really knew what behaviorism was.

Millich: You know, the human development and family life department at Kansas University, I think one of the ways—I'm not sure what you mean about projects—but I think one of the ways that behaviorism affected the Sunflower House was that there were all these structures. Of course, people don't like that. And I think, really, those structures can be freedom, once you're used to them. But it's easier to look at them . . .

Dakota: You know, like those lists on the wall. People at Twin Oaks would not have lists like that on the wall.

Q: Well, there are lists in the kitchen here, like how to do the cleanup after meals.

Millich: If that list were at Sunflower House, it would be longer, with many more things on it, all spelled out.

Dakota: And you would have to do this one thing first. [laughs]

Q: Who was influential in setting up the structures at Sunflower House?

Millich: Tom Welsh.

Q: And he did live there, right?

Millich: Yeah, for about ten years.

Dakota: I remember when Tom left, people were concerned, like, "Are things going to still run well?"

Millich: Yeah, sure. Like after the revolution, when the first leaders finally . . . Like, what is Cuba going to do after Fidel, you know?

Q: What originally drew you to living at Sunflower House?

Dakota: A cheap place to live. A peaceful, cheap place to live.

Millich: Also, where people live together.

Dakota: Right. [pauses] I think the Sunflower House actually was started, and was then taken over by the university, right? It wasn't a university thing to begin with, right?

Q: When you moved to the Sunflower House, in what ways was it different from living in a regular student dormitory?

Dakota: Well, if you think of it in terms of, "How much do people who live there have control of the house?" In a dorm, it's one extreme, like absolutely no control. And then the scholarship houses are sort of in between, together with sororities and fraternities, and then Sunflower House, and then living in your own apartment.

Q: While you were living at Sunflower House, did you have a sense of being part of a utopian experiment? Did it feel like building a better society?

Millich: I feel much more like that here.

Dakota: Actually, after I moved here, I was really surprised about Sunflower House. To read about it in *Communities* magazine. I just thought, "Wow, I didn't know it was like this famous place!" It was just a nice place to live. [laughs]

Millich: I think it became famous because people published about it.

Dakota: Yeah, right! I think it's famous maybe just because it's written about a lot.

# Works Cited

"Accord Reached on Autistic at R. I. School." *Evening Bulletin,* February 21, 1979, B8.

Altus, Deborah. "Roger Ulrich and Lake Village Community: 'The Experiment of Life.'" *Communities: Journal of Cooperative Living* 98 (Spring 1998): 52–54.

"Appletree." *Communities: Journal of Cooperative Living* 25 (March–April 1977): 51.

ASD Forum. Twin Oaks Papers (no. 9840). Special Collections, University of Virginia Library, Charlottesville.

Association for Social Design. Brochure. Twin Oaks Papers (no. 9840). Special Collections, University of Virginia Library, Charlottesville.

Baer, Donald M. "The Reform of Education Is at Least a Four-Legged Program." *Journal of Applied Behavior Analysis* 25.1 (Spring 1992): 77–79.

"Battling for the Disabled with Cesar Chavez in Mind." *Los Angeles Times,* June 12, 1995, B5.

"Bay States to Probe Death of Mass. Man at Providence Center." *Providence Journal,* November 22, 1980, A10.

Bellamy, Edward. *Looking Backward.* 1888; reprint, New York: Penguin, 1982.

Bethlehem, Douglas. "Scolding the Carpenter." In *B. F. Skinner. Consensus and Controversy.* Eds. Sohan Modgil and Celia Modgil. New York: Falmer Press, 1987. 89–97.

"Big Island Creek Folks." Incipient Groups. Twin Oaks Papers (no. 9840). Special Collections, University of Virginia Library, Charlottesville.

Bijou, Sidney W. "What Psychology Has to Offer Education—Now." *Journal of Applied Behavior Analysis* 3.1 (Spring 1970): 65–71.

Bjork, Daniel W. *B. F. Skinner: A Life.* New York: HarperCollins, 1993.

Callenbach, Ernest. *Ecotopia.* New York: Bantam Books, 1975.

———. Interview by Manfred Pütz. *Amerikastudien/American Studies* 41.3 (1996): 381–95.

Compendium of the ASD Forum. Twin Oaks Papers (no. 9840). Special Collections, University of Virginia Library, Charlottesville.

"Community Design." Incipient Groups. Twin Oaks Papers (no. 9840). Special Collections, University of Virginia Library, Charlottesville.

Couch, Richard W., et al. "Some Considerations of Behavior Analysts Developing Social Change Interventions." *Behavior Analysis and Social Action* 5.1–2 (1986): 9–13.

"Crabapple." *Communities: Journal of Cooperative Living* 30 (January–February 1978): 57.

"A Desert Group Lives by Skinner's Precepts." *New York Times*, November 7, 1989, B5–6.

Elms, Alan C. "Skinner's Dark Year and *Walden Two*." *American Psychologist* 36 (May 1981): 470–79.

Falda, Wayne. "Farm Commune Develops Nature and Human Nature." *South Bend (Ind.) Tribune*, March 12, 1988.

"Fantasy Farm." *Communities: Journal of Cooperative Living* 13 (1975): 54.

"Fantasy Farm." *Communities Directory* (1975): 27.

Feallock, Richard Arthur, and L. Keith Miller. "The Design and Evaluation of a Work-sharing System for Experimental Group Living." *Journal of Applied Behavior Analysis* 9.3 (Fall 1976): 277–88.

Fishman, Steve. "The Town B. F. Skinner Boxed." *Health* 5.1 (January–February 1991): 50–60.

Freedman, Anne E. *The Planned Society: An Analysis of Skinner's Proposals.* Kalamazoo, Mich.: Behaviordelia, 1972.

*General Description of Los Horcones Community.* Brochure. N.p., n.d. 1–8.

Graham, Richard. "Path with a Behaviorist Heart." *Communities: Journal of Cooperative Living* 103 (Summer 1999): 42–44.

Heyman, Ken. "Skinner's Utopia: Panacea, or Path to Hell?" *Time*, September 20, 1971, 47–53.

"Hidden Springs." *Communities: Journal of Cooperative Living* 14 (1975): 52.

———. *Communities Directory* (1977): 51.

Houriet, Robert. *Getting Back Together.* New York: Avon Books, 1972.

Huxley, Aldous. *Brave New World.* New York: Harper and Row, 1932.

"Implications of a Behaviorist Philosophy in Our Daily Life: Children Apply Behavioral Self-Management Programs." *Walhdos* 29 (April–June 1988): 10–11.

Israel, Matt. "Proposal for an Experimental Community." Behavior Research Institute. Twin Oaks Papers (no. 9840). Special Collections, University of Virginia Library, Charlottesville.

———. "'Rat Knows Best!' or, Some Proposed Characteristics of an Experimental School Based on Behavioral Psychology." ASD Forum. Twin Oaks Papers (no. 9840). Special Collections, University of Virginia Library, Charlottesville.

Johnson, Steven P., et al. "Participatory Management: Maintaining Staff Performance in a University Housing Cooperative." *Journal of Applied Behavior Analysis* 24.1 (Spring 1991): 119–27.

Jones, Tamara. "The Other American Dream." *Washington Post Magazine,* November 15, 1998, 12–19, 27–31.

"Judge Allows BRI Therapy to Continue Six Months." *Providence Journal,* June 24, 1987, A24.

"Judge to Receive Reports of Monitors of BRI." *Evening Bulletin,* June 22, 1987, A3.

"Julian Woods." *Communities Directory* (1975): 29.

Kanter, Rosabeth Moss. *Commitment and Community.* Cambridge, Mass.: Harvard University Press, 1972.

Keller, Fred S. "Good-Bye, Teacher...." *Journal of Applied Behavior Analysis* 1.1 (Spring 1968): 79–89.

————. *The Keller Plan Handbook.* Menlo Park, Calif.: Benjamin, 1974.

Kinkade, Kathleen. "But Can He Design Community?" *Communities: Journal of Cooperative Living* 103 (Summer 1999): 49–52.

————. *Is It Utopia Yet? An Insider's View of Twin Oaks Community in Its 26th Year.* Louisa, Va.: Twin Oaks, 1994.

————. "Power and the Utopian Assumption." *Journal of Applied Behavioral Science* 10.3 (1974): 402–14.

————. *A Walden Two Experiment: The First Five Years of Twin Oaks Community.* New York: Quill, 1973.

Kinkade, Lee Ann. "'Who's the Meta Tonight?': Communal Child Rearing at Twin Oaks." *Communities: Journal of Cooperative Living* 103 (Summer 1999): 45–48.

Klaw, Spencer. "Harvard's Skinner: The Last of the Utopians." *Harper's Magazine,* April 1963, 45–51.

Komar, Ingrid. *Living The Dream: A Documentary Study of Twin Oaks Community.* Louisa, Va.: Twin Oaks, 1989.

Krutch, Joseph Wood. *The Measure of Man: On Freedom, Human Values, Survival, and the Modern Temper.* Indianapolis: Bobbs-Merrill, 1953.

Kumar, Krishan. "The Utopia of 'Behavioral Engineering': B. F. Skinner and *Walden Two.*" In *Utopia and Anti-Utopia in Modern Times.* Oxford: Basil Blackwell, 1991. 347–78.

————. *Utopianism.* Milton Keynes: Open University Press, 1991.

"Larchwood." *Communities: Journal of Cooperative Living* 18 (January–February 1976): 57.

"Leaving Twin Oaks: A Conversation with Former Members." *Communities: Journal of Cooperative Living* 28 (September–October 1977): 20–28.

*Living the Reality: The New Member Survival Handbook.* Louisa, Va.: Twin Oaks Community, n.d.

"Los Horcones: An Adolescent Walden Two." *Walhdos* 31 (October–December 1988): 2–11.

Los Horcones. "Behaviorism at Los Horcones." *Communities: Journal of Cooperative Living* 32 (May–June 1978): 48–50.

———. "Natural Reinforcement: A Way to Improve Education." *Journal of Applied Behavioral Analysis* 25.1 (Spring 1992): 71–75.

———. "Natural Reinforcement in a Walden Two Community." *Revista Mexicana de Analisis de la Conducta* 9.1–2 (June–December 1983): 131–43.

———. "News from Now-Here, 1986: A Response to 'News from Nowhere, 1984.'" *Behavior Analyst* 9.1 (Spring 1986): 129–32.

———. "Personalized Government: A Governmental System Based on Behavior Analysis." *Behavior Analysis and Social Action* 7.1–2 (1989): 42–47.

———. "Pilot Walden Two Experiments: Beginnings of a Planned Society." *Behaviorists for Social Action Journal* 3.2 (1982): 25–29.

———. "Walden Two and Social Change: The Application of Behavior Analysis to Cultural Design." *Behavior Analysis and Social Action* 7.1–2 (1989): 35–41.

———. "Walden Two in Real Life: Behavior Analysis in the Design of a Culture." In *Human Behavior in Today's World*. Ed. Waris Ishaq. New York: Praeger Publishers, 1991. 249–55.

McLaughlin, Corinne, and Gordon Davidson. *Builders of the Dawn: Community Lifestyles in a Changing World*. Walpole, N.H.: Stillpoint Publishing, 1985.

Meyer, Michael. Introduction to *Walden and Civil Disobedience*, by Henry David Thoreau. New York: Penguin, 1983. 7–36.

Miller, L. Keith, and Richard Feallock. "A Behavioral System for Group Living." In *Behavior Analysis: Areas of Research and Application*. Ed. Eugene Ramp and George Semb. Englewood Cliffs, N.J.: Prentice-Hall, 1975. 73–96.

"Modern Utopian: Special Report." *First Walden Two National Convention*. 1.1 (n.d.): 4–27.

"Morningside." *Communities: Journal of Cooperative Living* 8 (1974): 54.

"Mother of Injured Autistic Girl Sues School for Negligence." *Providence Journal*, October 16, 1980, B11.

"Nasalam." *Communities Directory* (1978): 41.

*Newsletter of the Association for Social Design*, May 4, 1967, and August 16, 1969. Twin Oaks Papers (no. 9840). Special Collections, University of Virginia Library, Charlottesville.

"New York Threatens with Suit." *Evening Bulletin*, December 17, 1978, A8.

"New York to Remove Children from R.I. School's Care." *Providence Journal*, December 31, 1978, B12.

Pitzer, Donald E. "Developmental Communalism: An Alternative Approach to Communal Studies." In *Utopian Thought and Communal Experience*. Ed. Dennis Hardy and Lorna Davidson. Middlesex, U.K.: Middlesex Polytechnic Press, 1989. 68–76.

Plank, Robert. "The Modern Shrunken Utopia." In *America as Utopia*. Ed. Kenneth Roemer. New York: Burt Franklin, 1981. 206–30.

Rice, Berkeley. "Skinner Agrees He Is the Most Important Influence in Psychology." *New York Times Magazine*, March 17, 1968, 27, 85–90, 95, 98, 108–14.

Robinson, Juan. "Comunidad Los Horcones: Radical Behaviorism in Mexico." In *Communal Living around the Globe.* Ed. Bill Metcalf. Findhorn: Findhorn Press, 1996. 143–53.

Rockliff, Mara. "Yuppie No More: A Girl's Search for the Good Life." *The Leaves of Twin Oaks,* Summer 1998, 3–4.

Roemer, Kenneth. "Mixing Behaviorism and Utopia: The Transformations of *Walden Two.*" In *No Place Else: Explorations in Utopian and Dystopian Fiction.* Ed. Eric Rabkin et al. Carbondale: Southern Illinois University Press, 1983. 125–46.

Rogers, Carl, and B. F. Skinner. "Some Issues Concerning the Control of Human Behavior: A Symposium." *Science,* November 30, 1956, 1057–66.

Ruppert, Peter. *Reader in a Strange Land: The Activity of Reading Literary Utopias.* Athens: University of Georgia Press, 1986.

Ruth, David. "The Evolution of Work Organization at Twin Oaks." *Communities: Journal of Cooperative Living* 35 (November–December 1978): 58–60.

Schaub, Laird. "Federation History: Where We Come From and Where We Are Going." *Communities: Journal of Cooperative Living* 73 (1987): 53–59.

Skinner, B. F. *About Behaviorism.* New York: Knopf, 1974.

———. *Beyond Freedom and Dignity.* New York: Bantam, 1971.

———. *Cumulative Record.* New York: Appleton-Century-Crofts, 1959.

———. "The Design of Experimental Communities." In *International Encyclopedia of the Social Sciences.* Vol. 16. Ed. David L. Sills. New York: Macmillan, 1968. 271–75.

———. Foreword to *A Walden Two Experiment: The First Five Years of Twin Oaks Community,* by Kathleen Kinkade. New York: Quill, 1973. v–x.

———. *A Matter of Consequences: Part Three of an Autobiography.* New York: Knopf, 1983.

———. "News from Nowhere, 1984." *The Behavior Analyst* 8.1 (1985): 5–14.

———. *Science and Human Behavior.* New York: Macmillan, 1953.

———. *The Shaping of a Behaviorist.* New York: New York University Press, 1984.

———. "Utopia as an Experimental Culture." In *America as Utopia.* Ed. Kenneth Roemer. New York: Burt Franklin, 1981. 28–42.

———. "Walden (One) and Walden Two." *Thoreau Society Bulletin* 122 (Winter 1973): 1–3.

———. *Walden Two.* 1948; reprint, New York: Macmillan, 1976.

———. "Walden Two Revisited." In *Walden Two.* New York: Macmillan, 1976. v–xvi.

"Sonoran Commune Seeks Skinnerian Utopia." *Arizona Daily Star,* October 13, 1995, 1C.

Spudly. "An Open Letter to Kat Kinkade." *The Leaves of Twin Oaks,* November 1998, 6.

Starak, Yaro. "Living Prototypes for a Future Society." *Ekistics: The Problems and Science of Human Settlements* 313 (July–August 1985): 353–61.

Sulzer-Azaroff, Beth. "Is Back to Nature Always Best?" *Journal of Applied Behavior Analysis* 25.1 (Spring 1992): 81–82.

Sunflower House. Owner's Manual. Lawrence, Kans.: Sunflower House, 1997.

Thoreau, Henry David. *Walden and Civil Disobedience*. 1854; reprint, New York: Penguin, 1983.

"Twin Pines." *Communities: Journal of Cooperative Living* 16 (September–October 1975): 50.

Tyler, Alice Felt. *Freedom's Ferment: Phases of American Social History from the Revolution to the Outbreak of the Civil War*. New York: HarperCollins, 1962.

Ulrich, Roger. "In Search of Our Achilles Heel." *Behavior Analysis and Social Action* 6.2 (1988): 59–61.

———. Interview by David Ruth. *Communities: Journal of Cooperative Living* 30 (January–February 1978): 12–18.

———. "Operant Conditioning of Social Behavior and Society." In *Observe and Respect: The Experiment of Life*. Littleton, Mass.: Copley Publishing Group, 1989. 1–73.

———. "Some Moral and Ethical Implications of Behavior Modification." In *Rites of Life: A Book about the Use and Misuse of Animals and Earth*. Kalamazoo, Mich.: Life Giving Enterprises, 1989. 36–49.

———. "Toward Experimental Living." *Behavior Modification Monographs* 2.1 (1973): 1–74.

———. "Toward Experimental Living, Phase II: 'Have You Ever Heard of a Man Called Frazier, Sir?'" In *Behavior Analysis: Areas of Research and Application*. Ed. Eugene Ramp and George Semb. Englewood Cliffs, N.J.: Prentice-Hall, 1975. 45–61.

Ulrich, Roger, and Jacqueline Metheany. "Learning Village: You Just Can't Get There from Here; A Behaviorist Attempt to Establish a Model Day Care Center for Early Education." Unpublished manuscript in author's possession.

"Walden Group." *Communities: Journal of Cooperative Living* 4 (1973): 60.

"Walden Two for Real." *Synapsia* 3.3 (Autumn 1992): 32–33.

Watson, John B. *Psychology from the Standpoint of a Behaviorist*. Philadelphia: Lippincott, 1919.

Wenig, Mikki, and Chip Coffman. "Mothers and Daughters Break with Tradition." *Communities: Journal of Cooperative Living* 33 (July–August 1978): 32–39.

Wolfe, Peter. "*Walden Two* Twenty-Five Years Later: A Retrospective Look." *Studies in the Literary Imagination* 6.2 (1973): 11–26.

"Yarrow." *Commune Directory* (1974): 38.

Zimbardo, Philip G., and Richard J. Gerrig. *Psychologie*. Berlin: Springer, 1996.

# Index

HILKE KUHLMANN is assistant professor
in the American Studies program
at the University of Freiburg, Germany.

The University of Illinois Press
is a founding member of the
Association of American University Presses.

Composed in 10.5/13 Adobe Minion
at the University of Illinois Press
Manufactured by Thomson-Shore, Inc.

University of Illinois Press
1325 South Oak Street
Champaign, IL 61820-6903
www.press.uillinois.edu